The Iroquois in the Civil War

THE
Iroquois
AND THEIR
NEIGHBORS

LAURENCE M. HAUPTMAN, SERIES EDITOR

THE
IROQUOIS
IN THE
CIVIL WAR

From Battlefield to Reservation

LAURENCE M. HAUPTMAN

SYRACUSE UNIVERSITY PRESS

Copyright © 1993 by Syracuse University Press
Syracuse, New York 13244-5160

First Edition 1993
93 94 95 96 97 98 99   6 5 4 3 2 1

The paper used in this publication meets the minimum requirements
of American National Standard for Information Sciences — Permanence
of Paper for Printed Library Materials, ANSI Z39.48-1984. ∞™

Library of Congress Cataloging-in-Publication Data

Hauptman, Laurence M.
    The Iroquois in the Civil War : from battlefield to reservation /
Laurence M. Hauptman. — 1st ed.
        p.   cm. — (The Iroquois and their neighbors)
    Includes bibliographical references and index.
    ISBN 0-8156-0272-3 (cloth)
    1. Iroquois Indians — Wars.   2. Iroquois Indians — History — 19th
century.   3. Iroquois Indians — Government relations.   4. Indians of
North America — Wars — 1862-1865.   5. United States — History — Civil
War, 1861-1865.   I. Title.   II. Series.
E99.I7H335   1992
973'.04975 — dc20   92-3741

Manufactured in the United States of America

To
Harold and Freda Jacobs
and to the memory of
Cornelius Abrams, Jr.

Laurence M. Hauptman is Professor of History at the State University of New York College at New Paltz. He is the author of *The Iroquois and the New Deal* and *The Iroquois Struggle for Survival: World War II to Red Power* (both, Syracuse University Press) and has coedited *The Oneida Indian Experience* (Syracuse University Press) as well as three other books in Native American history. Hauptman has worked with the Wisconsin Oneidas and the Mashantucket Pequots in organizing historical conferences. He was the expert witness on the Seneca-Salamanca lease controversy, and he testified before committees of both houses of Congress in 1990. In May 1987 he received from the Iroquois the Peter Doctor Memorial Indian Scholarship Foundation Award for distinguished service in promoting goodwill and advancing the image of the American Indian.

Contents

Illustrations

CHARTS

MAPS

Preface

Historians have not sufficiently studied the effect of the Civil War on Native American communities. Most works on that watershed event are largely concerned with Indian-white relations, based almost exclusively on Interior and War Department records. Most scholarly writings on Native Americans in the Civil War era focus on five areas: the wartime involvement of Cherokee and other nations of the Five Civilized Tribes; biographies of prominent American Indian generals such as Stand Watie (Cherokee) or Ely S. Parker (Seneca) who fought in the conflict; wartime atrocities (such as Sand Creek and the Long Walk) committed against American Indians on the frontier during these years; the Great Sioux Uprising of 1862; and federal administration of Indian Affairs in the early 1860s.

Unlike earlier studies, *The Iroquois in the Civil War: From Battlefield to Reservation* is primarily a study of Iroquois communities. This book delves into Iroquois communities' perspectives about the Civil War, describes the wartime experience of Iroquois soldiers and sailors, details Iroquois existence on the home front, and measures the very significant impact of the war on Iroquoian life in the decades after the conflict. Part One focuses on Indian military participation, especially on the regiments that contained the two largest contingents of Iroquois soldiers — the 132d New York State Volunteer Infantry and the 14th Wisconsin Volunteer Infantry. Iroquois in the New York homeland are treated in more detail than those in Wisconsin and Indian Territory, largely because there were a greater number of Indian volunteers from a wider assortment of Iroquois communities. Part Two focuses on the "other war" — efforts by Iroquois to maintain their family and community existence, their lands, tribal governments, and cultural identity during and immediately after the Civil War.

Two caveats are needed at the beginning. This book does not provide another full-scale biography of General Ely S. Parker, the Seneca sachem who served prominently on General Ulysses S. Grant's staff and later became commissioner of Indian affairs. Although Parker is treated in one chapter, I refer readers to William Armstrong's excellent full-length biography, *Warrior in Two Camps: Ely S. Parker, Seneca Chief and Union General,* published by Syracuse University Press in 1978. Second, much of the documentation involving the Iroquois in the Civil War era relates to the Senecas, including the diary of Ordinary Seaman William Jones and several major collections of correspondence of Iroquois volunteers, including the papers of Sergeant Isaac Newton Parker and General Ely S. Parker. Senecas volunteered in greater numbers than the other Iroquois communities, but their overwhelming record is not just the direct result of their greater population. The Friends' missionary involvement with the Senecas was early and produced an extensive and valuable record, larger than for any other Iroquois nation. The location of the New York Indian Agency adjacent to the Senecas' Cattaraugus Indian Reservation led to voluminous records dealing with these Indians with less attention to more distant Iroquois such as the St. Regis (Akwesasne) Mohawk, some of whom served in the 98th New York State Volunteers. Moreover, few white officials' reports on the Indians of New York differentiated among the Iroquois residing on Seneca reservations, especially Cayuga residents, often grouping them all as "Seneca" throughout the Civil War period. Confusion reigned supreme in Indian Territory, where the designation of "Seneca" or "Seneca and Shawneee" was applied by War and Interior Department officials to all the diverse Iroquois populations resident there.

I wish to acknowledge the help of a few people who aided me in my research. George Hamell of the New York State Museum set me on the right path in search of letters in private and public collections related to Iroquois enlistment during the war. He also led me to the diary of Seneca sailor William Jones at the Rochester Museum and Science Center. I also thank Ken Poodry of the Tonawanda Indian Reservation as well as Charles Hayes III and Betty Prisch of the Rochester Museum and Science Center for allowing me access to this important diary. William Evans of the New York State Archives and Michael Meier of the National Archives pointed me toward the right Civil War military records. William Starna of the State University of New York College at Oneonta provided a helpful sounding board and encouraged me from day one of the project. Jack Campisi of Wellesley College also called materials to my attention, especially the Powless-Archiquette Diary written during and after the Civil War by two Wisconsin Oneidas. Mary Bell of the Buffalo and Erie County Historical Society, George H. J. Abrams, former director of the Seneca-Iroquois National Museum, and Tom Hill of the Woodland Indian Centre at the Six Nations Reserve helped me piece together the missing strands in Isaac Newton Parker's life. With the permission of their nation, three Wisconsin Oneida Indian historians — Gordie McLester of the Oneida Indian Historical Society, Judy Cornelius of the Oneida Library, and Jan Malcolm of the Oneida Nation Museum — generously provided photocopies of materials related to Oneida participation in the Civil War. I also thank Judith Greene, director of the Seneca-Iroquois National Museum, Duwayne "Duce" Bowen, the trustees of the museum, and the Seneca Nation of Indians Tribal Council for allowing me access to Civil War holdings and for providing photocopies of transcribed letters.

The State University of New York College at New Paltz contributed to this book in a variety of ways, including providing a series of internal grants to complete the manuscript. Joan Walker, the secretary of the History Department, typed all of the numerous letters of inquiry required in my research. Lynn Barley, Margaret Halstead, Jean Sauer, and the staff of the college's Sojourner Truth Library helped me obtain valuable secondary and primary materials for my research. Through the efforts of Jo Margaret Mano of the college's Geography Department, I was able to secure the excellent cartographic services of Ben Simpson. Katherine Fogden, a student at the college, also contributed her photographic expertise to the project.

Several friends helped make this project possible. David and Susan Jaman of Gardiner, New York, were of assistance, especially Susan for careful word processing of my handwritten transcriptions of original Civil War letters and word processing of the entire manuscript. My friend Roy Black graciously allowed me to talk about the project ad nauseam while we did true fieldwork — playing bogey golf. He deserves acknowledgment for giving me insights about Mohawk fighting men, but not for his putting.

Finally, my wife and two children excused my compulsive work habits and research travels, realizing that I was not suffering from "Civil War mania" but was merely acting out the reason why I became a historian in the first place. My interest in the subject during my undergraduate years, which occurred during the Civil War Centennial, propelled me to seek an advanced degree in history. Now, more than a quarter-century later, I was finally coming full circle!

Laurence M. Hauptman

New Paltz, New York
January 1, 1992

The Iroquois in the Civil War

Introduction

The Civil War was by far the most devastating event in the history of the United States. Approximately 618,000 of the 3 million Union and Confederate soldiers and sailors who fought in the war were killed. One in every three soldiers was a casualty and one in every five a fatality. During the War, 182 individuals per 10,000 population died. World War II casualties were one-sixth of the Civil War ratio, and the Vietnam War cost three American military deaths per 10,000. The Civil War touched every community in the United States, including those of the Iroquois Indians.

Iroquois involvement in the conflict was in some ways similar to white participation. Unlike African-Americans, Iroquois Indians served in integrated units in the Union army and navy and received the same pay as their white counterparts.[1] They served in the ranks as privates as well as commissioned and noncommissioned officers. Like most of their white counterparts, the Iroquois participants in the war were farmers. Country boys right off the farm, according to Bruce Catton, made very good soldiers because they "could stand more, they were more self-reliant, perhaps they were more used to handling weapons."[2] They also faced the same horrors of mid-nineteenth-century battlefield conditions. Two-thirds of Union deaths have been attributed to poor field sanitation, improper medical care, poor diet, and disease. Like their black and white counterparts, the Indians suffered physical disabilities and were emotionally scarred by the war.

Despite these similarities, contemporary popular accounts of the Civil War years portrayed a stereotyped image of the Iroquois. In the late spring of 1864, the *New York Herald* reported the heroism of a group of five or six Seneca soldiers, most notably Oliver Silverheels and Jacob Halftown of the 14th New York Heavy Artillery at the Battle of Spotsylvania. After

3

one of his regimental comrades was killed by a Confederate bullet, Silver-heels camouflaged his body from head to foot with the foliage of pine boughs. With a rifle in hand, he "sneaked" up behind a Confederate sharp-shooter who had perched in a tree before the Union lines, capturing the rebel soldier. Silverheels's action led the *Herald* to claim "that the wonders of Cooper's Indian heroes have not ceased," rivaling "the 'deviltry' of any of the Leatherstocking redskins."[3] Newspapers such as the *Warren Mail* recounted this famous capture throughout the rest of the nineteenth century, adding Tonto-like dialogue to Silverheels's activities: "You go heap straight[,] me no shoot; you look back[,] me kill you. . . . Drop gun, come down, or me shoot you dead. Me no tell again."[4]

Although this and other contemporary accounts emphasized individual prowess, Iroquois soldiers went off to war as representatives of communities, however different they were from other American communities. Recent Civil War historiography has focused increasingly on community studies. Historian Phillip S. Paludan has observed that the "attachment of communities to their soldiers endured throughout the war—linking community to the war in very personal ways." Another scholar, Maris A. Vinovskis, has chided the practitioners of the new social history for largely ignoring the impact of the Civil War on everyday life in America. Vinovskis insisted: "Groups of soldiers were often recruited from one locale and were usually formed into companies consisting of individuals from the same geographic area." He added, "The practice of creating units from the same locality had important implications for soldiers' life courses. Rather than being separated from their peers and getting a new start in the armed forces as American servicemen did in World War II and do today, most men served with friends and neighbors who were familiar with their social backgrounds and prior experiences."[5]

With the sole exception of Ely S. Parker, Vinovskis's conclusions are confirmed with regard to the Iroquois. These Indian communities faced racial discrimination in recruitment at the onset of the war. Eventually, Iroquois men went off to war together, often volunteering on the same day. They then fought side by side in combat from the Peninsula campaign of 1862 to the end of the war in 1865. As in the case of the 132d New York State Volunteer Infantry, they bonded together with other soldiers in their regiments, forging a connection that lasted for decades after the conflict.

The Iroquois military experience was not soon forgotten, and the camaraderie of war set these men apart from others in their communities. The Civil War was a turning point in men's lives. After the war, Iroquois like other Americans participated in the pageantry of the Grand Army of the Republic's regimental reunions and parades. Civil War Indian comrades were buried with military as well as Indian honors well into the 1920s, and Indian veterans' deaths were marked by elaborate obituaries detailing their Civil War records. Indian veterans helped widows and children of fallen comrades secure Civil War pensions; these applications extended well into the 1930s.[6]

Despite these similarities with non-Indian communities, Iroquois reservations were hardly identical to other American communities. The Iroquois had been victimized from 1784 onward, losing over 95 percent of their homeland. Many had been removed to Indian and Wisconsin territories or had sought refuge in Canada. In 1861, the Iroquois were not citizens of the United States, and most did not choose to be. They were historically, legally, and racially distinct communities set apart from other Americans.[7] Consequently, although at times their wartime experiences and attitudes about the "infernal rebels" paralleled those of many other Americans, they were not simply carbon copies of their non-Indian comrades in arms. Indians and non-Indians had distinctive reasons for joining military service and had varying experiences in the war. Most significantly, the Iroquois Indian experience was separate and distinct because they had to counter other challenges far from Southern battlefields. From 1838 to 1875, the Iroquois repeatedly had to fend off the grasping clutches of land speculators, railroad magnates, and state and federal officials intent on obtaining the Indians' shrinking land base. In effect, the Iroquois fought two wars, one in the South and the other on the home front.

PART ONE

THE IROQUOIS
GO TO WAR

1

The Call to Arms

IROQUOIS WARRIORS/VOLUNTEERS

On April 15, 1861, the day after the surrender of Fort Sumter, President Abraham Lincoln called seventy-five thousand state militia into ninety-day Federal service to suppress the insurrection. On May 3, the president, realizing the inadequacy of his earlier call, requested forty-two thousand three-year volunteers, thereby expanding the regular army by twenty-three thousand men. He also requested eighteen-thousand new sailors for the navy. After the secession of the final Confederate states, the Congress approved two laws in the summer of 1861, each calling for an additional five hundred thousand volunteers, chiefly for three-year service.

Recruitment officers were successful because of the wave of patriotism in 1861. Because each state had local authority for recruitment, the state governor's actions were all-important from the beginning. Only when a regiment reached its full strength of one thousand troops were the men sworn into federal service to become part of the Union army. Each infantry regiment had ten companies consisting of eighty-two privates, thirteen sergeants and corporals, two lieutenants, and a captain. Throughout the war, most regiments never approached their official full strength, and many had fewer than five hundred men in their companies.

The raising of regiments was a political process, as Bruce Catton has described it. The governors "naturally called on various and sundry leading citizens for help—men of stature and influence in village and city, in county and congressional district, and in the state as a whole." Many men who received commissions had little knowledge of the military, were not honest, and lacking experience, bungled their duties. Catton says:

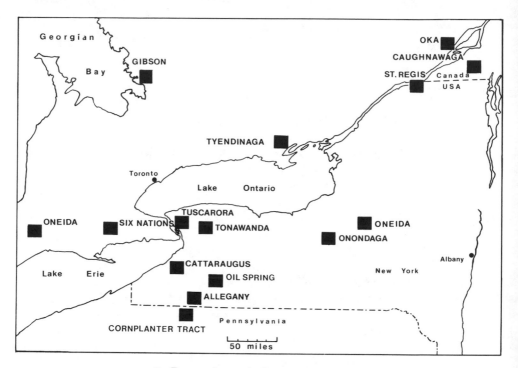

1. Eastern Iroquois Reservations, 1860.

In a typical northern county, for instance, there might be in the county seat or elsewhere, a man of some prominence—a lawyer, say, or a businessman, or miller, or a schoolteacher—who was tolerably well-known in his neighborhood and apparently gifted with some capacity for leadership. This man would be given a captaincy, and it was up to him to raise a full company of one hundred men. He began usually by finding a couple of local activists to serve as lieutenants, got the governor to commission them, and with them set out to get recruits. The recruits, of course, all came from the same neighborhood, often enough from the same township. Mostly, they knew each other and knew the captain and lieutenants, before they ever signed up. This process was repeated ten times, and presently there were ten companies off in boot camp, complete with colonel, field officers, company and platoon commanders, and all the rest; complete also with uniforms and with a sense that they were off on a great adventure. Presently, the whole outfit was mustered into Federal service, and the training could begin.[1]

CHART 1

Comparative Population of Iroquois Reservations
in New York, 1855 and 1865

Reservation	1855	1865
Allegany	754	825
Cattaraugus	1,179	1,347
Oneida	161	155
Onondaga	349	360
St. Regis (Akwesasne)*	413	426
Tonawanda	602	509
Tuscarora	316	370
TOTAL	3,774	3,992

Source: Derived from New York State, *Census of the State of New York for 1865,* compiled by Franklin B. Hough (Albany: Charles Van Benthuysen & Son, 1867), p. 603.

*According to the census of 1865, there were 413 St. Regis (Akwesasne) Mohawks on the so-called American side of the international boundary. Approximately 700 Mohawks living on the so-called Canadian side were not included in the census. There appear to be two errors in Hough's mathematical calculations. He incorrectly states there were 3,934 Iroquois in 1855 and 4,139 Iroquois in 1865.

Iroquois volunteers were recruited from widely separated communities. In 1860, reservations were scattered from Quebec to the northeastern part of Indian Territory. Besides the five reserves in Canada not involved in the conflict, there was one Iroquois reservation in Wisconsin, two in Indian Territory, nine in New York, and one in Pennsylvania, all affected by the Civil War. Iroquois and related Indians in Indian Territory numbered 310, 1128 in Wisconsin, and approximately 4700 in New York.[2]

The most famous of the Iroquois units in the Civil War from New York State was D Company of the 132d New York Volunteer Infantry. D Company was popularly referred to as the Tuscarora Company, because part of the unit was recruited by Lieutenant Cornelius C. Cusick, a Tuscarora Indian. In reality, the company was largely composed of German immigrants, mostly artisans recruited in Brooklyn, and twenty-five Iroquois farmers from western New York. The Iroquois Indians were mostly Senecas from Allegany, Cattaraugus, Cornplanter, and Tonawanda Indian Reservations with a sprinkling of Cayugas, Onondagas, Oneidas, and Tuscaroras. Iroquois recruits in the 132d New York Volunteer Infantry ranged in age from eighteen to thirty-eight, averaging approximately 26 years. The recruits had been born in the 1830s and early 1840s, an especially traumatic time in Iroquois history. The Treaty of Buffalo Creek of 1838 was at the center of Iroquois life, a fact that was not lost on youngsters growing up in reservation households or listening to elders in council meetings. The treaty would have consequences for Iroquoian life in New York, Wisconsin, and Indian Territory for a long time.[3]

The Treaty of Buffalo Creek, concluded between tribesmen in New York and the federal government, led to the loss of the Senecas' Buffalo Creek Reservation, the center of Iroquois traditional life after the American Revolution. The treaty, affecting all Six Nations and the Stockbridge-Munsees, led to the removal of many Indians from the state. The treaty was fraudulently consummated through bribery, forgery, the use of alcohol, and other nefarious methods. In it the Senecas ceded all their remaining New York lands to the Ogden Land Company and relinquished their rights to Menominee lands in Wisconsin purchased for them by the United States. In return, the Indians accepted a 1,824,000-acre reservation in Kansas set aside by the federal government for all the six Iroquois nations as well as the Stockbridge-Munsee. The Indian nations had to occupy these Kansas lands within five years or forfeit them. For their 102,069 acres in New York, the Indians were to receive $202,000, $100,000 to be invested in safe stocks by the president of the United States; the income earned was to be returned to the Indians. The United States was also to provide a modest sum to facilitate removal, establish schools, and purchase farm equipment and livestock for the Indians' use.[4]

The treaty had other far-reaching effects. Many Indians died of cholera, exposure, or starvation en route to or in Indian Territory. In addition, the bitter infighting over tribal policies after the treaty's consummation eventually led to the creation of a new political entity, the Seneca Nation of Indians, in 1848. Moreover, the treaty led to a Quaker-directed campaign to restore the Indian land base in New York and resulted in the United States Senate's ratification of a "compromise treaty" in 1842. The Senecas regained the Allegany and Cattaraugus but not the Buffalo Creek and Tonawanda reservations. Only in 1857 was the Tonawanda Band of Senecas finally allowed to purchase a small part of its reservation back from the Ogden Land Company. This land purchase as well as the confirmation of federal reservation status was acknowledged by the United States and the Tonawanda Band of Senecas in a treaty concluded the following year. American Indian claims under the 1838 treaty were not settled until the 1890s in a major United States Court of Claims award. Thus the

Buffalo Creek Treaty was the basis of much of federal-Iroquois relations throughout the nineteenth century.

Well after the 1838 treaty, the Iroquois faced efforts to remove them from their homeland. Philip E. Thomas, the prominent Baltimore Quaker philanthropist and advocate for the Seneca Indians, wrote George W. Manypenny, the commissioner of Indian Affairs, in June 1855, protesting the actions of "heartless" whites who were "determined to wrest from them [the Senecas] the land and drive them to destruction." Calling the Senecas a "cruelly wronged people," Thomas advocated federal intervention to protect the Indians. Despite this protest, the New York State comptroller in Albany the following year initiated tax foreclosure proceedings on 1,100 acres of the Cattaraugus Indian Reservation.[5]

Iroquois fears of being removed from their New York homeland continued unabated even after the formal Senate ratification of the Tonawanda Treaty in 1857. Councillors of the Seneca Nation of Indians drew up a petition on June 2, 1858, insisting that the "council is strongly opposed to any commissioner being appointed on the part of the United States for the purpose of negotiating any treaty with Seneca Nation respecting any proposed sale of their lands in the State of New York or elsewhere." The petition, which was forwarded to President James Buchanan and the Bureau of Indian Affairs, revealed that certain persons were circulating "petitions among our peoples" asking for negotiations encouraging emigration "in order to draw off our people from their present condition."[6] At approximately the same time, Thomas further elaborated on the plan to rid New York of Iroquois Indians by "rapacious land sharks that are hovering about them." He added that these forces aimed to "find means to corrupt and secure the co-operation of certain unprincipalled individuals among these Indians" to effect their removal to Kansas.[7] Thus the more important "impending crisis" for the Iroquois was not the approaching Civil War but the need to defend the Indian land base. Yet the secession crisis in 1860–61 was not merely a curiosity to the Iroquois. They feared its implications and worried about the future of their land claims, the continuation of the Indian Agency, and its impact on the New York Indian Agency.[8]

Why Indians sought to serve in the Union army is not easy to determine. George Snyderman, in his classic sociological study of Iroquois warfare in colonial times, has cautioned that "within a single war party, motivations were multiple and varied — men joined, fought, and died for different reasons."[9] Such was the case with Iroquois soldiers in the American Civil War. E. M. Pettit, the non-Indian superintendent of the Seneca state-financed schools, claimed in 1862 that a "large number of them [Indians] have enlisted in the army, and fight as bravely as other men to put down the rebellion, inspired by motives . . . truly patriotic, based upon an enlightened view of the cause of the rebellion and the importance of putting it down."[10] The trustees of the Thomas Asylum for Orphans and Destitute Indians insisted that the boys of the orphanage-school enlisted "full of enthusiasm for the service and abounding in expressions of loyalty and patriotism." Unlike those who sought ways out of service, the Indians, according to the trustees, never shirked their duty.[11]

Unlike many of their Iroquoian kin in Wisconsin, who were lured largely by significant bounty payments late in the war, Indians in New York attempted to join the Union war effort from the beginning. Despite the claims of white educators, the reason for Iroquois military service in the Civil War does not appear to be simple patriotism to the Constitution or to the flag of the United States, so evident in the North in 1861. Even though they referred to the South's "Devilism and Rebelism" in letters, they looked somewhat askance at white officers who rallied the troops solely on the basis of patriotic duty. Yet, like other Northerners, they perceived the attack on Fort Sumter, the secession, and the "War of the Rebellion" as an affront to them.[12]

What appears to whites as simply acculturative forces at work — in this case enlistment in a white man's war — was and is still viewed by the Iroquois as acceptable and logical Indian behavior. Most Iroquois people in New York do not choose to vote in off-reservation local, state, and national elections, choosing instead to participate in tribal referenda. Yet this separation does not prevent them from opening pow-wows with an American flag ceremony and a color guard to honor Indian veterans of past wars, including those who fought on the side of white men. However strange they seem to the dominant white society, these actions, which also include valued memberships in the Veterans of Foreign Wars and American Legion posts in nearly every Iroquois community, are all part of the complex that makes up Indian identity.[13]

Military service was and still is an honored profession in Iroquois ranks.[14] In protesting that Iroquois were first denied entrance into military service in 1861, Cayuga spokesman and physician Peter Wilson pointed this fact out. "Farmer's Brother was my Great Grandfather, Young King my Grandfather and he was a personal friend of General Porter. He was wounded in the leg at the skirmish at Black Rock. For his bravery and services he was [honored?] by a special act of Congress — I think in 1815. My father Col. Reuben James was a private during the War of 1812 and was present at the Battle of Chippeway, where his brother was killed."[15]

Despite religious proscriptions set in the early nineteenth century by the prophet Handsome Lake against entering white men's wars, Iroquois warrior-soldiers joined and excelled during this and later wars.[16] Moreover, validation of tribal leadership through war, which had been an important part of life in the seventeenth and eighteenth centuries, was still meaningful to Iroquois youth in mid-nineteenth-century America. As in the case of Peter Wilson, many fathers and grandfathers of Civil War volunteers had served proudly in the colonial wars, the American Revolution, and the War of 1812. Some such as Cornelius C. Cusick and Ely S. and Isaac Newton Parker were members of families with extensive military traditions and logically sought out service.

In an earlier era, ambitious individuals with talent such as Cusick and the Parkers were free to form war parties. War, then and now, had a key status function. The historian Barbara Graymont has noted that "war gave rise to a prominence of men who achieved their fame by ability rather than inheritance. . . . Prestigious titles were thus restricted to certain reigning families." Graymont added, "An ordinary man, however, might rise to note by merit alone if he had the proven qualities of courage and shrewdness required of a warrior." In 1776, 1812, 1861, 1898, 1917, 1941, 1950, 1965, and 1991 talented individuals could thus take their place in the community by gaining recognition and prestige on the warpath. A warrior, as well as other men of high ability, could become a pine tree chief, an elective office that was not hereditary as was that of sachem. They could serve as advisers to the sachems or might even become "far more noteworthy than sachems."[17] Although much had changed since the American Revolution, war served as a way to move up in the ranks of society well into the nineteenth century. Samuel George, the noted Onondaga runner and hero of the War of 1812, rose in prominence through military service, as did LaFort, Young King, Farmer's Brother, and others. By the time of the Civil War, Chief George of the Onondagas, had become the Great Wolf, the consensus builder, keeper of the wampum, and spokesman for the Iroquois Confederacy.[18]

Political conditions on the reservations also prompted youth to go off to war in 1861–62. This factor is described by anthropologist William N. Fenton.

> Scattered on reservations, they were dealt with separately and forced to act independently of each other. Reduction in size of territory increased population density, so that formerly autonomous tribes were thrown together on reservations, where the old lines of tribal distinction were soon obliterated. It was a new ball game with new rules. White farmers were settled among them, impeding communication further between scattered Indian homesteads. The felling of the forests spoiled the hunting of the warriors; their sport ruined, they turned reluctantly to farming, which

was traditionally women's work. The paths to self-respect were closed. There was no way that the young men could answer their elders, who had achieved distinction in the war out of Niagara. The body politic, moreover, was loaded with war chiefs, who, unable to validate their prestige on the warpath, became the frustrated leaders of factions.[19]

The claustrophobic quality of life and resulting factional behavior would be temporarily alleviated by the departure for war. The sense of adventure, found in the letters of the Indians in the 57th Pennsylvania Volunteer Infantry or in those written by recruit Isaac Newton Parker, was not just the feeling of average young men going off to war; it reflected the war alternative to a factional body politic. This outlet was built into Iroquois culture and recognized early by Euro-Americans.

Other aspects of the Iroquois worldview also promoted volunteering for military service. Most Iroquois see themselves as citizens of their own Indian nations, not New York or the United States. They generally perceive themselves as Indian allies of the United States going to war to help as part of treaty obligations. In the Civil War era, the president was seen as the Great Father, however fickle and unreliable, protecting the Indians from the mercenary interests of their enemies — the Ogden Land Company and New York State politicians. The Parker family, along with their able attorney John Martindale, were mostly responsible for lobbying for the restoration of Tonawanda lands in the Tonawanda treaty which reinforced the Iroquois view that Washington was their only protector. Their friend Martindale became the military commander of the District of Columbia during the Civil War, a fact not lost on the Indians.[20]

The Iroquois in New York made every effort to enter military service in 1861 but were repeatedly rejected on the basis of race and the absence of specific laws about enlisting Indians. Admission of Indians into Union service varied from locale to locale and state to state. Although Native Americans were allowed entry in other areas of the North, they were constantly rejected in New York State.[21] Isaac Newton Parker wrote his wife, Sara Jemison, in October 1861, "I. N. Parker is not accepted in the volunteers services for the 'U.S. Army.' The officer of the 'Mustering Office of the U.S. Office' could not accept *me* because there is no regulation, that is no law for accepting the 'red man' in 'U.S.' law on the subject."[22]

Parker and other Tonawandas went to Geneseo to join General Samuel W. Wadsworth's Wadsworth Guards but were discharged because they were Indians. Before Parker's enlistment was rejected and he was dismissed from service for a second time, he returned to his home at Tonawanda, proudly dressed in his military uniform. He made the faux pas of entering church in his army uniform, which caused a commotion in the small community. Other Iroquois also met with little success. In the fall of 1861, several Tuscaroras recruited by Cusick attempted without success to enlist in Buffalo. Fifty Mohawks, who had volunteered with the 98th New York State Volunteer Infantry, were also discharged "all on account of they being Indians."[23]

Shortly thereafter, Peter Wilson began a series of appeals to military officials and prominent Buffalo businessmen to overturn the decision excluding Indians. Wilson wrote General Gustavus A. Scroggs, the provost general of New York State, on November 11, 1861, that "some of our people the red men the native born of the Six Nations are anxious to join some regiments." Suggesting that he could arrange an Indian ball game to prove "their great agility and their powers of endurance," Wilson protested the policy of excluding Indians "in this present contest to put down the infernal rebellion." After mentioning with pride the loyal services of his father, grandfather, and great-grandfather in the War of 1812, Wilson volunteered his own services as a physician and surgeon.[24]

Wilson and a Buffalo teacher, Chauncey C. Jemison, a Seneca whose father was a wealthy farmer on the old Buffalo Creek Reservation, even appealed to the nefarious Orlando Allen, the former tavern keeper who had been involved in the swindles of 1838 under the Treaty of Buffalo Creek. By the 1860s, Allen and other land sharks had emerged as "respectable citizenry," leading members of Buffalo society with all the right connections.[25] Wilson reported every step of his lobbying efforts to Allen.

Upon hearing about the recruiting of General Francis B. Spinola's Eagle Brigade, Jemison asked Allen to inform him how to secure entry of one or two Indian companies. He insisted that the Indians "are a handy race of people; we get our living by the sweat of our brow tilling our farms, and we would equally work as hard for our country should our services be in demand." Jemison added: "We are anxious to go forth, serve our country and defend the stars and stripes as our white brothers have done around us."[26]

On November 13, 1861, Allen wrote William Wilkeson, an ironworks magnate, whose father, Judge Samuel Wilkeson, was a hero of the War of 1812, an abolitionist, and founder of the city of Buffalo. Allen told Wilkeson of a "movement among the N.Y. Indians in relation to enlisting, or rather volunteering, in the service of the state" in the "struggle now going on for the preservation and maintenance of the Union." He asked Wilkeson to help him in the drive to recruit Iroquois by getting the secretary of war's approval. In the letter, Allen revealed that he had seen Wisconsin regiments pass through Buffalo and knew they contained American Indian volunteers, "one of whom was a non-commissioned officer." He questioned why New York was resistant to Indian soldiers. Allen also told of meeting Indians who wished to volunteer their services on their way to "the ancient council ground of the Six Nations at Onondaga." According to Allen, "They say and truly, that the Gov't did not refuse their services in the war of 1812 and patiently ask 'Why should it now refuse our aid?'" He lauded Wilson and Jemison for their efforts and for showing that Indians were "not the dissolute vagabond set" they were thought to be in the popular white mind of the time, but men of fine abilities "comparing favorably with an equal number of white farmers around them." Allen maintained that he could raise as many as three companies from among them "which would stand head and shoulders above any company" recruited. He concluded that he could "see no valid reason why the services of these men may not be secured particularly when men are needed."[27]

.When efforts at enlistment failed in New York in the fall of 1861, eight Iroquois men, later followed by four others, went to Harrisburg and enlisted at the Pennsylvania capital.[28] All calls by prominent Iroquois for the right to enlist in New York proved futile. On November 21, N. T. Strong, a Seneca, wrote to William D. Dole, commissioner of Indian affairs, saying that the Senecas were anxious to enlist and "they care not whether they go as 'Indian Warriors' or as soldiers." Suggesting that the Senecas were unaware of any legal requirements against their service, Strong adamantly questioned why Dutch, Irish, French, Germans, and English had been allowed into the Union army when Indians were excluded.[29]

In March 1862, after no action had been taken on these appeals, Ely S. Parker wrote to the commissioner of Indian affairs. It was no accident that Parker addressed his appeal. His title in the Iroquois Confederacy of "Do-ne-ho-ga-wa" or the "Open Door" or "Keeper of the western door" delegated him as the Iroquois leader who dealt with outsiders. As a man of noble lineage, restorer of the Tonawanda lands, and a highly educated attorney and engineer, he was long recognized as a spokesman. Explaining that the Senecas were getting the runaround from New York officials and that loyal officers were not enrolling Indians into service allegedly because of "special orders of the War Dept," Parker asked the commissioner to help resolve the matter and explain the Bureau of Indian Affair's policy on the matter. In a coordinated effort, Cusick, with the aid of Colonel John Fisk of the 2d New York Mounted Rifles, then flooded congressional offices with protests against restricting Iroquois from war service. On March 12, 1862, the commissioner responded that there was "nothing to forbid the Indians from volunteering." Fisk wrote to Parker three weeks later informing him that the War Department had ordered the mustering offices at Buffalo to accept Indian recruits. Fisk proposed to work with Cusick, Jemison, and Parker to recruit the Indians. Comparing the three hundred potential Indian recruits to Leonidus's three hundred Spartan heroes of the ancient world, Fisk melodramatically appealed to Parker to lead the call, "seize upon your countries flag as it is extended to you and bear it aloft, *onward and upward to Victory* and immortality."[30]

Between May and July, the two Parkers, Cusick, and Jemison raised Iroquois troops for service. The process was not without controversy and bickering among the four men. Apparently, Cusick was never completely trusted by the others. By the spring of 1862, a special committee in western New York was appointed, and "they gave permits to persons to raise companies," including an "Indian company." When Cusick received a commission for his efforts, Jemison accused him of dastardly acts. Calling him "that *Tuscarora rascal*," Jemison alleged that Cusick had received credit for mustering Senecas raised by Jemison himself. Jemison even suggested that Cusick sold "our Seneca brothers" into service with the assistance of "that other *sneak Waite*" for $115 and that several angry Cattaraugus Seneca "would like to get hold of him." Jemison asked Newt Parker to keep him "posted on their *darn* speculation operation." He bemoaned, "When will we Indians cease to be tools for these white devils?" Ironically, a similar unsubstantiated charge had been leveled at Newton Parker by an unknown Seneca in the fall of 1861.[31]

On July 23, 1862, Colonel Peter J. Claassen received authority to raise the 132d New York State Volunteers. Part of the regiment, including the Indians, had been previously recruited as the 53d New York State Volunteer Infantry or the D'Epineuil Zoaves, a fancily dressed outfit with a decidedly French flair. According to the *New York Tribune*, the soldiers of this unit were "complete with short-hooded cloaks, yellow-tasseled red fez, tan colored leggins, white gaiters, blue sash, vests, jacket and baggy trousers. . . . It is a dress which gives the human figure a barbaric picturesqueness." The unit was known for its brawling in addition to its distinctive and somewhat gaudy dress. The 53d New York State Volunteer Infantry was eventually disbanded because its commander showed "incompetency, conduct unbecoming an officer and a gentleman, conduct prejudicial to good order and military discipline, destruction of government property and disobedience of orders." He had also "lied about his previous military service, but falsely encouraged enlistments, treated his officers like enlisted men, physically abused his troops, illegally kept his wife in camp dressed as a male, and had thrown government property into Chesapeake Bay."[32]

After many false starts, this major Iroquois contingent of fighting men was finally ready for war by midsummer of 1862. Much had happened in the sixteen months since the fall of Fort Sumter, both in the Indian world and on distant Civil War battlefields. By denying Indian entry into Union military service because of racial prejudice, New York State officials had not only produced bitterness but also reinforced Iroquois determination. Undoubtedly, it had reinforced their long-held views about the separation of the two worlds. The Civil War, nevertheless, helped provide Iroquois young warriors an alternate path to distinction and status, as no other since the War of 1812. Faraway battlefields such as Atlanta, Cold Harbor, and Spotsylvania became important in their life cycle just as the War of 1812 battlefields at Black Rock, Chippewa, and Lundy's Lane had been for their fathers and grandfathers. The country had already witnessed the First Battle of Bull Run, the Battle of Shiloh, the Peninsula campaign, Jackson's Shenandoah Valley campaign, the Battle of Seven Pines or Five Oaks, and the Seven Days' Battle. Yet the Civil War, a "total war," still offered, for the "munificent" sum of $13 a month, later $16, more fighting than even young Iroquois volunteers expected or sought in their desire for glory in the manner of their forefathers in the wars out of Niagara.

Despite the many false starts in New York State in the first year of the war, the twelve Iroquois soldiers, who had enlisted at Harrisburg, Pennsylvania, in the fall of 1861, quickly received their fill of war. Although a sense of group adventure, male bonding, and camaraderie were reflected in their early accounts of the war, few realized the hardships they were soon to face, nor did they accurately predict the length of the conflict. After celebrating in grand style, these volunteers were assigned to K company of the 57th Pennsylvania Volunteer Infantry. It is apparent that the men, who included Wooster King, Willet Pierce, Cornelius Plummer, and Levi Williams, had a false sense of reality. In his exuberance after signing up, King insisted that the "southern men are now laying down thier guns and are begging for peace [and that] we understand that they are burning all their rice and other articles down south for fear the United States Army will get it all." The Iroquois soldier confidently boasted: "There are thousands and millions of soldiers on our side [and] there is not much danger of being got and beated[;] there is a good hope that we shall conquer the south and come back to native homes rejoicing[.]"[33] On the same day, after informing his brother that he had "become a brave United States Soldier,"

Plummer predicted that the South was about to surrender since there were just "to many of our union men."[34]

The Iroquois soldiers, mostly Senecas from the Allegany Reservation, continued to write of pleasantries throughout the winter months of 1862 and predicted an early return home. In February near Manassas, Plummer wrote home that the "Indians are going off picket duty" and that it was his hope that he would not have to fight at all.[35] Yet, by April, an Indian rifleman of the 57th Pennsylvania reported that he and his Indian friends were bogged down in heavy fighting during the Peninsula campaign, five miles from Yorktown. Sixty men of the regiment had already been killed; nevertheless, the Iroquois still had time for developing new culinary delights, including oystering offshore during the periodic lulls in the fighting.[36]

Disaster awaited the men at Fair Oaks (Seven Pines) from May 31 to June 1, 1862, where Union casualties numbered 5,000. Even in tragedy, the Indian soldiers' sense of community was displayed. Williams was delegated by the men to write home about the death of Plummer, who was killed in the battle. Williams, who later that month was killed at Charles City Crossroads, wrote Plummer's father:

> I will trry [sic] and write a few lines to you this morning in behalf of yesterday's great Battle[.] I cannot say much this morning because I am so sorry for my friend your son Cornelius Plummer. He is now dead [since] he got shot yesterday as they were marching upon the rebels[.] The ball struck him in his mouth and came out near his ear [and] he fell sudden and died in an instant.[37]

At Fair Oaks, King was severely wounded, "shot through both legs between his hip and his knees.[38] King was later discharged from service for wounds suffered in the battle. Immediately after the conclusion of the fighting, Willet Pierce informed his own father of the intense fighting, the death of Plummer, and the wounding of King, events which brought home the horrors of war to his Seneca community. With a sense of relief, Pierce added that "the rest of our Indian soldiers are well."[39] Pierce's analysis proved optimistic. Of the twelve Iroquois soldiers in Company K, two were killed in action, one died of tuberculosis, four were discharged for disabilities incurred in service, and at least two were classified as deserters.[40]

Despite the initial enthusiastic response to Union military service by a sizable number of Iroquois youth by the fall of 1862, some Iroquois chiefs were less than enthusiastic about their men volunteering in another white man's war. At a council of Six Nation chiefs from Canada and New York held at the Newtown Longhouse at the Cattaraugus Indian Reservation on November 29, 1862, a delegate expressed opposition to involvement in the war. In metaphoric style, an unidentified chief stated that, just as the Indians had buried their tomahawks below the sacred tree, "white men have put guns in the earth also." Nevertheless, "now white men have found his rifle again, perhaps their refle [sic] are carried away by the spring and perhaps they found theirs near the ocean and took them up again and are now fighting at the south," a phrase interpreted by anthropologist J. N. B. Hewitt, himself of Tuscarora ancestry, as the Civil War. The unknown chief warned: "If any one should see a rifle at the spring where they draw water, they should let it alone but turn your face away and dont look at it."[41] Despite the warning, Iroquois youth, as in the War of 1812, ignored this advice and volunteered by the hundreds.

The initial exclusion of Iroquois in New York from military service seems hard to fathom, especially when seen in the context of their impressive performances during the war as attested in studies of Civil War veterans conducted by the War Department and the United States Sanitary Commission. In 1864, the Sanitary Commission appointed Benjamin A. Gould, a member of the National Academy of Sciences and president of the American Association for the Advancement of Science, to assume direction of anthropometric statistics. This branch of the Sanitary Commission produced a report in 1869 entitled *Investigation in the Military and Anthropological Statistics of American Soldiers.*[42] By collecting statistics from physical examinations of thousands of Union military personnel from different racial groups, the Sanitary Commission attempted to construct "Quetelet's average man," named after the scientist who invented this methodology. The examiners, most of whom were poorly trained and had been hired through circular advertising, used andrometers, spirometers, dynometers, facial angles, platform balances, calipers, and measuring tape to determine the "most important physical dimensions and personal characteristics" of each group.[43] According to a modern physical anthropologist's study of the Sanitary Commission's report, "measurements were largely designed for clothes sizing determinations" and were "not wholly in accord with modern racial anthropometry."[44] Moreover, the Sanitary Commission reflected the "scientific racism" of the age in its culturally myopic analysis of black soldiers.

Despite much that was naïve, intellectually unsound, and racist about the Sanitary Commission's report, it provides a valuable portrait of 517 Iroquois Indian males of military recruitment age of the 1860s. Unlike other commission studies that were undertaken by incompetents, it sent Dr.

George F. Buckley, the most experienced anthropometrist and chief examiner of the Sanitary Commission, to western New York. In 1865, Buckley examined 503 Iroquois Indians, most probably Seneca and Cayuga, on the Allegany, Cattaraugus, and Tonawanda reservations. Fourteen other Indians had previously been measured while serving in the Army of the Potomac. These men ranged in age from nineteen to forty-seven. They appeared to Buckley "to have no mixture of white blood." The mean male Iroquois stature was five feet eight inches, approximately the same as the soldiers of the Tuscarora Company, and their mean weight was 162.8 pounds. Although their height was approximately the same as that of the average Union or Confederate soldier or sailor in the Civil War, the Indians' mean body weight was 20 pounds heavier. Buckley found that the Indians showed an average lateral body build but had longer trunks and arms relative to stature. He claimed that the Indians tested had greater lifting strength than the average soldier. One of the Indians he examined was a blubbery forty-seven-year-old weighing a whopping 276.8 pounds. Yet he was atypical because the Indians' greater body weight was the result of muscular development: "Yet the group hip breadth and the chest, waist and hip circumferences bespeak the laterality of average body build in the Seneca beyond simple fat accumulation." The Sanitary Commission report of 1869 noted that, besides their superior strength and weight, the Indians had wider faces and jaws and better visual acuity than their white and black counterparts in the Union military.[45] Despite its limitations, this evidence suggests that efforts at keeping Iroquois Indians out of military service were foolhardy at best because physically they were apparently the match of any soldier or sailor in the Union military service.

The performance of the Tuscarora company in the war was also to prove that New York State officials had erred in their initial decision to exclude Iroquois from serving the Union. Two non-Indian veterans of the 132d New York State Volunteer Infantry made that clear in letters about the war. According to Dudley Beekman of New York City, "as near as I can remember there were some 25 Indians in Co. D all of this state and all could talk *american* for I was often with them and considered them pretty good fellows[.] it was these same indians that taught me to swim." A second member of the GAR observed that they were "as much civilized as any other person in the Reg't." He added that the Indians were "more charitable than many other comrades in the Reg't. They were honest, brave, fearless and obediant soldiers, and they never committed any act to disgrace themselfs or the Reg't."[46] By examining the company and its leadership in the forthcoming chapters, the accuracy of these two post-war veterans' assessments can easily be seen.

2

The Tuscarora Company

THROUGH THE EYES OF ISAAC NEWTON PARKER

The wartime letters of Isaac Newton Parker provide an excellent glimpse of Iroquois life during the Civil War. Unlike his famous brother General Ely S. Parker, Newt, as he called himself, was not in a lofty position at Grant's headquarters. He was a third sergeant and color-bearer of the Tuscarora Company, which contained twenty-four other Iroquois volunteers, and his writings reflect the common foot soldier's perspective of army life and the Civil War.[1]

Yet Newt was no ordinary man. Born in 1833, he was the son of Chief William Parker, Jo-no-es-sto-wa, a leading Seneca who had been wounded in battle in the War of 1812. His mother, Elizabeth Johnson, Ga-out-gwut-twus, was the niece of Jimmy Johnson, the major disciple of Handsome Lake. Newt was the second youngest child of six brothers and a sister. Moreover, he had been well-educated in the Seneca world of Tonawanda, reservation schools, and the New York State Normal School at Albany. Before his enlistment in the war, he had been a farmer and a teacher and had traveled extensively throughout the eastern half of the United States as an entertainer in a troupe with his brother Nicholson.[2]

With his brothers Ely and Nicholson and their attorney John Martindale, he had spent considerable time in the 1850s fighting to regain the Tonawanda Indian Reservation from the clutches of the Ogden Land Company. He had also aided the noted Lewis Henry Morgan, father of American anthropology, in his ground-breaking ethnographic study *The League of the Ho-de-no-sau-nee, or Iroquois* (1851).[3]

Newt Parker, however, was a "black sheep" of his famous family. According to Arthur C. Parker, his grand-nephew, Newt Parker received a

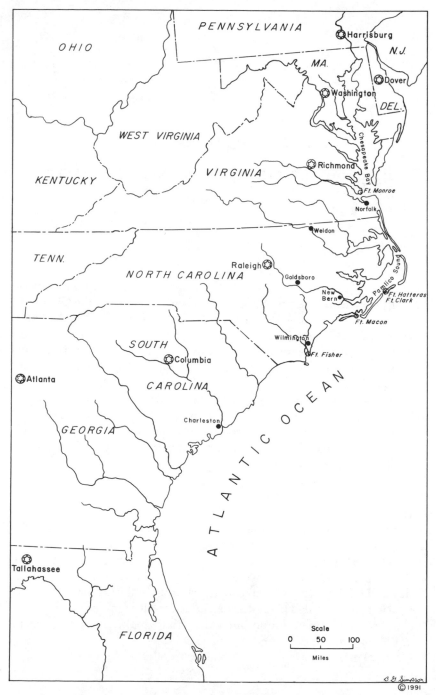

2. The Military Operations of the Tuscarora Company, 1864,
based on a map by George Annand.

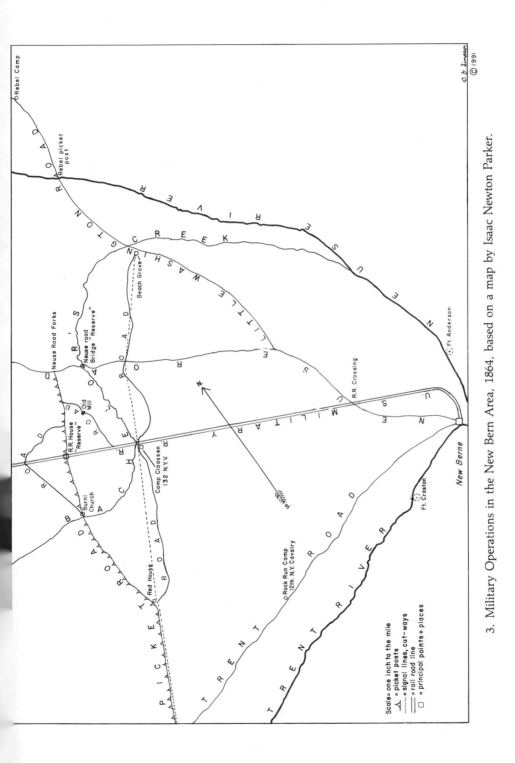

3. Military Operations in the New Bern Area, 1864, based on a map by Isaac Newton Parker.

"polished education" and was a "keen student of fine literature," but he had a drinking problem that "brought with it unreliability" and hindered his success in life. In the 1850s, his amorous escapades, his wanderlust, and the ne'er-do-well side of his character proved embarrassing to his family.[4] Despite his checkered career, Parker was a keen observer of the Civil War. He served as the scribe, the resident intellectual, as well as the "Indian trickster" of the Tuscarora Company.

The twenty-five Indians who served in the Tuscarora Company were recruited from May 12 to August 26, 1862. All were credited to Cusick's or Jemison's efforts. From their dates of enlistment, it is clear that they joined in clusters, on or just off their reservation communities at Lewiston, Suspension Bridge (Niagara Falls), or in Buffalo. Seven men from the Cattaraugus Indian Reservation volunteered on the same day, May 24, 1862. Isaac Newton Parker and two other Senecas — Benjamin Jonas of Cattaraugus and Henry Sundown of Tonawanda — volunteered on June 18, 1862 at Buffalo (see Chart 2).

The D Company of the 132d New York State Volunteer Infantry came into existence when the 53d New York State Volunteer Infantry was disbanded in the late spring of 1862. Although referred to as the Tuscarora Company, it contained more Germans than Iroquois and had four times as many Senecas as Tuscaroras. Despite its polyglot nature, it is clear from Parker's letters that the men of the company bonded together as a fighting unit and there was little, if any, race discrimination directed toward the Indians. Newt Parker's comments reflected regimental pride. On August 15, 1863, he wrote: "We commenced our (apparent) good name in N.Y. The N.Y. press praised us as in fact of being the best regiment of General Spinola's Brigade and second to none of the N.Y. City regiments that had then left for the seat of war." He noted that the regiment "kept ascending the ladder of fame slow, but apparant sure." Parker proudly told his sister-in-law that the 132d "are the exterior out post from and the key to Newbern which in a military phrase is called a post-of-honor, that is, a post of the highest trust entrusted to a body of soldiers in active campaign."[5]

After receiving assurances that they would receive a $25 bounty, a $2 premium, and a month's pay of $13 for enlisting, the twenty-five Indians were sent to Camp Scrogg in New York City. There they trained on the parade grounds and received regimental inspection. When their payment was delayed, Colonel Claassen, with the fervent patriotism typical of the early Civil War, told his troops to stop complaining but to go out and "defend the lives of thousands — the *Union* and the *Constitution*." Although

Claassen's rhetoric was meant to stir the men, Parker saw it more in religious terms. As a Seneca Indian influenced by the famous Presbyterian missionary Asher Wright, who is mentioned affectionately in his letters, Parker expressed his moral commitment to help the Union cause: "In this, it's a country's call to save a country in danger — and to wipe away Devilism & Rebelism — having *God* for our shield, our protector, and our spiritual adviser."[6]

On September 28, 1862, the 132d New York State Volunteer Infantry was sent to Washington. On October 4, the Indians were mustered into service for three years and sent to Suffolk, Virginia, for duty at Camp Hoffman at Fortress Monroe under General John Peck of Syracuse, New York. Parker, who had enlisted for "3 years or sooner shot," served in a variety of positions. He was assigned to headquarters, serving as a copyist, then was "promoted" to orderly sergeant, which meant camp duty, not picket posting, and "lying in my tent wallowing over in my perspiration."[7] Finally, he was made sergeant color-bearer, which was a dangerous position because the Confederate forces always shot at the color-bearer to prevent Union advance. One of the greatest threats to his life during the Civil War, however, occurred when a Union storehouse of mines accidentally exploded, killing thirty-five men in the 132d New York State Volunteer Infantry and throwing Parker nearly fifty feet.[8]

In December 1862, Parker was assigned to the signal corps to "talk on the fields of battle by means of flags." He noted that "it is not the regular American flag, but it is a flag made expressly for [a] signal flag. In the field of battle, I am to be with the Genl and whatever he commands, I am to transmit his commands to the Cols of the different Regts in the Brigade by means of signal flags." Later in the war, Parker wrote that he liked "to learn something new every day in the way of doing business in the army and of tactics, and of the life *out* and *in* camp, in garrison, in the field and on the march."[9] The war was to give Parker a cram course in the geography of the Upper South.

At Christmas in 1862, the 132d New York State Volunteers and the entire brigade were ordered to prepare to leave Fortress Monroe for North Carolina. Under a cloak of secrecy, the regiment was ordered to New Bern, North Carolina, a major railroad terminus that had been captured by General Ambrose Burnside and his Union forces in an amphibious landing nine months earlier. The troops were moved by steamer. On board ship, they faced a major storm that stranded them on a sandbar, caused them to be lost on several different occasions, and resulted in twenty additional miles of passage. The regiment made up lost time in a series of

CHART 2

D Company, 132d New York State Volunteer Infantry: The Iroquois Indians of the Tuscarora Company

Name	Rank	Age	Height	Occupation	Joined for Duty and Enrolled			Term	Discharge
					When	Where	By Whom Enrolled		
Bailey, Smith	pvt.	23	5'5"	farmer	7/22/1862	Buffalo	C. C. Cusick	3 years	6/29/1865
Cusick, Cornelius C.	lieut.	27	5'7"	farmer	5/12/1862	New York City	Col. Buckingham	3 years	6/29/1865
Garlow, George	pvt.	32	5'7"	farmer/musician	5/31/1862	Lewiston	C. C. Cusick	3 years	5/25/1865
Green, Edward	pvt.	23	5'5"	farmer	6/28/1862	Buffalo	C. C. Cusick	3 years	Disability discharge 9/15/1863
Halfwhite, James	pvt.	25	5'9"	farmer	5/24/1862	Cattaraugus	C. C. Jemison	3 years	5/25/1865
Hudson, Foster	sgt.	23	5'7"	farmer	5/24/1862	Cattaraugus	C. C. Jemison	3 years	Shot Jackson's Mills, N.C.; died
Isaacs, Samuel G.	pvt.	26	6'1"	farmer	5/24/1862	Cattaraugus	C. C. Jemison	3 years	5/25/1865
Jacobs, Hewlitt	pvt.	20	5'6"	farmer	5/31/1862	Lewiston	C. C. Cusick	3 years	5/25/1865
Jameson, Cyrus	cpl.	27	5'10"	farmer	6/24/1862	Buffalo	C. C. Cusick	3 years	Transferred to U.S. Navy
Jameson, George W.	pvt.	23	6'1"	farmer	5/24/1862	Cattaraugus	C. C. Jemison	3 years	5/25/1865
Jameson, Jesse	pvt.	22	5'8"	farmer	7/22/1862	Buffalo	C. C. Cusick	3 years	6/29/1865
Jonas, Benjamin	pvt.	27	5'9"	farmer	6/18/1862	Buffalo	C. C. Cusick	3 years	6/29/1865
Kennedy, William	pvt.	19	5'4"	farmer	7/16/1862	Buffalo	C. C. Cusick	3 years	Died at Andersonville Prison of scorbutus 9/27/1864

Continued on next page

Chart 2—*Continued*

Name	Rank	Age	Height	Occupation	Wher:	Where	By Whom Enrolled	Term	Discharge
						Joined for Duty and Enrolled			
Mason, William	pvt.	18	5'3"	farmer	6/13/1862	Tonawanda	C. C. Cusick	3 years	6/29/1865
Moore, Charles	pvt.	35	62"	farmer	6/13/1862	Cattaraugus	C. C. Cusick	3 years	6/29/1865
Parker, Isaac Newton	sgt.	29	5'8"	farmer	6/18/1862	Buffalo	C. C. Cusick	3 years	6/29/1865
Peters, Jeremiah (Jerry)	pvt.	21	5'7"	farmer	6/1/1862	Lewiston	C. C. Cusick	3 years	—
Peters, John	pvt.	22	5'3"	farmer	5/31/1862	Buffalo	C. C. Cusick	3 years	5/25/1865
Powles, Abram	cpl.	26	5'9"	farmer	8/26/1862	New York City	Capt. A. W. Smith	3 years	6/29/1865
Redeye, Martin	pvt.	25	5'8"	carpenter	7/22/1862	Buffalo	C. C. Cusick	3 years	Disability discharge 3/26/1863
Snow, George	pvt.	32	6'	farmer	5/24/1862	Cattaraugus	C. C. Jemison	3 years	5/25/1865
Sundown, Henry	pvt.	24	5'8"	farmer	6/18/1862	Buffalo	C. C. Cusick	3 years	6/29/1865
Titus, John	pvt.	22	5'9"	farmer	7/22/1862	Buffalo	C. C. Cusick	3 years	6/29/1865
Warmee, Jacob	pvt.	38	6'	farmer	5/24/1862	Cattaraugus	C. C. Jemison	3 years	5/25/1865
Wilson, George	pvt.	34	5'10"	farmer	5/24/1862	Cattaraugus	C. C. Jemison	3 years	5/25/1862

Source: Descriptive Muster Rolls, NA and NYSA, and Iroquois community records.

forced marches through low-lying terrain. The three-day adventure totaled sixty-eight miles, leading Parker to calculate proudly that his regiment out-shone the *"Army of the Potomac,"* which averaged only some "4 to 8 miles a day."[10]

Throughout the expedition, Parker carefully observed the route, not-ing disappointedly: "No Indians on the entire route." His comments reveal that army life and Indian identity were not mutually exclusive in the Civil War era. His sense of Indianness was not lost after a half-year of military service.[11]

In mid-January 1863, the 132d was transferred from Spinola's brigade to the 2d Brigade commanded by General James Jourdan. The brigade was headquartered about one-half mile southwest of the city of New Bern on a fifty-acre cornfield. D Company fronted on Trent Road, and the center of the field was used for "squad drills and our Dress Parades." The area was surrounded by swamps that served, in Parker's words, as "company sinks." Parker noted that six or seven married Irish immigrant women served the brigade, presumably as cooks and seamstresses. Camp life of the 132d in North Carolina included parade drills, forced marches with little conse-quence through ankle-deep mud, delayed payment, and rumors, as well as dreams of leave and a brief return to a loved one's arms.[12]

Work details relieved both the anxiety and the monotony of army life. While guarding the rails, Parker recounted how his men, in makeshift fash-ion, mounted a two-rifle iron Parrott gun on a boxcar on wheels, which he humorously called their "Monitor," for the famous Union ironclad. In the fall of 1863, Parker described how his men worked at building winter quarters, raising small logs, "clotting the chinks with clay," and construct-ing a chimney.[13]

Some of the Indians in the company received acclaim for their special skills. Although Parker is rarely mentioned in the regiment's official rec-ord, many of his Iroquois colleagues are cited in the Tuscarora Company's morning reports. Private Samuel G. Isaacs, known as "Big Ike" because he towered over all but one of the Indians, was the most frequently men-tioned of the volunteers. He was such an accurate sharpshooter using the telescopic sight on his rifle that he picked off an entire Confederate gun battery that had pinned down his company. In February 1863, the morn-ing report noted that "Sam Isaacs made the best target-shot yet made in the company." Later, he and James Halfwhite were detailed to "pioneer duty," a hazardous assignment that required the Indians to serve as rail-road track construction and repair workers with their backs to the enemy at the front. In February 1864, Isaacs was cited for being "Brave and manly" while "under heavy fire of the enemy" at the Battle of Batchelder's Creek.

By the summer of 1864, Isaacs had returned from "Detached service" and was soon detailed to serve as a scout.[14]

Another Indian, Abram Powlis (Powles) from the Onondaga Reservation, became well-known for his skill as a scout. He was frequently permitted to venture well beyond the New Bern area, cross the Neuse River, and even visit the Confederate army camp commanded by one Major Whitford. Powlis was "accorded immunities by the enemy; he was free to come and go, and had the freedom of the country beyond our lines. He was truthful, brave and loyal, was a useful and honorable scout."[15]

The camp had another, more pleasant side than soldiering. Despite the macabre conditions of war, the camp had a bowling alley and theater. Anxiety about the war was broken by parties and entertainment. On one occasion, Parker reported the visit of "Negro singers or minstrels, 3 violins, banjo, 1 tambourine and a bass violin who performed for the troops." On another occasion, troops came together to honor their captain, Thomas Green, with a party and the presentation of a "gold watch with a silk guard clasped with a gold slide" worth $140, which had been raised by company subscription.[16]

At other times, the tension of war was broken by brawling. On four separate occasions, Indians found themselves in the stockade for such extracurricular activities. George Jameson and John Peters were temporarily confined in 1863. Cyrus Jameson, Henry Sundown, and John Titus were sentenced in March of the same year to "20 days hard labor," but their crime must have been minor because they were released after only one day. George O. Garlow, who was absent without leave but soon returned, was also punished with a short stay in confinement.[17]

The all-pervasive fear of death bonded Indian and German troops in the company. Fear led Parker to ask his sister-in-law for "encouragement" and empathy for a soldier who is "battling the storm and front of a rebellion such as any *enlightened* nation never saw." In August 1863, this constant fear led Parker to observe: "Death reigns amongst us. He sways his sceptre of death in our ranks, regardless of positions."[18] Two Senecas in the Tuscarora Company—Foster J. Hudson and William Kennedy—were killed in the war. Other Indian soldiers suffered from recurring illnesses. Martin Redeye, who had earlier served in the 57th Pennsylvania Volunteers, was discharged with a disability less than a year after enlisting in D Company. Jerry Peters suffered throughout his three-year military service and was in and out of the major Union hospital at Fortress Monroe.[19] On several different occasions, Newt Parker reported about the progress of his own illnesses and those of his men, whom he called the "victims of the southern clime."[20]

Battlefield casualties and camp illnesses were not peculiar to the Indians in the company. After the Battle of Batchelder's Creek in February 1864, Parker empathically reflected on the gruesome death of First Lieutenant Arnold Zenette, the acting quartermaster of the Tuscarora Company, describing it in grisly detail. "The Rebs burried him after stripping the body to its very cotton knit-shirt. He had on a splendid suit of clothes [and] fine silver watch, high boots, $7.00 woolen shirt—and all your [illegible] except the shirt, and burried with *toes* and *hands sticking* out of the ground, and all *crampt* up at that."[21]

Parker also had personal fears and misfortunes that weighed on him heavily. Both his father and mother died while he was away at war. Although he received a furlough to Buffalo to attend his father's last rites, his earlier letters reflect concern for his parents' failing health and his distance from them. Equally if not more vexing was his separation from his wife, Sara Jemison. As the war continued, their relationship became increasingly strained. Newt, who corresponded frequently, was chagrined at not receiving letters from his wife. On two occasions, he blamed her failing eyesight and illness for her failure to write. On another occasion, he accused "somebody on the Res," no doubt a reference to an Indian trickster "who is playing a *dead beat* upon our letters, making good use of *these, his* or *her* long fingers in cabbaging us." The strain was evident by the early months of 1863, when Parker ended his letters "From Your Dear Husband I. N. Parker," instead of his usual "From Your Newt."[22] By the spring of 1864, Parker was writing to other relatives as often as to his wife. Although Parker's wartime correspondence, with the exception of one letter, ended in June 1864, after the war he married a Cherokee and lived in Indian Territory. The fate of his wife, Sara, after 1864 remains a mystery.[23]

Parker was homesick for reasons unrelated to family. Army life required precision, and his valued imported German watch was in disrepair in 1863. Disliking not having a proper working timepiece, he sent the watch for fixing to his wife in Buffalo because North Carolinian watch repairers were like the "unfinished apprentices of our northern cities." He claimed that some did not even know "the difference between a 'balance wheel' and mainspring." He also pointed out that a "large class" of the civilian population "tagging after the federal army" were simply "money suckers" taking advantage of Union soldiers.[24]

By the fall of 1863, Parker's enthusiasm for military service had cooled. When Cusick returned from furlough and brought news from the Cattaraugus Reservation, Parker's changed attitude became apparent. Parker's sister Caroline informed him that an Indian named Ed Green had reenlisted for military service. Parker, increasingly discouraged by service, the distance from Tonawanda, and the lack of letters from his wife, reacted by labeling Green a "Great Fool," who must have reenlisted "for money I reckon." After being promoted to "Sergeant Color Bearer" on December 20, 1863, and once again receiving letters from his wife, Parker rebounded, his spirits rose, at least temporarily.[25] Parker's later attempts to secure a commission as captain failed despite a personal recommendation from Lewis Henry Morgan praising Parker's character, leadership qualities, and pedigree, which Morgan forwarded to General Benjamin Butler.[26]

Parker differentiated enemy Confederates from the general populace of the South. Enemy "rebs" were capable of any atrocity:

> I have found out to my dreaded satisfaction what will become of me, if I ever fall into the hands of the enemy — either with a whole skin or in a wounded state. Neither will help me. If I am captured "whole," *the first* thing will be they (the captors) will demand and if I don't accede, they will take every thing of any value, in money and articles, off from my person and then they will conduct me to the "rear" of their forces — If the Enemy should find me on the field in a wounded state, unable to help myself they will riffle me of every thing about me, and either leave me to die, or take me to the "rear," or, and which is the worst of all, either dispatch me to the "unknown regions" — to which place, I might not be in none to much hurry to go to — Or, and which is the last of all, if I am shot dead upon the field, and the Enemy gets to me, they will take *every thing* down to my shirt.[27]

He viewed local North Carolinians as thoughtful, friendly people who served the Union army's needs as cooks, seamstresses, and grocers. The state of North Carolina was a hotbed of dissent in the Confederacy during much of the fighting of the Civil War. When Parker was "perfectly tired of government rations," he visited "two good families" on Batchelder's Creek, where he would "invariably partake of a good hearty meal and it would be four times out of six that I wouldn't be charged anything at all." After asking that his sister send him his moccasins to relieve the suffering from his "heavy government shoes" that were "unbearable" during the hot summer months, Parker made an unusual request. He asked his sister to send him two Iroquois pudding sticks and two ladles, which he planned to give as presents to these local families.[28]

At the Battle of Batchelder's Creek, Union forces, composed of the 99th and 132d New York State Volunteers and 12th New York State Cavalry, faced a Confederate three-pronged attack. Under the command of Colonel Peter J. Claassen, the Union forces held their ground until the

Confederates brought up their artillery pieces. At 2:30 A.M. on February 1, the Confederates launched their surprise attack against the Union picket post holding access to Batchelder's Creek on the Neuse Road Bridge. Claassen described the heroism of the Indians of the Tuscarora Company in the ensuing engagement:

> I found it so foggy that signals could not be used. I dispatched Company D. One hundred and thirty-second New York, Capt. Thomas R. Green commanding, double-quick to the Neuse Road bridge. First, Lieut. Abram P. Haring, of the One hundred and thirty-second New York, commanded at the time of attack the reserve at the Neuse bridge, consisting of 11 men, who heroically held that all-important point for over one hour against thousands of the enemy. Captain Green arriving while Lieutenant Haring was firing his last round of ammunition. Company D threw themselves (composed mostly of Indians) promptly behind the breastworks, and did so effectually resist the enemy that they (the enemy) had to bring up artillery.[29]

The Indians as well as Company D as a whole paid a heavy price. Union forces had to fall back after setting fire to their own camp. They also suffered five deaths, six wounded, and eighty captured.[30] Newt Parker, in shorthand fashion, described the intensity of the fighting in the pitch-pine timberlands interspersed with swamps:

> On February 1st 1864 — Fight — the most fighting was at the "Neuse Road Bridge" from 2:30 till 9:30 a.m. They drove us down the road and R.R. like hot cakes. Our train ran their battery at the R.R. crossing. The Enemy came down the "Neuse" and Trent *roads.* — On the 3rd the little garrison at "Beech Grove" surrendered. Kennedy boy with them. Along *all* the *rivers* and *creeks* it is very *swampy* and all the *open* places on the map is *pitch pine timber* interspersed with *swamps* come large and small — so that it is impassible for troops.[31]

William Kennedy, a nineteen-year-old Seneca lad who was captured on the battlefield, later died in Andersonville Prison.[32] We know little of his experiences as a prisoner of war in this Confederate hell except for his twelve-day stay in the hospital; however, we do have a description of the death of John B. Williams, another Iroquois Indian and a member of the 24th New York State Cavalry, who was captured at Cold Harbor in June 1864 and sent to Andersonville. Sergeant Daniel G. Kelley of Buffalo described the camp's miserable, overcrowded conditions, the stench, the putrid water and food, and the "maggots crawling in the mouths and ears of living men." He then described the death of his trusted Indian comrade from western New York:

> At the time of his [Williams'] capture, he was a strong, hearty man, but having neither blanket or shelter, and being constantly exposed to the sun and rain, wore heavily on his constitution. His feet became swollen, and his form wasted to a mere skeleton.
>
> At last I lost sight of him, and did not see him for two days. Becoming alarmed about his absence, I went to look for him, and found him in the valley, by the brook, unable to walk or stand alone, so I procured assistance and took him back to his detachment. During the two days of his absence he had not tasted food. I found him on the 24th of August, and from that time till his death I took care of him.
>
> The 25th and 26th of August were extremely hot, and he lay with a burning fever exposed to the sun and unable to move, only as I helped him. He had no appetite, and not till I strongly urged him, would he eat a little poor corn bread, which was the best I had, or could procure for him.
>
> How many times during those two long days did I pour cold water on his fevered brow, and give him of the same to drink. How many times during those two long days of countless suffering, did he speak of him and loved ones. Of the father who had guided him with gentle hand, instructing him in the ways of honor, integrity and manhood; of the mother who had early taught him to remember his Creator in the days of his youth; of the kind, loving woman he had chosen to be the companion of his life, and the childish prattle of the little one he should never more behold. Yes, it was sad to stand by the side of him whose life was thus passing away in a rebel prison, far from all that he held dear on earth, and hear him speak of loved ones and the comforts of home and be able to administer no relief for his sufferings. But they were destined to be of short duration, for, on the morning of the 27th of August, he expired, after giving me messages to carry to his kindred.[33]

Despite his youth, Kennedy, like Williams, left a widow behind as well as a widowed mother who was dependent on her son's military pay.

Newt Parker's correspondence to his family ends after a skirmish at Jackson's Mills, North Carolina, in the third week of June 1864. The Tuscarora Company's last major encounter with Confederate forces occurred on March 7–10, 1865, at Wise Fork's, North Carolina. One of the casualties at the skirmish was Foster J. Hudson, seventh sergeant of the company and a Seneca Indian from the Cattaraugus Reservation. Parker was the one who conveyed the bad news to his fellow Senecas, perhaps because of his education, literary skills, and prominent family. He graphically described Hudson's death. On March 7, 1865, his Seneca comrade was shot in the left knee joint at Jackson's Mills. When he lay wounded, Confederate soldiers robbed him of his watch. D Company then recaptured him, and he was sent to the military hospital at New Bern, where the military surgeons amputated his left leg "half way up the thigh" because the bullet was lodged deep in the joint. Hudson died on March 23 of a hemorrhage.[34]

Instead of writing directly to Hudson's mother, Parker wrote to Asher Wright, the trusted Presbyterian missionary, asking the clergyman to convey the sad news to his mother, Louisa Hudson. After describing how the soldier died and mentioning that Captain Thomas Green of his company would forward Hudson's few possessions, Parker compassionately wrote, "Please tell the bereaved mother that Foster was respected & beloved by all in the regiment and especially by those who knew him best & his loss is deeply mourned and more particularly in the company of which he was an Acting Orderly—His loss is deeply & sincerely felt and I can assert with much assurance that our sympathies & prayers are with her. Look up to God who *giveth* & taketh away."[35] Thus, eight days before Lee's surrender at Appomattox, Senecas were paying the price of war with their lives.

Isaac Newton Parker and eight other Iroquois of the Tuscarora Company were mustered out of service on June 29, 1865. Benjamin Jonas and Henry Sundown, who had volunteered with Parker at Buffalo on the same day in 1862, left service together. Nine other Indian members of the Tuscarora Company had been mustered out a month earlier (see Chart 2). Although there were between twenty-eight and thirty deserters in Company D during the Civil War, only one Indian was among them.[36] Much of the credit for the Indians' excellent record belongs to Lieutenant Cornelius C. Cusick, the military leader of this remarkable company of Iroquois.

Isaac Newton Parker's post–Civil War existence is shrouded in mystery. He frequently sought out his brother Ely's help for employment or a special favor. After the Civil War, he challenged the power of the Tonawanda Council of Chiefs and soon found himself out of favor on the reservation. Although offered a military commission in the regular army at war's end, Parker went west as a teacher. He later married for the second time, wedding a Cherokee woman during Reconstruction in Indian Territory. In his last years, Parker worked in Montana, "where he contracted a fatal malady. He fell dead from his horse as he journeyed over the prairie and was buried on the plains near the spot where he died."[37]

Parker's letters reveal much about Indian life in the Union army; however, the story of the Tuscarora Company cannot be told in its entirety without focusing on its extraordinary Iroquois commander, Cornelius C. Cusick.

3

"War Eagle"

LIEUTENANT CORNELIUS C. CUSICK

Lieutenant Cornelius C. Cusick was the most important Iroquois commander of Indian troops during the American Civil War. Ely S. Parker held a higher rank, that of brigadier general, by war's end; however, Parker, unlike Cusick, never led Iroquois soldiers into combat. Because of Cusick's demonstrated leadership abilities, he received a commission in the regular army at the end of the Civil War and served for more than a quarter of a century as an officer on the trans-Mississippi frontier.

Despite being a "peace chief," having been appointed Turtle Clan sachem after the death of his uncle Chief William Chew around 1857, Cusick was the archetype of the classic ambitious war chief who raised war parties in seventeenth- and eighteenth-century forest combat. His leadership was based on his abilities as well as his prestigious lineage, which for decades had been associated with success on the warpath. Warrior volunteers followed him because of these all-important qualities. Known as War Eagle, he was the recognized leader of the Tuscarora Company. It was no coincidence that the commanding officers of the 132d New York State Volunteer Infantry frequently alluded to "Cusick's Indians" and their military prowess during the latter stages of the Civil War and that the Tuscarora oral tradition is filled with references to Cusick's military exploits.[1]

Cusick was born on the Tuscarora Indian Reservation in western New York on August 2, 1835, the son of James and Mary Cusick. His was the most prominent lineage in Tuscarora history. Like the Parker family among the Seneca, the Cusicks were part of a leadership elite who shaped community existence. Cusick's grandfather was Nicholas Kaghnatsho (Cusick),

39

the bodyguard and interpreter for General Marquis de Lafayette, who faithfully served the patriot cause in the American Revolution. Cornelius's father, James Cusick, was the Baptist minister on the Tuscarora Indian Reservation, but because of his leadership of the pro-emigration party and family support for the Treaty of Buffalo Creek, James and his religious efforts fell into disfavor on the reservation during the 1840s. Cornelius C. Cusick's uncle David was a noted scholar, author of *Sketches of Ancient History of the Six Nations,* the "first major work written by an Iroquoian," which was published in 1828.[2] Cusick's grandnephew Clinton Rickard was the founder of the Indian Defense League of North America and a passionate spokesman for Indian treaty and civil rights who fought, until his death in 1971, for the Indians' right of free and unlimited passage across the international boundary between Canada and the United States. His great-grandnephew William Rickard led the unsuccessful fight against Robert Moses's and the New York State Power Authority's condemnation of Tuscarora lands in the 1950s.[3]

Cornelius Cusick belonged to a family tradition directly related to American military service. Clinton Rickard was one of ten soldiers detailed to protect Vice-President Theodore Roosevelt on a visit to Buffalo in 1901. Later, Rickard served with distinction in the United States cavalry during the Philippine insurrection after the Spanish American War. In his autobiography, Rickard described his family's military tradition:

> Many of my ancestors were soldiers and warriors. I was following in this tradition. My great great grandfather was Lieutenant Nicholas Cusick of the Revolutionary War. He took part in the Battle of Saratoga and also served as an interpreter and as bodyguard to General Lafayette. He was one among many of our Indian people who helped these United States achieve their independence. My grandfather's half-brother, Captain Cornelius Cusick, was a professional army man and fought in the Civil War. Also, my father's eldest brother was on guard at the White House the night Lincoln was shot.[4]

Cornelius Cusick was a mediator between cultures. He was a member of the educated leadership elite that has been part of Iroquoian society since the seventeenth century and has served as liaison and broker between the Indian and non-Indian worlds. He spoke eight Indian languages and was recognized in the non-Indian world as an authority on Iroquoian culture, as evidenced by his appointment as assistant director of archaeology and ethnology for the Columbian Exposition in Chicago in 1892.[5] Despite his family's support of the Buffalo Creek Treaty, Cusick apparently was back in favor on the reservation by the Civil War. One source indicates that at the age of twenty-five, Cusick was "installed as a sachem of the Confederacy." Throughout the war and after, his superior officers referred to him as a Tuscarora chief.[6]

In his appeals to federal officials to allow recruitment of "Iroquois warriors" (Cusick's words), he was imitating earlier war chiefs' routes to prestige among his people. The "war path" (Cusick's words) was his route to fame just as earlier Tuscarora warriors served the American government in 1776 and 1812.[7] Because of their strategic location along the Niagara River, which connects Lake Erie and Lake Ontario, the Tuscaroras served the United States as allies during the War of 1812. Three of the thirty-five warriors listed in the records were named Cusick — Joseph, John, and David.[8]

Cornelius Cusick was one of twenty-three Tuscaroras to volunteer for Union service in the American Civil War. In part as a result of Cusick's and Fisk's petitions in the early spring of 1862, Congressman Burt Van Horn of western New York interceded on behalf of the Indians' "right" to serve in the Union army. Seventeen of the twenty-five Iroquois in the Tuscarora Company were credited to Cusick's enlistment efforts.[9]

The records of the 132d New York State Volunteer Infantry reveal very little about Lieutenant Cusick's Union military service before February 1864. A man of dark complexion and five feet seven inches tall, he volunteered on May 12, 1862, and was promoted to first lieutenant on July 1, 1863. It was ironic that Cusick was sent with his warriors in December 1862 to the New Bern area of North Carolina, where they guarded a rail terminus depot at Tuscarora, the precise spot from which his tribesmen had been forced to flee 150 years earlier during the so-called Tuscarora Wars. Despite the paucity of records concerning Cusick in the first half of the war, the Tuscarora lieutenant was to make his mark dramatically from February 1 to June 24, 1864, when the general calm of the New Bern theater of the war was shattered.[10]

In early January 1864, General Robert E. Lee recommended that the Confederate armies march on the Union forces at New Bern. Seeking to capture the "large amounts of provisions and other supplies," Lee informed Confederate president Jefferson Davis about his estimate of Union forces there:

New Berne [*sic*] is defended on the land side by a line of entrenchments from the Neuse to the Trent. A redoubt near the Trent protects that flank, while three or four gun-boats are relied upon to defend the flank on the Neuse. The garrison has been so long unmolested, and experiences such a feeling of security, that it is represented as careless. The gun-boats are small and indifferent and do not keep up a head of steam. A bold party could descend the Neuse in boats at night, capture the gun-boats, and drive the enemy by their aid from the works on that side of the river, while a force should attack them in front.[11]

Lee was also intent on recapturing the railroad at New Bern, which had been guarded by the Tuscarora Company and other Union forces since General Ambrose Burnside's seizure of the area in 1862; however, Lee badly underestimated his enemy's abilities and chose the wrong commander, General George E. Pickett, to lead the strike.

With thirteen thousand men and fourteen navy cutters, General Pickett moved on New Bern on January 30, 1864, dividing his troops into three columns. Confederate General Seth M. Barton and his men were to cross the Trent River near Trenton and proceed on the south side of the river to Brice's Creek below New Bern. He was to take the forts along the Neuse and Trent rivers and then enter New Bern via the railroad bridge, thus preventing Union reinforcement by land or water. Colonels James Dearing and John N. Whitford and their men were to move down the Neuse River and capture Fort Anderson. Generals Robert F. Hoke and Pickett and the remainder of the expeditionary force were to "move down between the Trent and the Neuse, endeavor to surprise the troops on Batchelder's Creek, silence the guns in the star fort and batteries near the Neuse, and penetrate the town in that direction." The Confederate navy was to descend the Neuse, capture Union gunboats, and cooperate with the three Confederate columns.[12]

General Pickett "bungled the New Bern operations," although he shifted blame to Generals Barton and Hoke. Pickett had failed in planning beforehand, underestimating, as Lee did, the task at hand. General Hoke moved quickly to reach Batchelder's Creek before the bridge was taken out by Union forces, but the firing of pickets had warned the Union forces of the enemy's approach. The Union troops then destroyed the bridge to prevent the Confederates' advance. Hoke also failed to capture the Union train and enter the city by rail. Nevertheless, Hoke's men adapted to the circumstances and cut down some trees. Two of Hoke's regiments then crossed over the creek. Despite Union reinforcements, Hoke routed them once his troops crossed Batchelder's Creek. His men then marched to within a mile of New Bern waiting to join Barton's forces.[13]

General Barton's men never reached Hoke. After passing through low swamp country with vast mud holes caused by winter showers, Barton came in view of the enemy's breastworks close to Brice's Creek at 8:00 A.M.

on February 1. Instead of attacking immediately, which might have caught the Union forces by surprise, he ordered a reconnaissance while bringing up his artillery. The reconnaissance found that Union forces were more entrenched than previously thought. Barton concluded, and then reported to General Pickett, that his troops were "unprepared to encounter so serious" and "insurmountable" a defense. In the meantime, Union forces were alerted and their artillery began to hit Barton's position. Pickett then ordered Barton to join the troops before New Bern for an assault on that front. Yet to do so, Barton had to cross the Trent River and retrace his steps, which would have taken more than two days. When Pickett was informed that Barton and his men could not reach him until February 4, Pickett withdrew on February 3 and admitted failure. Although the Union forces suffered more than twice as many casualties — one hundred compared to the Confederate forty-five — the Confederates failed to capture the supplies they so desperately needed and sought.[14]

Cusick's Indians excelled in this battle at Batchelder's Creek and in subsequent military engagements in North Carolina in 1864. Captain Charles G. Smith, the general officer of the day on February 10, 1864, of the 132d New York State Volunteer Infantry, commended Cusick and several other commanders at Batchelder's Creek for their "individual instances of coolness and heroism." After lauding one "Lieutenant Haring" for his bravery in defending the Neuse bridge, Smith added, "In this he [Haring] was nobly seconded by Capt. Thomas B. Green, Lieutenant Cusick, and Companies D and G, with Lieutenants Gearing & Ryan, who were both badly wounded, the respective companies losing heavily."[15] Later, Captain R. Emmett Fiske, also of the New York State Volunteer Infantry, wrote of the fight at Batchelder's Creek: "Lieutenant Cusick with some thirty of his warrior soldiers of his tribe, engaged the rebel advance in a sharp skirmish for several hours and by desperate fighting prevented the dislodgement of the picket reserves and the capture of the outpost camp."[16]

Iroquois veterans of the Battle of Batchelder's Creek had to contend with vicious rumors disparaging their military service for the next thirty-five years. Colonel John N. Whitford and his brother Major Edward Whitford, who were in the command of the 67th North Carolina Volunteer Infantry in the vicinity of New Bern at Beech Grove, North Carolina, later accused the Indians of the 132d New York of "scalping" the Confederate wounded at the Battle of Batchelder's Creek. These efforts to discredit Cusick's troops were finally laid to rest when Hugh Hastings, the New York State historian, published an exposé of the alleged affair in 1897, discounting the accounts as war propaganda because none of the Confederate wounded were left behind on the battlefield. Colonel Claassen once again praised Cusick's Indians for their valor at Batchelder's Creek and other military engagements.[17]

In June 1864, Colonel Claassen's men were sent on an expedition from Batchelder's Creek to the vicinity of Kinston, North Carolina. While on reconnaissance "into the enemy country," Lieutenant Cusick, "leading his Indians in a flank movement, distinguished himself by materially assisting in the capture of the commandant of Kinston, N.C., Col. Foulke [Folk], (6th N.C. Cav.), together with five of his officers and upwards of fifty of his rank & file." The regiment's captain, Thomas B. Green, and his officers and men were cited in the official record for the success of the operation, which was attributed to their "endurance and determination."[18] Claassen later wrote that at Jackson's Mills, North Carolina, Cusick and his "dusky warriors," lying in wait in a "roadside thicket, with instructions to closely guard the rear," trapped the rebels.[19]

The ambitious Tuscarora chief soon began to promote his exploits. Even before the end of the war, his goal was to receive a commission in the regular army. In January 1865, he wrote President Lincoln asking for an appointment as second lieutenant in the regular army. In seeking the promotion, Cusick mentioned that "with the assistance of Colonel John Fisk, late Colonel 2nd NYM Rifles, I sent a petition to the Secretary of War" requesting that Indians be allowed to volunteer. As a result of their efforts, "300 sturdy warriors" took the "war path."[20] The same month, Cusick's colonel, Peter J. Claassen, recommended him for the regular army because of his "soldier qualities," "demonstrated proof of his bravery and courage in action," "upright character, temperate habits and considerable talent." Claassen further stated that "his retention in the military service of the Government would be for the interest of the Country."[21] These early efforts at securing a commission failed; the next year, however, Cusick secured the backing of prominent politicos, who facilitated his securing of a commission. E. L. Porter, the son of General Peter B. Porter, hero of the War of 1812 and former secretary of war, wrote on Cusick's behalf, describing him as "an hereditary chief of the Tuscarora and the grand-son [sic] of a brave man who fought under Washington."[22]

On June 22, 1866, the Tuscarora soldier, who had been mustered out of Civil War service almost exactly a year earlier, received a commission as second lieutenant in the 13th United States Infantry. On August 24, Cusick took the oath of allegiance to "support and defend" the Constitution of the United States and bear "true Faith and Allegiance to the same." Less than a week later, he was on duty in Kentucky. Eight months later, he was transferred to the 31st United States Infantry and sent with his regiment to fight Red Cloud's Lakota warriors in Dakota Territory.[23]

For most of the next quarter-century, Cusick was stationed on the trans-Mississippi frontier. His assignments read like a road map of the Indian wars: Forts Buford, Randall, Rice, Stevenson, Sully, Dakota Territory; Lower Brule Indian Agency; Fort Gibson, Indian Territory; Fort Keogh and Tongue River, Montana Territory; Forts Clark and Duncan, Texas; Fort Lyon, Colorado. As an officer in the frontier army, he was involved in campaigns of conquest and pacification against Plains Indians. Some of his own Tuscarora people resented Cusick's action in fighting other Indian nations. Others perceived him as a great warrior in the Iroquoian tradition. His frontier military service was not without risk. In August 1868, he was wounded in the right shoulder by a Plains Indian war club while fighting the Sioux.[24]

Eight months later, Cusick was transferred to the 22d United States Infantry, rising to the rank of first lieutenant in August 1872 and captain of Company E in January 1888. He served under Nelson A. Miles's command, fighting in the Sioux War of 1876–77 in Montana and Dakota Territory and, once again, was cited for heroism; he also was a participant in the Ute War of the late 1870s. Despite recurring medical problems—gastrointestinal and eye disorders—Cusick served with distinction until his retirement from military service on January 14, 1892.[25] In 1890, his commanding officer, Lieutenant Colonel J. S. Conrad, wrote a summary report of his military service performance in which he described Cusick as "generally conversant with his profession," rating "good" in "attention to duty, conduct and habits, discipline and care of men."[26]

Cusick died of hepatic disease "biliary obstruction," considered to be a service-related gastrointestinal disorder, on January 2, 1904, and was buried with military honors at Old Fort Niagara, only a few miles from his birthplace on the Tuscarora Indian Reservation. He was survived by his widow, Lizzie Barnes, whom he had married in 1879, and at least one child, Alton.[27] His career had led him far from his Tuscarora community; yet his path was not altogether strange to Iroquois warriors who had traveled sizable distances to fight Pawnees and Hurons in the seventeenth century or Cherokees and Ojibwas in the eighteenth century. However paradoxical his career, Cusick had followed a time-honored route to fame: the warpath. Ely S. Parker, a Seneca, was to choose a similar route and achieve even greater fame as a result of his Civil War service and his association with General Ulysses S. Grant.

4

"Grant's Indian"

ELY S. PARKER AT THE BATTLE OF CHATTANOOGA

Ely S. Parker, Newt Parker's brother, had a Civil War experience unlike that of any other Iroquois Indian. After his initial efforts to secure a commission were rejected, Parker finally received a captaincy in the Union army in May 1863. He served as assistant adjutant general, division engineer, and military secretary to General Ulysses S. Grant, whom Parker had known before the outbreak of hostilities. By the end of the war, he had been promoted to brigadier general and served as Grant's scribe, drawing up the articles of surrender which General Robert E. Lee signed on April 9, 1865, at Appomattox Court House. Sylvanus Cadwalader, the war correspondent for the *New York Times* covering General Grant's campaigns, described Parker's role at that fateful event: "The terms [of Lee's surrender] being fully understood and agreed to, were written out in duplicate by Col. E. S. Parker, in whose possession I saw the original, written on yellow manifold paper in 1890."[1]

Parker was no ordinary man in background, intellect, or physical appearance. His great uncle Jimmy Johnson, or Sose-ha-wa, was a nephew of the celebrated Seneca orator Red Jacket and the leading disciple of the great Seneca prophet Handsome Lake. Moreover, it was no coincidence that the Parkers' two-story log homestead at the Tonawanda Reservation became the center of political activity against the Treaty of Buffalo Creek and that Parker, Do-ne-ho-ga-wa, devoted more than a decade of his life to that effort.[2]

Parker's intellect was extraordinary. He was widely versed in both the Indian and non-Indian worlds. He had an encyclopedic mind, acquiring

47

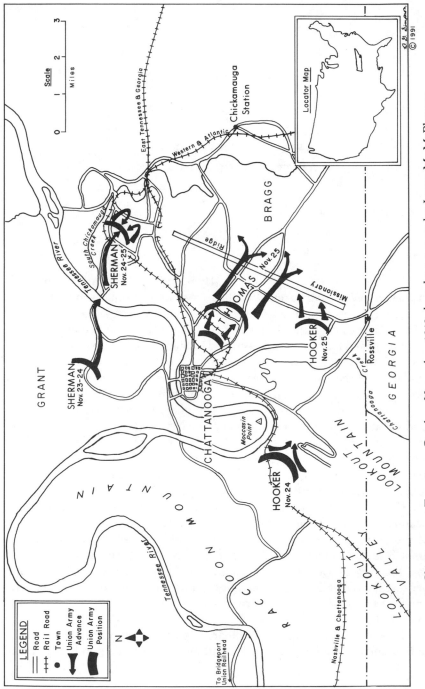

4. Chattanooga, Tennessee, October–November 1863, based on a map by James M. McPherson.

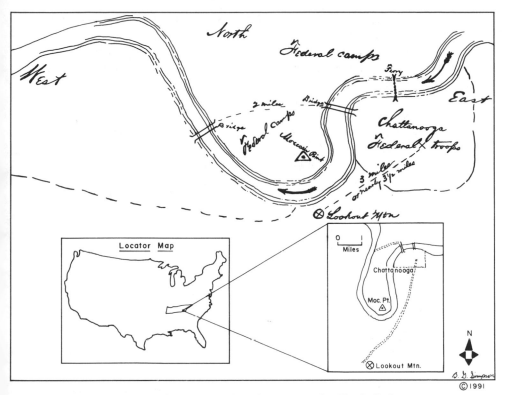

5. Battle of Chattanooga, based on a map by Ely S. Parker.

knowledge of the Gaiiwio or Old Way of Handsome Lake from his great uncle; at the same time, he was a Christian, educated in the new ways of his white teachers at the local Baptist school and Cayuga Academy in Aurora, New York. By the late 1840s, he was reading law at Ellicottville, near the Allegany Indian Reservation, and receiving on-the-job engineering experience on the Genesee Valley Canal. As early as 1853, he was adding to his growing résumé by serving in the New York State militia as a captain of engineers with the Rochester regiment. It is little surprise that this resident reservation intellectual and sachem of the "Great Peace" became the major informant for Lewis Henry Morgan, whom he met in a bookstore in Albany in 1844. Morgan was a welcomed guest at the Parker homestead at Tonawanda and was soon introduced into the rituals and lifeways of the Seneca peoples, which resulted in his publishing the first great ethnography in North America, *The League of the Ho-de-no-sau-nee, or Iroquois,* in 1851.³

Parker was a physically imposing figure. Although he was slightly above average height at five feet eight inches, he carried two hundred pounds on a wide, muscular frame. During the war, he was frequently referred to in camp by officers and enlisted men as "the Indian" or "Grant's Indian," as well as "Big Indian" and "Falstaff." Fluent in English and in several of the Iroquoian languages, he seldom used his lower lip in talking, but rather seemed to talk from his throat. This manner of speaking was because the Seneca language has no labials. Thus, although he spoke English without a trace of an accent, his intonation as well as his physical appearance separated him from Grant's staff and troops. Although Parker had one opportunity to speak Seneca during the war—to Assistant Secretary of War Charles Dana, who had been raised in western New York—his work duties were such that he basically was a lone Indian in a white world, which happened to be at the power center of the Union military command.⁴

At a council at Tonawanda in June 1863, some six hundred Senecas gathered to bid him well in the white man's war. Parker then left to join General John E. Smith's command as division engineer of the 7th Division, 17th Army Corps. By the time he arrived at Smith's headquarters at Vicksburg on July 7, the great battle for that strategic city was over and the Union forces under General Grant had control of the Mississippi River. On September 18, Parker was assigned as assistant adjutant general on Grant's personal military staff, where he largely functioned as an aide-de-camp at headquarters.⁵ For the next two months, Parker's combat experience was limited. All this was to change in November 1863 at Chattanooga, Tennessee.

The city of Chattanooga had considerable strategic value, guarding a gap in the Cumberland Mountains and dominating the Tennessee River. It was also a major railroad terminus connecting two major east-west railroads, thereby serving as a gateway to the rich farmlands of the South and the industry of Atlanta. The Confederates held a seemingly impregnable position along Missionary Ridge, the four-hundred-foot-high garrison along a six-mile front, as well as holding two-thousand-foot-high Lookout Mountain, south of the ridge. General Grant realized that a direct frontal assault on the Confederate positions would be suicidal. General Braxton Bragg's forty-five thousand Confederate forces occupied Missionary Ridge east of the city and had artillery fieldpieces on the top of Lookout Mountain, which commanded approaches to the city from the east and west. Grant, who had been named commander of all Union military departments between the Mississippi and the Appalachians in October

1863, had seventy-seven thousand troops. Grant went to Chattanooga after placing General George Thomas in command of the Army of the Cumberland.

Grant's strategy was to prepare a three-pronged attack: General Joseph Hooker and his three divisions were sent to outflank the Confederates from the south, come over and around Lookout Mountain, cross the intervening valley, and attack Missionary Ridge on the left flank; General William Tecumseh Sherman and his four divisions were to attack the northern end of Missionary Ridge; and General George Thomas was assigned the command of the center to prevent the Confederates from reinforcing their positions. When the plan was finally implemented, Hooker successfully advanced, but Sherman was soon bogged down. Grant then ordered Thomas to advance up the center and take the Confederate rifle positions at the foot of Missionary Ridge. Instead, Thomas's men, much to the surprise of the Union command, advanced all the way to the top of Missionary Ridge, sending Bragg's men in flight. The battle, which included some of the heaviest combat of the war, was marked by skirmishes in heavy fog, broken-down chains of command on both sides, impromptu orders and advances, and substantial slaughter. In the end, Grant could claim a victory that led to his being named supreme commander of all Union forces in March 1864. The battle, along with Union victories at Vicksburg and Gettysburg in the same year, contributed immensely toward the ultimate Northern victory in the Civil War.

Ely Parker described the momentous events from the days just before the battle to two months after the bloody event in great detail. His letters to his older brother Nicholson and his sister Carrie tell much about Parker, his views about Civil War combat, his perceptions of the South, and his observations of white Southerners and black freedmen. Parker's letters often parallel the views of other Union officers during this bloody conflict. Historian Reid Mitchell has accurately observed that Union soldiers saw the South as "unredeemed" and the Southern landscape as "strange and un-American. The Northern soldier in the South felt himself in a bizarre and hostile environment."[6] The same feelings were reflected in Ely Parker's writings. The Seneca officer also presented a Native American perspective of the South and its inhabitants because of his residence on an Iroquois reservation, his prominent Seneca background, his growing up in the era of the Buffalo Creek Treaty, and his knowledge of Native American history.

On November 18, 1863, Parker wrote a revealing letter to Nicholson from Grant's headquarters near Chattanooga, an area which he referred to as a "God forsaken country." Accurately predicting a major battle, Parker insisted that General Bragg's Confederates, the "flower and bulk of the Southern Army," would be wise to flee before the Union forces drove them out of the region. He added that the enemy was "here within speaking distance in one front." Graphically describing the situation, the Seneca officer suggested that Nicholson and others in the North, "who are out of the reach of the noise, excitement, and hardships" of army life, "cannot begin to realize what war is." According to Parker, war was two armies face to face, whose "whole study and object is to destroy one another," with scouting parties, heavy cannonade, and deadly missiles scattering in every direction. He admitted that he was no longer afraid because he had been numbed by the experience and that he could go to "regular battle as calmly as I would go to my meal when hungry." Despite casual references to death, he specified his will and his intentions about the distribution of his property if he fell in battle. He indicated, however, that he had every plan "to come home and settle down once more upon my farm, and go to work as all honest men do."[7]

His letter of November 18 also revealed several other key points. Parker was well-respected and had the rank of captain, but he turned down an offer by General William Smith to remain on Smith's engineering staff. Parker indicated his loyalty to and admiration for Grant in stating that his goal was to provide "services desirable to the best Generals in the Army."[8] Parker then asserted, "As for the common soldier, he does his duty and pays respect to my shoulder straps." Although James Harrison Wilson, the Union army's inspector general, expressed racist sentiments in his writings about Parker, the Seneca officer's words in his letter of November 18 suggest that common soldiers deferred to him and that racial prejudice did not affect his relationship with the troops. Parker's special position as "Grant's Indian" unquestionably led to his acceptance in most situations despite the prejudice of the time.[9]

Parker also indicated that he had been seriously ill and had lost thirty pounds but was recovering on a diet of "beef, bread and coffee 3 times a day." His health was apparently suffering because army conditions forced him to sleep "almost anywhere." This illness was to plague Parker throughout the Battle of Chattanooga and for several months afterward. Although his father's health was in decline, Parker regretfully said he had no money to send home and he was heavily in debt. In concluding his letter, he sent his regards to his family and to Asher and Laura Wright, the respected Presbyterian missionaries to the Senecas. Parker added that he believed that a "great commotion is about to take place among these hills."[10]

In a letter to his sister Caroline on November 21, 1863, Parker first expressed his concern about his father's failing health, the serious crop failures at Tonawanda, his own slow recovery from illness, the treacherous battle terrain of the Cumberland Mountains, and the death of his trusted steed, which he had foolishly lent to a fellow Union officer. Parker then warned that the "rebel army are south, east and west of us. In fact they almost surround us." He drew a map of the city and the position of the Federal troops, suggesting that the "mountainous country and the summits of the mountains are almost inaccessible." According to the Seneca officer, Union and Confederate armies were so close to each other that "our pickets can talk with the rebel pickets." As the Union command often did during the war, Parker seriously underestimated the number of enemy troops, putting them at sixty thousand strong. "They fire us every day with cannon from the top of Lookout Mountain which hangs over our city one-half mile above the plain we occupy." Union guns at Moccasin Point, twelve hundred feet below the Confederates on the mountain, responded in kind, leading Parker to comment: "No day passes that the cannons are not engaged." Although the battle for Chattanooga did not formally begin until several days later, Parker estimated that five or six hundred men had already been killed in the vicinity of the city.[11]

In the same letter, Parker discussed the war's impact on the South and his perceptions of the region and its people. He suggested that rural Southerners "do not live as well or as comfortable as the Tonawanda Indians," not really a surprise after three bloody years of conflict. He insisted that "the negroes, once slaves, of course are all with us and are our servants to pay." He then went on to describe the Southerners' round log country houses, mostly deserted at the time, claiming that "any Indian house is better and more comfortable and cleaner." Parker noted that textiles manufactured in the North before the war were no longer available and that Southern women were wearing "coarse homespun dresses very much like our old-fashioned flannel, usually called domestic flannel." The Seneca officer bemoaned the fate of the South, while chiding Confederate leaders such as General Bragg: "O Carrie! This is a most desolate country, and no human being can realize or comprehend the dreadful devastation and horrors created by war, until they have been in its track." The ruins of war were nearly everywhere. He added that just one hundred miles from Louisville, all that could be seen was "lone chimneys standing where once may have been a fine mansion." Parker believed that only one acre out of one hundred was still being cultivated in this region and weeds dominated the landscape.

As a man of chiefly lineage and Western education, Parker reflected some of the biases common to those of his status. In and around Chattanooga, the Seneca sachem found "only poor 'white trash'" who were "so poor that they can hardly speak the English language" and who have a "blind infatuation" for the Confederate cause. He observed that in other areas of the South blacks were now occupying great mansions and had stripped these homes of their fine mahogany and rosewood furniture to furnish their own cabins. Fine dresses "that white ladies once bedecked themselves with, now hang shabbily upon the ungainly figure of some huge, dilapidated Negro wench," wrote Parker sadly, reflecting both his elitism and his own racist attitudes. Thus Parker, a man of limited wealth who was frequently in debt, identified with the white planter class of the South whose lifeways were being shattered by the American Civil War more than either the lower white classes who largely composed the Confederate armies or the black freedman.[12]

In concluding his letter of November 21, Parker revealed another side of his thinking. He informed his sister that "[we] are here in the ancient homes of the Cherokees, and our present quarters are only about 12 miles from John Ross' old home." To Parker, a Seneca Indian attorney who had resisted emigration west under the Treaty of Buffalo Creek and had fought fervently to win back the Tonawanda lands, Ross, the head of the Cherokee antiremoval party, was a living legend and his homestead was a shrine, worthy of pilgrimage.[13]

There was no time to write during the intensity of the battle, and Parker delayed corresponding to his sister until December 2, one week after the Union victory. "We have had a big fight here, which commenced on the 23rd ult. and lasted 5 days." He recounted the engagement in detail:

> The first day our troops moved on our left towards Missionary Ridge capturing their first line of rifle pits and between 2 and 300 prisoners. The next day we took Lookout Mt'n, capturing from 1500 to 2000 Gray backs. The 3rd day the fighting was terrible because it was a general engagement along the whole line, and every available man and gun upon both sides were brought into use. The length of the line of battle was about 8 miles. The Comd'g Genl and staff occupied a position that overlooked the whole battle. This day we took Missionary Ridge and captured over 40 cannon and 3 or 400 prisoners. It was a most terrific battle. The cannonading was like continuous thunder and the rattle and crash of musketry was deafening and any thing but pleasant—You may have heard of the music of the spheres, which to those who have heard it may be exceedingly pleasant and harmonious, but the music of the screaming shell and the sharp whiz of the bullet are sounds and agreeable or harmonious to a civilized ear. It was the latter kind of music that we listened to the live long day—until long after the shades of night had spread her pall over the bloody battle field—Upon the next day we pursued the re-

treating enemy in 3 lines, Hooker on the right, Thomas in the center and Sherman on the left. Neither Hooker or Thomas did much this day. The enemy's hats being a little too lively for our folks to overtake them — Sherman however overtook their rear guard at Chickamauga Station, on the Chattanooga and Atlanta R.Rd. This place has been a principal supply or provision depot for the rebel army, and large amount of stores had been collected here. This they could not remove because they were pressed for time, and they therefore determined to destroy them the best way they could. They opened sacks of corn meal and emptied them upon the ground, then they opened sacks of shelled corn and emptied that upon the ground until the ground was covered with corn meal about 2 feet deep, and it looked as pretty and white as a snow bank. The distance the ground was covered in this way would reach from our house to Levi's and was 3 to 4 rods in width. Then there were large store houses filled with corn in the ears, and taken all together would make a heap as large and as high as our barn, and these they set fire to. But before they could complete their work of destruction our troops were upon them, and after a very pretty little fight the enemy were driven off. We again overtook them just before sun down about 2 miles this side of Graysville, and had another fight, which lasted until after dark, driving the enemy from his positions as before. Genl Grant and staff then returned to Chattanooga reaching it at 2 o'clock in the morning. After breakfast we again mounted our war steeds and went to our right after Hooker. At noon we overtook him at Ringgold, 20 miles from here. Long before we reached him, the booming of cannon and the rattle of musketry informed us that he was fighting. The enemy had gone through the village and taken a position beyond it; our folks occupied the village, and the enemy were throwing shell, shot and bullets into the village in a perfect storm. We rode through the principal street and almost through the town before we halted. It was very interesting to one's feelings to have the shrill scream of the fearful shell pass near him or to see it explode in his immediate vicinity—The worst of all [of the] shooting is to hear the spark, quick and momentous whiz of the bullets as they pass in showers all around you. It is no use to attempt to come the dodge upon them, for the very act of dodging might cost you your life. The best way is to pay no attention to them, but turning neither to the right or left, we proceed to discharge our duties as soldiers. Our men were severely handled here, but we again drove the enemy and remained over night masters of the field. The next day we rode through the country we had taken over to Graysville and so on home by way of Chickamauga Station—We have captured 7000 of the enemy and wounded and killed probably 4 or 5000 more. We shall also have about 60 or 70 cannon. Of small arms no estimate can be made, for the roads, the sides of the roads, the wells and the creeks are filled with them. Of wagons and harness there are also plenty.[14]

Parker concluded his letter by describing the Confederates' wounding of a fellow staff officer from Batavia, a town only fifteen miles from the Tonawanda Reservation. The officer was struck between the shoulders by a shot from an Enfield rifle, "which passed around his neck, coming out in front of the shoulder joint above the collar bone."[15]

In a letter to his brother Nicholson written from Nashville on January 25, Parker revealed further details about his illness, the Battle of Chattanooga, his impressions about the South, and his admiration for John Ross. His illness nearly resulted in his death because "my pulse apparently died out and my extremities began growing cold." After recovering, he spent four days during the Battle of Chattanooga constantly on horseback, which ultimately led to a major "relapse of the shakes." Parker was "greatly reduced in flesh" as a result of this unidentified but debilitating illness, but he insisted that he had finally recovered and apparently he had no more major health problems during the war.[16]

Parker further elaborated on the Battle of Chattanooga, where the "enemy slaughtered our men dreadfully." Because he was not in General Hooker's first advance, Parker was "compelled to ride more than a ½ a mile under the enemy's fire" to get to Hooker's headquarters. Although the "bullets, shot and shell did whistle fearfully and wickedly all around us," Parker insisted that he "was not in the least alarmed, but on the contrary was at the time greatly pleased at being in the midst of a battle." The Seneca officer admitted that he had become hardened to the immense tragedy of the battlefield with its stacked bodies and putrid smells. "I have at no time experienced any unpleasant sensations in riding over a battle field, among the dead, dying and wounded. I admit that it is a most shocking sight to look upon, but generally we have other and more important matters to think of, that does not permit us to yield to feelings of sympathy and pity."[17]

Iroquois warriors in the beaver wars and wars out of Niagara were taught emotional restraint. Perhaps Parker's stoicism was as much a product of his Seneca heritage as of his Civil War experiences.[18] The war did, however, transform human beings into part of a vast army war machine intent on destruction, not simply winning battles.

Grant's Indian continued to write about John Ross and his Cherokee people in most appreciative terms. He pointed out to Nicholson that Chattanooga was only four miles from Rossville, "the birth place and ancient home of John Ross." In the letter of January 25, he mentioned that he had conversed with many local people who had been associated with the Cherokees "previous to their removal from this country." Parker, whose views had been shaped by his own crusade to win justice for his Tonawanda

Seneca people in the 1840s and 1850s, found Ross a Native American patriot, one worthy of high praise. Referring again to rural white Southerners, he insisted that the farmers of the South "have never at any time been as comfortable or as good houses as our New York Indians. They live here in miserable log or blockhouses with the chimneys stuck on the outside." He added that they made use of "old fashioned fireplaces and sleep upon the floor." Although his remarks betrayed his elitism, Parker acknowledged that some "villages" such as Huntsville, Alabama, were a "great deal handsomer" than Batavia and that other places in the South looked far different and more prosperous than those of the rural South. Yet he blatantly generalized that residents of Southern rural communities "are not as civilized as our Indians."[19]

Thus Parker, like other Union diarists and correspondents in the Civil War, expressed in his writing his own perspective based on his background and education. Not all of Parker's thoughts reflect a cultural relativistic point of view. His comments add to our understanding of Native Americans as well as to the Battle of Chattanooga. Yet his letters reveal more about Seneca thinking than about the military engagement. Memories of the nefarious Treaty of Buffalo Creek haunted Indians. To the Senecas, blood lines determine status, as they do in many societies. During the Civil War, Parker's frame of reference was always Seneca country and the Tonawanda Reservation, and he measured the South and Southerners by those standards, which reflected his affection for the Indian path he had taken in the first half of his life.

Ely S. Parker's life dramatically changed as a result of the Civil War. Remaining in military service, Parker parlayed his military fame at Appomattox and his close association with Grant into a postwar career. Grant served as best man at Parker's wedding to Minnie Sackett, a white woman, in 1867. Two years later, President Grant appointed Parker commissioner of Indian affairs, the first Native American to hold that position. At a time of the so-called Grant peace policy, Parker had unremitting faith in the American military. He favored the unsuccessful attempt to transfer the Bureau of Indian Affairs to the War Department, which antagonized the newly created United States Board of Indian Commissioners, headed by William Welsh, a leading Philadelphia Friend.[20]

Parker soon became caught up in the allegations of corruption that characterized the Grant administration. Parker was accused of and tried for illegally signing private contracts for about four million pounds of beef and large amounts of flour; wasting funds for unnecessary materials, excessive freight rates, and improper tribal allocations; bypassing the Board of Indian Commissioners and violating laws on accounting, advertising, and notification of purchases.[21] Eventually, the House Committee on Appropriations acquitted Parker, finding "no evidence of any pecuniary or personal advantage." Although Parker acknowledged mistakes of judgment, he vehemently denied official wrongdoings and fraud.[22]

Privately blaming Grant for his troubles, Parker left office in disgrace in June 1871. Although he made a significant fortune in business in Connecticut, he lost much of it in the Panic of 1873 and its aftermath. He died two decades later in Fairfield, Connecticut, "an obscure, disabled pensioner with a low-paying minor job in the New York City Police Department," surviving in his later years largely through the favors and handouts from military colleagues on General Grant's staff.[23]

Ironically, in 1871, during Parker's term as commissioner of Indian affairs, the United States government ceased making treaties with the Indian nations. Parker, whose family had led the fight against the Buffalo Creek Treaty and who personally led the fight for the Tonawanda Treaty, had journeyed far down the white man's road. Moreover, as an official advocate of the so-called civilization program from 1869 to 1871, Parker advocated American citizenship for Iroquois and other Indians, which ran counter to Seneca tradition.[24] Although still interested in the welfare of his Seneca people, Parker's direct influence in Tonawanda affairs had largely ended by the early 1870s. Unlike his Tonawanda Seneca contemporary William Jones, an "Ordinary Seaman" in the Union navy, Parker's post–Civil War career was far from his roots.

5

Ordinary Seaman William Jones
in War and Peace

William Jones was a Seneca seaman in the Union navy, serving from August 29, 1864, until his honorable discharge on October 13, 1865. His diary of the 1860s and his Civil War pension record provide a fine portrait of two sides of Iroquois participation in the Civil War: naval combat and postwar adjustment to reservation life. Jones's diary reveals that he was largely monolingual, thinking in Seneca and often reversing his words in English. His diary includes his penmanship lessons in English letters and reveals his struggle to learn a foreign tongue. It also contains his skillful artistic renderings of his adventures as a whaler in the South Pacific.[1]

Jones was born on the Tonawanda Indian Reservation in 1833. In his Civil War pension records, Jones is described as weighing 150 pounds and being between five feet seven and ten inches in height. Unlike most Seneca of the era, he is listed as a laborer, not a farmer. His wife was Maria Skye, although the date of their marriage is uncertain. She certified that she married her husband in December 1860 in a ceremony conducted by the local Presbyterian minister, but at that time, according to his diary, Jones was aboard a whaling ship heading for the Pacific Ocean. Many Seneca had common law marriages at this time so one may surmise that Maria Jones intentionally fabricated the truth to cover up this fact or to facilitate receiving her widow's pension, thus avoiding bureaucratic hurdles. Their marriage lasted over twenty years until William Jones's death in 1882. The couple had one child, Jennie, born in August 1875.[2]

The Senecas and other Iroquoian peoples were long involved in the Euro-American maritime trades. The Seneca Nation's Cattaraugus Reservation borders Lake Erie; the Tuscarora Reservation is adjacent to the Ni-

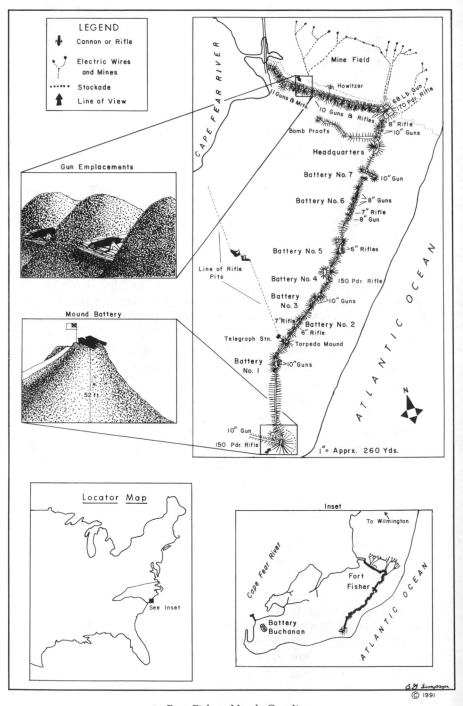

6. Fort Fisher, North Carolina.
Data from Col. William Lamb, Rowena Reed, and the Fort Fisher Historical Site.

agara River, which connects Lake Erie with Lake Ontario; the St. Regis (Akwesasne) Mohawk Reservation is along the St. Lawrence River; and William Jones's Tonawanda Reservation is less than thirty-five miles from both Lake Erie and Lake Ontario. Mohawks served as valuable canoemen for the Hudson Bay Company and in British military expeditions and voyages of exploration in the nineteenth century from the Sudan to the Arctic Circle. Senecas were employees in the Allegheny River logging trade based in Pittsburgh in the years after the American Revolution. Seven Iroquois Indians in Company K of the 57th Pennsylvania Volunteer Infantry listed their occupation as raftsman. Mohawks also served as raftsmen along the St. Lawrence River and on the rivers of the Adirondacks.[3]

The Erie Canal was opened in 1825, and the city of Buffalo was founded six years later. Buffalo soon became a major Great Lakes port with a population exceeding eighty thousand by 1860, making it one of the leading urban centers of the nation.[4] Senecas, Cayugas, and Tuscaroras from nearby reservation communities soon became associated with the Great Lakes trade, serving in capacities from ordinary seamen to pilots. During this period, Iroquois Indians became whalers, as mentioned in a 1982 publication that states that the "son of a nineteenth-century Cattaraugus Seneca whaling crewman preserved his father's collection of scrimshaw."[5]

Jones arrived in New York Harbor in the summer of 1864 after a three-and-a-half-year whaling expedition. On August 29, he enlisted for three years as an ordinary seaman in the Union navy and was assigned to the USS *Ohio.* On October 1, he was transferred to the USS *Rhode Island,* soon shipping out for enemy waters off the South Atlantic coast. Despite his Seneca ancestry, he is identified in the *Rhode Island*'s logbook as a "West Indian-born Negro." His discharge papers identify Jones as a "mulatto." Apparently because of racist perceptions the military improperly classified the dark-skinned, nonwhite sailor.[6]

The *Rhode Island* took part in the successful Union blockade of Confederate ports, which by 1864 had resulted in much travail for the South. Confederate blockade runners were largely stymied except near Wilmington, North Carolina. By December, Jones's ship was off the Carolina coast. Soon Jones and his shipmates were to face the full fury of the most intense naval fighting of the Civil War.[7]

The Union navy's assault on Fort Fisher in December 1864 and January 1865 was to prove the major sea engagement of the Civil War. By mid-December General Robert E. Lee's undermanned and ill-supplied Army of Northern Virginia was in desperate straits, although it managed to hold onto besieged Petersburg and Richmond until the first days of spring 1865. The Confederate Army of Tennessee had been decimated at the battles of

Franklin and Nashville. General William Tecumseh Sherman had captured Atlanta and was carrying out his destructive march to the sea. Thus the Mississippi River and its tributaries, the Gulf of Mexico, and Mobile Bay were fully under Union control. One of the few remaining supply lines for the Confederacy was in and around the port of Wilmington. This port was protected by a network of Confederate forts at the mouth of the Cape Fear twenty miles below the city.[8]

Fort Fisher was the most important of these defenses. The fort, which was known as the Gibraltar of the Confederacy, was a huge earthenwork with seventy-five heavy guns, including two 150-pounders. Fort Fisher was shaped like the letter *L* with the angle pointing to the sea in a northeasterly direction. Union forces had unsuccessfully attempted to seize the fort in the fall of 1864, but formidable defenses and treacherous currents made it an almost impregnable bastion. The fort, which had been built with the aid of black slaves from 1861 to 1864, was one of the "strongest installations in the world" by the time of its completion. With the largest earthenwork in the Confederacy, its horizontal arm extending nearly seven hundred yards across a peninsula, and its superior mound battery with long-range guns, the fort seemed secure. Although it looked impregnable, however, its garrison of fourteen hundred Confederate troops in December 1864 included nearly five hundred junior reserves under the age of sixteen.[9]

The Union's North Atlantic Blockading Squadron was under the command of Rear Admiral David D. Porter, who had prepared for the assault by sending J. S. Bradford of the Coastal Survey to make an extensive beach reconnaissance. The navy planned to open attack on Fort Fisher by blowing up an old steamer, the *Louisiana*, filled with gunpowder, close to the beach off the fort's east angle. After one fiasco after another, the *Louisiana* was blown up off Fort Fisher on December 23. Unfortunately for the Union forces, the 215 tons of gunpowder did not ignite simultaneously but in succession and most did not burn at all. Fort Fisher remained intact.[10]

The *Rhode Island*, along with other Union vessels, began firing on Fort Fisher from its starboard battery at 2:50 P.M. on December 24 and maintained "a brisk and continuous fire" upon the Confederate bastion. After five hours of bombardment, Porter realized that the enemy had been alerted to the attack by the Union's abortive plan and that his ships were too far out of range to do much damage; nevertheless, two crew members of the *Rhode Island* were missing in action and eight were wounded in this first naval engagement. William Jones reported in his diary on the next day, Christmas, that the fighting had died down, presumably because it was "foggy like hell."[11]

The next Union assault on Fort Fisher came on January 14–15, 1865. Ironically, many of the fifty-eight ships in the Union armada carried Native American names—the *Cherokee, Chippewa, Huron, Osceola, Mohican, Pequot, Powhatan, Sassacus, Seneca, Shenandoah, Susquehannah,* and *Tuscarora.*[12] This time, Admiral Porter, calling on his Mexican War experience, conceived of a combined land-sea operation employing his large fleet and ten thousand Union troops. Although the Confederacy had six thousand troops under the command of General Braxton Bragg, the Union efforts were to prove successful. After five hours of bombardment by Union ironclads and two hours by the rest of the fleet, sixteen hundred sailors and four hundred marines made an amphibious landing, along with artillery, other siege guns, and horses, and assaulted the fort's seaward bastions. At the same time, four thousand army troops under General Alfred Terry circled around and swarmed over the fort's rear parapets.[13]

The *Rhode Island* participated in the combined operation. On January 14, the crew engaged in landing troops, horses, and artillery. The next day, they opened fire at 11 A.M. with their starboard battery of seven guns and blasted Fort Fisher for four hours. According to one estimate, the Union fleet used a thousand pounds of metal explosives for every linear yard of the fort. The *Rhode Island*, under the command of Stephen D. Trenchard, used 302 rounds alone, employing 30-pound and 12-pound guns during the battle. Eight of the crew were wounded and two were missing in action. In the bloody hand-to-hand combat that ensued at the fort, the Union suffered 659 casualties, more than the Confederate total of 400 to 500. In capturing the fort, the Union forces seized 112 Confederate commissioned officers, 1,971 enlisted men, 169 artillery pieces, and 2,000 small arms.[14]

Despite the greater number of casualties, the Battle of Fort Fisher was an overwhelming victory for the Union. Bragg was forced to retreat to Wilmington, which was abandoned by the Confederate army on February 21, 1865. Naval historian Rowena Reed has observed that the military engagement at Fort Fisher was successful because the Union had finally abandoned General Henry Halleck's "wasteful and ineffective continental strategy," substituting a "waterborne offensive. By doing so, the Union not only took full advantage of its superior manpower and material resources, but it exploited the Union's command of the sea to bring about the rapid collapse of enemy resistance and the end of the war."[15]

Jones's diary provides a glimpse of the Battle of Fort Fisher. From January 13, 1865, onward, the *Rhode Island* was involved in supply and evacuation off the coast opposite Fort Fisher. On January 15, Jones reported that his ship carried ashore thirty-six mules. He realized that something dramatic was happening: "I think great fight . . . with whole fleet." He reported that by 6:00 P.M. his ship was taking in Confederate prisoners, but that there was still "a hard time" left in the fight. By 7:00 P.M., the fleet had assumed control over substantially more Confederate prisoners. Triumphantly, Jones reported, "At 11 o'clock [we] took the fort." Although slightly over two thousand Confederate enlisted men and officers were captured, Jones's exaggerated estimates were that the Union had seized seven thousand Confederates. He indicated that the Union forces had killed five hundred men, although that was the total number of Confederate casualties.[16]

The events of December 1864 and January 1865 permanently affected William Jones's life. As a result of his exposure to cold and wet while on watch in December 1864, Jones contracted bronchial pneumonia, which was to plague him off and on until his death. Besides "pulmonary consumption," the Seneca sailor was injured in the naval bombardment between the *Rhode Island* and the Confederate steamer *Vixen*. His left side was crushed during one of the salvos that hit his ship. Jones was sent to various naval hospitals after the *Rhode Island* returned to New York Harbor in March 1865. He was eventually released from the United States Naval Hospital in Brooklyn in October, by that time on assignment with the USS *Vermont*. On the thirteenth of the month, Jones was mustered out of the navy with $66.62 in wages. He was awarded an "invalid pension" of $8 per month because of his pulmonary condition; he was described as being "totally disabled from obtaining his subsistence by manual labor."[17]

On October 15, he returned to Iroquoia, traveling for thirteen hours by train from New York City to Syracuse. After a four-hour stopover, he took a one-hour train ride to Batavia. He then traversed the fifteen-mile route, presumably by carriage, from Batavia to Tonawanda, which took approximately four and a half hours. Upon arriving at Tonawanda on October 16 at 5:00 P.M., he wrote, "I step on Indian land and [see] my folks about 6 p.m. Also hear [that] 97 men died [in the past] 3 years. [Left] March 26, 1860. Come home Oct. 15, 1865 [actually October 16]."[18]

Although his diary entries dwell on the weather, Jones's activities over the next four months illustrate the cultural resilience of Seneca identity during this time of travail. The day after his return, Jones participated in Iroquois traditional ceremonies. He took the train to Syracuse, reaching the Onondaga Reservation at midnight. On the morning of October 18, he commented: "I see all [the] Indians." The following two days, Jones participated in Green Corn festivities: "I see Green Corn Dance . . . and [next] morning I see war dance . . . and Six Nation[s] [in] council." Sadly, he noted, "21 men quite drunk." After spending a week at Onondaga, he returned to his father's house at Tonawanda.[19]

In late January and early February 1866, he attended the Seneca Midwinter Ceremony at Newtown Longhouse on the Cattaraugus Indian Reservation. His delight was evident: "I see Indian New Years [with] Big Head[s] [the "uncles" who herald the new year and stir the ashes of the hearths of traditionalists' homes] and [have] fine . . . day." Thus Seneca identity, at least for one sailor, was strong enough to survive the lengthy hunt for the great whale in the South Pacific and the firefight of General Bragg's Confederate forces at Fort Fisher.[20]

In the years following the war, Jones fought a constant battle with the Pension Board to retain his meager annuity. Despite producing witnesses to his infirmities, attending a white physician in Gasport, New York, and relying on "Indian medicines for said consumption," Jones was denied his pension in 1871, when his examining surgeon reported "no evidence of disability." Jones attempted to overturn this decision. In 1880, he was restored to half pension of $4 per month because of a severe cough and bronchial condition that were attributed to his Civil War service.[21] On October 3, 1882, William Jones, apparently totally deaf, was killed while crossing the tracks of the West Shore Railway in the town of Newstead, not far from the Tonawanda Indian Reservation. His wife and surviving daughter received a widow's pension of $8 per month until Maria Jones's death in 1909.[22] The Jones's experiences epitomize the way the Civil War shattered Indian lives and had long-term effects on community existence in Iroquoia.

6

The Oneidas of the
14th Wisconsin Volunteer Infantry

For the Wisconsin Oneidas, the Civil War years were a disaster, ranking next in importance to the Oneida removal to Wisconsin and to allotment under the Dawes General Allotment Act of 1887. Estimates of Oneida enlistment in the Civil War range from 111 to 142 out of approximately 1,100 reservation residents. At least 46 of these volunteers for the Union were killed, missing in action, or died of disease while at war. Two tribal historians estimate that as many as 65 Oneidas were fatalities of the war.[1] Moreover, the Oneida Indian Reservation in Wisconsin was ravaged by a major smallpox epidemic, which raged from November 1864 through March 1865 and claimed 15 tribal members. White communities that suffered in the war were soon replenished with immigrants, but the Wisconsin Oneida Indian community faced a 4- to 5-percent population decline, which had severe and debilitating repercussions well into the future.[2]

In contrast to the Iroquois Indians of D Company of the 132d New York State Volunteer Infantry, who eagerly sought entry into the Union army, most Wisconsin Oneidas were reluctant combatants who were latecomers to military service. Many Oneidas enlisted in late 1863 and early 1864, nearly three years after the conflict had erupted at Fort Sumter; nevertheless, their contributions were extensive.

Reginald Horsman has written that the Oneidas' participation in the Union effort was a logical extension of their past history and worldview: "Most of the Oneidas still thought of themselves as allies rather than enemies of the United States. . . . The Oneidas felt they had a tradition of fighting with the Americans because of their service in the Revolution, and patriotism is a theme that runs through many Oneida petitions and letters

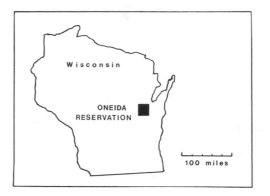

7. The Oneida Indian Reservation in Wisconsin, 1860.

in the nineteenth century."[3] Although Horsman is accurate in his assessment of Oneida pride in past military service, especially in the American Revolution, he ignores a major factor in motivating Civil War enlistment—the bounty system. Going against the advice of some of the chiefs and Episcopal missionary E. A. Goodenough, Oneida youth were enticed by large monetary payments to become loyal recruits for the Union. By October 1863, the federal government provided a $300 bounty for three-year recruits. By early 1864, it was possible for a volunteer to receive even more money in federal, state, and local bounties. Encouraged by bounty brokers working on commission, the Oneida "dirt farmers" from north-central Wisconsin, like other poor country folk, saw the economics of fighting for the Union. M. M. Davis, the United States Indian agent of the Green Bay Agency, wrote to the commissioner of Indian affairs on May 31, 1864. "The Oneidas who have enlisted in the military service have done so of their own free will. They have received Government and local bounties and I have no doubt that they are much better provided for in the service than they have ever been heretofore. The families of these enlisted men are also much better off than heretofore. They already received large bounties and they receive $5 per month from the state."[4]

Oneida reluctance to enter the war was based in part on their history since 1776. They had participated in two other "wars of white brothers"—the American Revolution and the War of 1812—but received little in return. More significantly, they had been lured away from their New York homeland in the three decades following the War of 1812. They had been swindled of their lands by the Ogden Land Company and other land speculators and had been enticed to go west by the machinations of nefarious missionaries such as Eleazar Williams and corrupt Indian agents such as Jaspar Parrish. Although they were proud of their military successes at Oriskany in the American Revolution and at engagements in the War of 1812, they had the bitter memories of frauds such as those perpetrated on them in the Treaty of Buffalo Creek of 1838. Besides the pain of removal, the Oneidas in Wisconsin were a divided people who could not reach consensus throughout much of the nineteenth century. Politically divided into three separate factions from their days in New York—the First and Second Christian and Orchard parties—the Oneidas remained divided in Wisconsin. Leaders of these groups attempted to assert their hereditary rights, chiefs' prerogatives, and other claims to power that they had had in New York, resulting in the continuation of factional behavior. Further contributing to chaos, a sizable number of so-called homeless Indians settled at Oneida after moving west from New York and Canada. The status of these newcomers remained bitterly debated until the tribe accepted them at the end of the nineteenth century.[5]

Intratribal conflict was exacerbated by timber cutting and proposed land sales. By the 1850s, Green Bay and environs had become of prime interest to lumbermen. After the surrounding area was denuded of white pine, lumbermen sought the timber of the nearby Oneida Indian Reservation, which contained sixty-five thousand acres of virgin land. Soon the possibilities of hauling timber for quick cash sales to adjacent white-owned sawmills put new pressures on tribal unity. Individual Oneida entrepreneurs seeking a steady income and tribal leaders protecting the tribal inheritance or feathering their own nests fought it out. The commissioner of Indian affairs reported in 1864: "Greatly to the injury of the common property of this tribe [Oneida], some of its more shiftless members have been engaged, contrary to the direct orders of the agent, issued by direction of this office, in cutting and hauling away for sale much of its valuable timber."[6]

Tribal leaders debated the wisdom of proposed land sales. Oneidas such as Daniel Bread, Jacob Cornelius, Cornelius Hill, and Elijah Skenandore appealed to Washington for assistance. During the height of the Civil War, one group headed by Chief Hill of the First Christian party petitioned President Lincoln, referred to as "the emancipator of slaves and the protector of the oppressed," protesting proposed Wisconsin land sales, including one to the Stockbridge Indians.[7]

Besides intratribal squabbles, there were other reasons for the Oneidas' hesitation to join the Union military effort. From the 1830s onward, some Wisconsinites attempted to remove the Oneidas from their midst. In 1845, Henry Dodge, the territorial governor of Wisconsin, began negotiations with Oneidas to facilitate their removal.[8] At the beginning of the Civil War, Commissioner Dole suggested the consolidation of all the Indians of the Green Bay Agency "onto a single reservation" and the assignment to them of "a proper quantity of land to be held in severalty." In 1863, Dole advocated removal of the Oneidas, in the "best interests of the Indian," to the upper Missouri on lands "obtained from loyal Indians of the Southern Superintendency."[9]

The state of Wisconsin did not immediately seek out Indian recruits for the army, largely because of increasing Indian-white tensions caused by the eruption of the so-called Great Sioux Uprising in neighboring Minnesota in August 1862. Within seven days of the war's inception, 737 white men, women, and children had been killed. The war resulted in the exodus of 40,000 refugees from Minnesota to Wisconsin. Rumors spread that the Santee Sioux and other Indians had burned the Wisconsin communities of Manitowoc and Sheboygan and were advancing to Fond du Lac. Governor Edward S. Salomon of Wisconsin contributed to the hysteria by suggesting that his state's Indian population had been influenced by rebel agents who were in collusion with the Santee. He encouraged the formation of home guards and requested reinforcements from Secretary of War Edwin Stanton. The situation was further exacerbated by the murder of a white woman and the attack on another by Winnebago Indians near New Lisbon, Wisconsin. Indian-white tensions remained high in the state, and Madison authorities continued to talk of Indian removal, especially of the Winnebago, as a solution to the "Indian problem" well into 1863.[10]

The initiation of conscription had a dramatic impact on Oneida life during the Civil War. Although Indians were not United States citizens and hence not eligible for the draft, they were soon to be seen as satisfactory replacements by white individuals, hamlets, towns, communities, and district enrollment boards. In the first year of the war, thousands of new recruits flocked to the Union cause in the flurry of patriotism that surrounded the initial battles. After news of heavy losses at the Union victories at Shiloh and of General George B. McClellan's failure in the Peninsula Campaign, however, recruitment slackened. Consequently, on July 2, 1862, President Lincoln called for 300,000 three-year volunteers, assigning each state a quota based on population. When Northerners failed to respond to patriotic calls for civic duty and enlistment did not reach the desired numbers, Secretary of War Stanton issued a requisition for an additional 300,000 nine-month militiamen under a provision of the Militia Act of July 17, 1862.[11]

On August 4, the secretary of war warned that states failing to reach their quotas would be subject to military conscription and issued a complicated formula intended to put pressure on states such as Wisconsin to stimulate volunteers. On August 8, the secretary ordered the states to enroll all able-bodied citizens between the ages of eighteen and forty-five by districts. If the states did not provide officers, the secretary authorized the governors to appoint them, and the federal government would pay all reasonable expenses. The draft of August 1862 was the first and only draft made by state authorities. All subsequent ones were supervised by the provost marshal general in Washington. Some states allowed drafted men to hire substitutes, while states and localities began the practice of paying bounties of $100 or more to three-year volunteers, "justified" because these men had to leave their families and jobs behind to fight for the Union cause. Although the calls to service during the summer of 1862 produced the requisite numbers in the North, they introduced in Wisconsin as elsewhere a mercenary factor into volunteering that would become worse over time.[12]

In Wisconsin the draft of 1862 and later drafts resulted in massive popular resistance as well as civil disturbances at Green Bay in the late summer of 1862. Belgian-Americans marched on the home of the United States senator, whom they blamed for the Militia Act. He escaped before they exacted their wrath. In Ozankee County, 150 people were arrested after the governor sent in eight companies of militia to quell a riot. The draft in Milwaukee had to be suspended for fear of riot; the draft commissioner was beaten by a mob and his house ransacked.[13]

A worse crisis materialized in 1863. Because fewer and fewer recruits were coming forward, Congress passed the Enrollment Act of March 3, 1863, making every able-bodied male citizen and resident alien who had filed for naturalization aged twenty to forty-five eligible for the draft. Wisconsin was divided into six draft districts, coinciding with congressional districts. Each district acquired a set of federal draft officers — a provost marshal, a commissioner, an examining physician, and a board of enrollment. The enrollment boards were to make up lists of eligible conscripts for military duty, leaving off those they considered exempt on physical or other grounds. Once a man's name was drawn, he had ten days in which to report for duty, furnish a substitute, or buy exemption by paying a $300 fee. The War Department assigned each congressional district a quota based on a percentage of its eligible males minus the number of men who had already served in the army. A district would be given fifty days to fill its quota, and conscription would be a last resort in case of a shortfall after other methods — bounties, substitutions, and commutations — failed to meet the quota.

The bounty system became the chief means of stimulating volunteering. Districts competed for volunteers by offering greater bounties. Wealthier districts enticed men away from their home districts. Although the Enrollment Act contained no occupational exemptions and exempted only the infirm or those who were the sole support of widows, indigent parents, orphan siblings, or motherless children, conscripts were allowed to provide substitutes. This practice led to the enrichment of so-called substitute brokers. A drafted man could also pay a $300 commutation fee which exempted him from that particular draft but not from future drafts. In response to growing criticisms, Congress abolished commutation in July 1864, except for conscientious objectors.

Enrollment in Wisconsin began in May 1863. Before the end of 1863, some Wisconsin counties and municipalities began to offer additional bounties. The War Department continued to pay $300 for new three-year recruits, but volunteers also received a bounty from the localities in which they enlisted, helping fill the quota of that locality. Although the Wisconsin state legislature passed a law in 1864 limiting local bounties to $200, the bounty system paid more to the men who joined the war latest and served the least time.[14]

The area around the Oneida Indian Reservation, Brown and Outagamie counties, was a hotbed of draft resistance in 1862 and 1863. The city of Green Bay, which borders the reservation, was the headquarters for the state's fifth district. Outagamie County was among the five Wisconsin counties most resistant to the draft, and no residents there could be found to serve as enrolling officers. According to historian Eugene C. Murdock, the provost marshal's men "covered most places in the district, but few current names were obtained." The provost marshal conceded that the draft was a failure, and he was forced to secure "names from poll lists, tax lists and from confidential statements of the few loyal men who could be found." Murdock concluded that "Green Bay, Wisconsin, and the rest of Wisconsin's Fifth District, was one of the most difficult areas in the entire country for enrolling officers and draft officials." In two towns in Brown County "the feeling was so strong that not a single man could be found who would even assist the enrollment board in conducting the enrollment." After the provost marshal sent four squads of twenty soldiers to aid in enrollment, potential conscripts fled with their families into the heavily timbered country. The Wisconsin provost marshal as well as local enrollment board members were threatened with assassination in Outagamie and Brown counties. Green Bay area attorneys would lie about age, residence, or use other excuses to get their clients exempted from service. Here as well as in other areas of the state, collusion between brokers and examining surgeons resulted in men in vibrant health being rejected for imaginary infirmities.[15]

Their white neighbors in Brown and Outagamie counties began to view poor Oneida Indians as replacement soldiers. The Indians also saw it as a viable option. From 1860 through 1863, the Oneida economy was in shambles. Agriculture, largely of a subsistence level, had been the basis of the Oneida economy before the Civil War. Oneidas had supplemented their farming with hunting game, fishing in Duck Creek, and gathering wild berries. Leasing land to whites and selling timber became increasingly important. During the early 1860s, the Oneidas suffered two years of drought, were affected by severe winters leading to livestock losses, and even witnessed a June frost. The *Annual Report* of the commissioner of Indian affairs for 1864 indicated that many were destitute and that school-age children did not have clothes to attend the Indian school. Hence, for the Oneidas, military service, despite the risk, became a way out of their desperate economic condition. War bounties and the substantial relief efforts of the Quakers in early 1864 enabled the Oneidas to survive.[16]

Most of the Oneida recruits in late 1863 and early 1864 filled the ranks of existing units. Although a sprinkling of Oneidas joined other units such as the 3d Wisconsin Volunteer Infantry, 49 men joined the 14th Wisconsin Volunteer Infantry, 39 of them assigned to F Company and 10 to G Company. The 14th had served with distinction at the battles of Corinth and Shiloh and during the Vicksburg Campaign. Despite heavy losses in 1862 and 1863, more than two-thirds of the regiment reenlisted on December 11, 1863, making it a veteran unit. To make up for its losses and restore it to its original strength of 970 men, the regiment began enlisting Oneida Indians from December 15, 1863, onward while it was on veteran furlough at Madison, Wisconsin.[17]

The descriptive muster rolls provide a statistical portrait of the Oneidas. Nineteen of the Indians were recruited by Captain C. R. Merrill, the Wisconsin state provost marshal, at Green Bay during a twelve-day period in December 1863 and early January 1864. The Oneidas volunteered for service together, enlisting in clusters of five on December 31, 1863, and six on both January 4 and 7, 1864, at the recruitment office at Green Bay. In addition, twelve Oneidas, recruited by one Captain Phillips, volunteered on March 4, 1864, at Fond du Lac. At least thirty-nine of the Indians gave Oneida, Wisconsin, as their residence. Nearly all of them were credited for enlistment purposes to nearby white communities around the reservation, including DePere, Fort Howard, Green Bay, and Lomira; a few were counted to Wisconsin communities such as Oshkosh and Sheboygan, which are a considerable distance from the Oneida Indian Reservation. The records reveal substantial personal information about the Oneida recruits, all of whom had the rank of private. Nine of the forty-nine were

14th Wisconsin Volunteer Infantry F Company Oneidas

Name	Rank	Occupation	Birthplace	Residence	Age	Marital Status	Height
Antone, Abram	pvt.	farmer	Wisconsin	Oneida	19	unknown	5'7½"
Archiquet, Aaron	pvt.	farmer	Wisconsin	Oneida	18	unknown	5'10½"
Archiquet, John	pvt.	farmer	Wisconsin	Oneida	19	unknown	5'10½"
Archiquet, Solomon	pvt.	farmer	New York	Oneida	40	married	5'11"
Baird, Thomas	pvt.	farmer	Wisconsin	Oneida	40	married	5'5"
Bread, Daniel	pvt.	farmer	Wisconsin	Oneida	22	unknown	5'9"
Chrisjohn, Daniel	pvt.	farmer	Wisconsin	Oneida	25	married	6'
Coulon, Henry	pvt.	farmer	Wisconsin	Oneida	20	unknown	5'9"
Danforth, Cobus F.	pvt.	farmer	Wisconsin	Oneida	18	married	5'10"
Danforth, John	pvt.	farmer	New York	Oneida	46	married	5'10"
Doxtator, Cornelius	pvt.	farmer	New York	Oneida	46	married	5'10"
Doxtator, George S.	pvt.	farmer	Wisconsin	Oneida	29	married	5'10"
Doxtator, Jacob S.	pvt.	laborer	New York	Oneida	36	married	5'7½"
Doxtator, Paul C.	pvt.	farmer	Wisconsin	Green Bay	22	unknown	5'9"
Hill, Abram	pvt.	farmer	Wisconsin	Oneida	20	unknown	5'6½"
Hill, Abram C.	pvt.	farmer	Wisconsin	Oneida	23	unknown	5'11½"
Hill, David	pvt.	farmer	Wisconsin	Oneida	20	unknown	5'8½"
Hill, Henry	pvt.	farmer	Wisconsin	Oneida	19	unknown	5'8"
Hill, Lewis	pvt.	farmer	Wisconsin	Oneida	28	unknown	5'10"
James, Antoine (Anthony)	pvt.	farmer	Wisconsin	Oneida	20	unknown	5'7"
Johnson, Peter	pvt.	farmer	Wisconsin	Oneida	29	unknown	5'9½"

Continued on next page

Chart 3A—*Continued*

Name	Rank	Occupation	Birthplace	Residence	Age	Marital Status	Height
King, Adam	pvt.	farmer	Wisconsin	Oneida	28	unknown	5'8"
King, Nicholas	pvt.	farmer	Wisconsin	Oneida	24	unknown	5'11"
King, Simon	pvt.	farmer	Wisconsin	Oneida	19	married	5'4"
Nimham, Anthony	pvt.	farmer	New York	Oneida	23	married	5'10½"
Nimham, James	pvt.	farmer	Wisconsin	Oneida	19	married	5'11"
Powlas, Anton[y]	pvt.	farmer	Wisconsin	unknown	29	single	5'10"
Powlas (Powless), George	pvt.	farmer	Wisconsin	Oneida	21	single	5'7"
Powlas (Powless), Moses	pvt.	laborer	New York	Oneida	29	married	5'10"
Powlas (Powless), Peter I	pvt.	farmer	Wisconsin	Oneida	32	married	5'9½"
Powlas (Powless), Peter II	pvt.	farmer	Wisconsin	Oneida	24	married	5'11½"
Silas, Abram	pvt.	farmer	Wisconsin	Oneida	22	married	5'6"
Silas, Isaac	pvt.	farmer	Wisconsin	Oneida	23	single	5'6½"
Skenandore, Jacob	pvt.	farmer	Wisconsin	Oneida	21	single	5'6"
Stephens, Henry	pvt.	farmer	New York	Oneida	46	married	6'
Thomas, Thomas	pvt.	farmer	Wisconsin	Oneida	26	single	5'9"
Webster, Augustus	pvt.	farmer	Wisconsin	Oneida	29	married	5'10"
Webster, Edgar E.	pvt.	farmer	De Pere	Lawrence	20	single	5'4"
Webster, Lewis B.	pvt.	farmer	Green Bay	Lawrence	25	single	5'4"

Source: Descriptive Muster Rolls, SHSW and NA, and the records of the Oneida Nation of Indians of Wisconsin.

CHART 3B

14th Wisconsin Volunteer Infantry F Company Oneidas

Name	Enlistment Credited to	Place of Enlistment	Recruiting Officer	Date/Length of Enlistment		Date of Discharge
Antone, Abram	Fort Howard	Green Bay	Capt. E. R. Merrill	1/4/1864	3 years	Died at Vicksburg 6/11/1864 of chronic diarrhea
Archiquet, Aaron	Fort Howard	Green Bay	Capt. E. R. Merrill	1/4/1864	3 years	5/18/1865
Archiquet, John	Sheboygan	Fond du Lac	Capt. Phillips	9/8/1864	3 years	10/19/1865
Archiquet, Solomon	Fort Howard	Green Bay	Capt. E. R. Merrill	3/8/1864	1 year	5/31/1865
Baird, Thomas	Oshkosh	Green Bay	Capt. E. R. Merrill	4/19/1864	3 years	Died at Big Shanty, Ga., 6/16/1864 of typhoid
Bread, Daniel	Lomira	Fond du Lac	Capt. Phillips	3/4/1864	3 years	Disability discharge 10/1865
Chrisjohn, Daniel	Sheboygan	Fond du Lac	Capt. Phillips	3/11/1864	3 years	10/9/1865
Coulon, Henry	Lomira	Fond du Lac	Capt. Phillips	3/4/1864	3 years	10/9/1865
Danforth, Cobus F.	Fort Howard	Green Bay	Capt. E. R. Merrill	1/4/1864	3 years	Died in service 8/24/1864
Danforth, John	Lomira	Fond du Lac	Capt. Phillips	3/5/1864	3 years	10/9/1865
Doxtator, Cornelius	Oakfield	Fond du Lac	Capt. Phillips	2/3/1864	3 years	Deserted 11/30/1864; returned 4/26/1865; Discharge –
Doxtator, George S.	Lomira	Fond du Lac	Capt. Phillips	3/4/1864	3 years	10/9/1865
Doxtator, Jacob S.	Lomira	Fond du Lac	Capt. Phillips	3/4/1864	3 years	Deserted 11/30/1864 Dishonorable discharge 4/16/1869
Doxtator, Paul C.	Lawrence	Green Bay	Capt. E. R. Merrill	1/2/1864	3 years	Deserted 11/23/1864; returned 4/1865 Discharge 10/9/1865
Hill, Abram	Lomira	Fond du Lac	Capt. Phillips	3/4/1864	3 years	10/9/1865
Hill, Abram C.	Lomira	Fond du Lac	Capt. Phillips	3/11/1864	3 years	10/9/1865
Hill, David	Lomira	Fond du Lac	Capt. Phillips	3/4/1864	3 years	Deserted 2/5/1865; returned 4/22/1865; discharge 5/15/1865

Continued on next page

Chart 3B − Continued

Name	Enlistment Credited to	Place of Enlistment	Recruiting Officer	Date/Length of Enlistment		Date of Discharge
Hill, Henry	Lomira	Green Bay	Capt. E. R. Merrill	1/10/1864	1 year	Killed while serving as sharpshooter at Spanish Fort 9/10/1864
Hill, Lewis	Fort Howard	Fond du Lac	Capt. Phillips	3/4/1864	3 years	10/9/1865
James, Antoine (Anthony)	Fort Howard	Green Bay	Capt. E. R. Merrill	6/4/1864	3 years	10/9/1865
Johnson, Peter	Fort Howard	Green Bay	Capt. E. R. Merrill	1/4/1864	3 years	Deserted 10/10/1865
King, Adam	Fort Howard	Green Bay	Capt. E. R. Merrill	1/4/1864	3 years	10/9/1865
King, Nicholas	Fort Howard	Green Bay	Capt. E. R. Merrill	4/29/1864	3 years	10/10/1865
King, Simon	Casco	Green Bay	Capt. E. R. Merrill	4/29/1864	3 years	Killed − musket ball through head at siege of Atlanta 7/22/1864
Nimham, Anthony	Lomira	Fond du Lac	Capt. Phillips	3/4/1864	3 years	10/9/1865
Nimham, James	Lomira	Fond du Lac	Capt. Phillips	3/4/1864	3 years	Died of disease at Keokuk, Iowa, 2/9/1865
Powlas, Anton[y]	Fort Howard	Green Bay	Capt. E. R. Merrill	9/12/1864	1 year	7/18/1865
Powlas (Powless), George	Green Bay	Green Bay	Capt. E. R. Merrill	1/2/1864	3 years	10/9/1865
Powlas (Powless), Moses	Fort Howard	De Pere	Charles Beattie	12/15/1863	3 years	Deserted at St. Louis 11/19/1864
Powlas (Powless), Peter I	Fort Howard	Green Bay	Capt. E. R. Merrill	1/4/1864	3 years	10/9/1865
Powlas (Powless), Peter II	Lomira	Fond du Lac	Capt. Phillips	3/4/1864	3 years	10/9/1865
Silas, Abram	De Pere	Green Bay	Capt. E. R. Merrill	1/7/1864	3 years	10/9/1865
Silas, Isaac	Green Bay	Green Bay	Capt. E. R. Merrill	1/7/1864	3 years	10/9/1865
Skenandore, Jacob	New Holstein	Green Bay	Capt. E. R. Merrill	9/10/1864	1 year	6/1/1865
Stephens, Henry	Lomira	Fond du Lac	Capt. Phillips	3/4/1864	3 years	10/9/1865
Thomas, Thomas	Fort Howard	Green Bay	Capt. E. R. Merrill	1/7/1864	3 years	Died at Brownsville, Ark., 10/4/1864
Webster, Augustus	Oshkosh	Green Bay	Capt. E. R. Merrill	4/20/1864	3 years	10/9/65
Webster, Edgar E.	Holland	Green Bay	Capt. E. R. Merrill	2/22/1864	3 years	10/9/1865
Webster, Lewis B.	De Pere	Green Bay	Capt. E. R. Merrill	1/1/1864	3 years	10/9/1865

Source: Descriptive Muster Rolls, SHSW and NA, and the records of the Oneida Nation of Indians of Wisconsin.

CHART 4

14th Wisconsin Volunteer Infantry G Company Oneidas

Name	Rank	Occupation	Birthplace	Residence	Age	Marital Status	Height	Enlistment Credited to	Place of Enlistment	Recruiting Officer	Date/Length of Enlistment	Date of Discharge
Anthony, John 1st	pvt.	farmer	New York	Oneida	19	single	5'8"	Green Bay	Green Bay	Capt. E. R. Merrill	12/31/1863 3 years	10/9/1865
Anthony, John 2d	pvt.	farmer	Wisconsin	unknown	42	unknown	5'6"	unknown	Green Bay	Capt. E. R. Merrill	8/18/1864 1 year	7/21/1865
Anthony (Antone), Thomas	pvt.	farmer	New York	Oneida	43	married	5'6"	De Pere	Green Bay	Capt. E. R. Merrill	12/30/1863 3 years	Died in service 6/26/1865
Bread, Peter	pvt.	farmer	Wisconsin	Oneida	18	single	5'5½"	Green Bay	Green Bay	Capt. E. R. Merrill	12/31/1863 3 years	10/9/1865
Doxtator, Charles	pvt.	farmer	Wisconsin	Oneida	28	single	5'8"	De Pere	Green Bay	Capt. E. R. Merrill	12/31/1863 3 years	Presidential discharge 11/13/1864
Doxtator, Paul	pvt.	farmer	Wisconsin	Fort Howard	20	married	5'9"	unknown	Green Bay	Capt. E. R. Merrill	12/31/1863 3 years	Died of disease in service of dysentery 5/3/1864
Powlas, August	pvt.	farmer	Wisconsin	unknown	18	single	5'9½"	De Pere	Green Bay	Capt. E. R. Merrill	12/31/1863 3 years	Died of disease in service 8/18/1864
Powlas, Cobus	pvt.	farmer	Wisconsin	unknown	25	married	5'6"	Green Bay	Green Bay	Capt. E. R. Merrill	1/ 5/1864 3 years	10/9/1865

Source: Descriptive Muster Rolls, SHSW and NA, and the Records of the Oneida Nation of Indians of Wisconsin.

born in the Oneida homeland in New York, which is not surprising because seven of the Indians were over forty years of age at the time of their
enlistment. Their ages ranged from eighteen to forty-six; their average age
was twenty-six. The Oneida soldiers were of average height, ranging from
5 feet 4 inches to 6 feet. At least twenty-one were married, and forty-seven
listed their occupation as farmer (see Charts 3a, 3b, and 4).[18]

In the first months of 1864, the regiment was temporarily divided, with
part of the unit, Worden's Brigade, remaining behind for training. From
March 1864 onward, the 14th Wisconsin's itinerary reads like a road map
of the Deep South, stretching from Georgia to Arkansas. In the first year
of their enlistment, the Oneidas participated in some of the most intense
fighting and forced marches of the Civil War. The 14th Wisconsin was under the overall command of General William Tecumseh Sherman during
the Atlanta Campaign and General George A. Thomas at the Battle of
Nashville.[19]

During the march toward Atlanta, the Oneidas received significant attention for their manner of fighting, their exploits, and their personal
sacrifice. Private Elisha Stockwell, Jr., a white man in the 14th Wisconsin,
observed the skill of "F Company Indians." At Kennesaw Mountain, an
Oneida outfoxed his Confederate enemy and took a rebel prisoner much
to the Southerner's amazement as well as embarrassment:

> He [the prisoner] was the most disgusted Reb I ever saw. He was behind
> some rails they had piled up to protect them, and out in front was an
> open field with big stones, some higher than a man, and near the woods,
> which were big trees and no underbrush. He said he saw the Indian go
> behind the stone, and was waiting for him to come out to get a shot at
> him, when the first thing he knew the Indian's gun came over the end
> of the rails and there was nothing to do but surrender. He asked the In-
> dian if he was the one that went behind the stone. The Indian said he
> was, but wouldn't tell the Reb how he got out without being seen. The
> Reb said he had read of the Indians doing such things, but didn't believe
> such yarns, but had to believe it this time. He said he didn't care so much
> about being taken prisoner, but hated to have such a game as that played
> on him. The Indian just laughed at him.[20]

During the Atlanta Campaign on July 19, 1864, an advance party was sent
to the southeast around the Confederates' right flank. These were mostly
Company F Indians serving as skirmishers off to one side of the road, just
behind a low ridge. The skirmish was soon over, and the Indians resumed
their march to Atlanta.[21] These actions were costly. Daniel Bread was a
casualty, permanently disabled from wounds that later led to his military

discharge. Others were less fortunate. Tribal records indicate that Simon King, an Oneida recruit, was "shot in the head while lying on the ground at Kennesaw Mountain."[22]

According to historian Richard Current, "the shared experience of the Civil War reinforced rather than modified the mental stereotypes that already prevailed among the native white Wisconsinites when thinking about immigrants, or Indians or blacks." Although Indians were usually given more credit than black troops, officers commanding Indians recruits repeated that they were "good soldiers, being unsurpassed for scouting or picket duty, but quite unable to stand a charge or artillery fire."[23] Provost Marshal Merrill perpetuated this simplistic picture by suggesting that "the Oneida Indians, always a warlike people, organized a company of sharpshooters [3d Wisconsin Volunteer Infantry] under command of Cornelius Doxtator."[24] The same stereotype appears in Elisha Stockwell's account, but he also provides insights into special problems faced by Indians. Stockwell described an incident during the Atlanta Campaign in which an Oneida recruit could not understand or speak English. Another Oneida had to translate orders given to the recruit by a corporal on picket duty. One of these two Oneidas decided to proceed on his own "down the road some forty rods to woods, where he could get out of sight, as it was open ground where I had posted him." Stockwell falsely generalized that the "Indians were good skirmishers, but didn't like the open country or pitched battle."[25]

The Wisconsin Oneidas participated in frontal assaults and defended their position as did the Tuscarora Company in North Carolina. On July 22, 1864, during the Battle of Atlanta, certain units, including D, E, and F companies of the 14th Wisconsin, were cited for heroism in the official record by Lieutenant Colonel John C. Abercrombie of the 11th Iowa Volunteer Infantry. After returning from picket duty, they turned back an assault on a small fort on a hill and on the immedite line of works connected with it. Abercrombie insisted: "Many acts of bravery were performed by officers and men of the regiment which might be mentioned if time and opportunity permit."[26] General John McArthur, who commanded the 1st Division at the Battle of Nashville, cited the regiment "for their promptness in moving forward to support my left on the first day's battle and securing many prisoners."[27]

The Oneida troops were members of a much traveled unit; some were on detached service in different theaters of the war. Indians died at Cairo, Illinois; Vicksburg, Mississippi; Atlanta, Big Shanty, and Rome, Georgia; Montgomery and Spanish Fort, Alabama; Keokuk, Louisiana; and Memphis, Tennessee. In 1864, some Oneidas from the 14th Regiment took part in the ill-fated Red River Expedition. They encountered rebels at Pleasant

Hill Landing, Simmsport, Clouterville, Marksville, Yellow Bayou, and Tupelo. In a series of futile forced marches into Arkansas and Missouri, they failed to capture Confederate General Sterling Price's elusive army. In 1865, they routed Confederate General Lawrence Ross at Corinth and joined in Union operations at Mobile. Under General Edward Canby's command, they participated in the Battle of Spanish Fort. Tragically, Oneida Henry Hill, wounded at that battle on April 2, was one of the last casualties of the Civil War, dying on April 9, 1865.[28]

The Oneida casualty rate in Company F was especially high. Seven of the twenty-seven deaths suffered by the unit were Oneidas. In addition to the deaths of King and Hill in combat, five died of disease, including dysentery and typhoid. Of the ten Oneidas identified as members of G Company, one died from dysentery and one, according to pension records, from whiskey.[29]

The records of the 14th Wisconsin Volunteer Infantry clearly indicate that Union army life for the Wisconsin Oneidas was much harsher than that experienced by soldiers of the Tuscarora Company. The Oneidas engaged Confederate forces more times than their New York counterparts and lost more men in war. The Oneidas of F and G companies were all privates in rank. There was no one like Cornelius C. Cusick, Newt Parker, or Foster J. Hudson among them. They were Indians in a white man's army. Of the twelve members of F Company who were counted as deserters, four were Indians. A fifth Oneida returned from being AWOL on April 9, 1865, and was not counted as a deserter. In Company G, one of the deserters was an Oneida. Although these figures appear excessive, the Oneida 10 percent desertion rate was approximately the same as that for the Union army as a whole.[30] Approximately 200,000 of the 776,829 people called in the four drafts between the summer of 1863 and spring of 1865 deserted. Nevertheless, the records clearly indicate that the Oneidas were reluctant combatants. Three of the Indians were formally listed as substitutes. Another, Charles Doxtator, was apparently drafted illegally. He later was discharged by presidential order "because he was an Oneida Indian."[31]

The Oneidas had an important impact on regimental life. They appear to have been resourceful in securing food and in influencing the culinary direction of camp life. As a diversion from writing about combat, Stockwell described how one of the F Company Indians, armed with his Belgian rifle, went squirrel shooting and came back to camp "with all the squirrels he could handily carry, all shot in the head."[32] Squirrel soup, an Iroquois favorite, was a welcome substitute for stale hardtack.[33] Yet the Oneidas were not credited with contributing to the overall improvement of camp life. Lieutenant James K. Newton of De Pere, commander of Company F, never specifically mentioned the Indians, but by reading between the lines of Newton's account, one can see the Oneida presence. Newton, who lived adjacent to the Oneida Indian Reservation, made reference to a culinary delight "discovered" by recruits:

> You would not believe how many ways we can cook our corn so as to have a variety. We have parched corn, boiled Do. mush, corn coffee etc. but the latest invention to make it go down good is to half parch it, and then grind it coarse like hominy and then boil it with a small piece of pork to season it. If you have to live on corn altogether, by reason of this war's continuing for a great length of time longer I advise you to cook it in the way I last mentioned.[34]

Parched hominy seasoned with salt pork is a typical Iroquois recipe, "Onon'daat." It has been described as an Indian dish since earliest European contact and is often referred to as sagamite, sapaen, or suppawn.[35]

After a six-month respite at the end of the war in the heart of Dixie at Eastport, Mississippi, and Montgomery and Mobile, Alabama, the Oneidas came marching home in the fall of 1865. The 14th Wisconsin returned on October 26, and the reservation community celebrated their return with a veterans' party six days later.[36] The war had weakened the already divided community by permanently taking away so many of the youth. News of leasing to whites, a suspicious fire that destroyed a saw and shingle mill in the summer of 1865, the cutting and sale of timber by individual Oneidas, and talk of the need to institute a new tribal governmental elected system greeted the returning veterans.[37]

Anthropologist Jack Campisi has insisted that the Oneida political system from 1820 to 1870 "never had time to solidify; the precipitous changes in the surrounding white society, which in the 1870s controlled the political destinies of the tribe, precluded any adjustment."[38] The Civil War made this adjustment less likely if not impossible. The white citizens of Brown and Outagamie counties soon had collective amnesia about the role of the Oneidas in the Civil War as "replacement soldiers." Oscar Archiquette, an Oneida tribal leader from the 1930s until 1971, frequently suggested that Green Bay's white citizens be reminded of the Indian contribution by putting up a statue in downtown Green Bay honoring the Oneidas who served in their ancestors' places during the Civil War.[39]

There had been only a few white settlers on the west side of the reservation in 1850; but after the Civil War the Oneidas found themselves surrounded by an aggressive non-Indian world desirous of Indian lands. Led by Morgan L. Martin, "one of the most important entrepreneurs in early

Wisconsin history," who also served as Indian agent, the citizens of Green Bay began calling for the allotment of the Oneida Indian Reservation as well as for removal of the Oneidas. Although Chief Cornelius Hill responded angrily to Martin's initiative, the movement to allot the Oneidas was soon begun in earnest. In 1870, a bill to accomplish Martin's objective was sent to Congress by the Indian agent. Although this effort failed, it set in motion efforts that culminated in the passage of the Dawes General Allotment Act of 1887 and the allotment of the Oneida Indian Reservation in 1892, a policy that resulted in the loss of nearly all of the sixty-five-thousand-acre tribal estate.[40]

Although the Civil War was a tragedy of immense proportions for the Oneidas, it was far less of a debacle than the Iroquois faced in Indian Territory when they found themselves caught in the middle of the war between Union and Confederate armies.

7

The Iroquois in Indian Territory

The Civil War had devastating effects on Indian Territory, determining the future for Iroquois and other Indians in the area. The Iroquois in Indian Territory, referred to in the records by numerous names — Cayuga, Western Cayuga, New York Indians, Seneca of Sandusky, Neosho Seneca, Cowskin Seneca, Seneca Nation, Mixed Seneca and Shawnee, and Seneca and Shawnee — were forced by their location to sign a treaty with the Confederate States of America. Although Union officials recognized during the war that the Iroquois had little choice but to sign this treaty, Washington policy makers used the treaty as a convenient excuse for forcing Iroquois land cessions during Reconstruction. The Civil War also led to the near total destruction of Iroquois property, resulting in extreme poverty, refugee status in Kansas, and substantial loss of life for these Indians.

The trek by two bands of Iroquois Indians residing in Ohio to the trans-Mississippi West began in the early 1830s. These Iroquois tribesmen, who besides Senecas and Cayugas, included Mohawks, Oneidas, Onondagas, and refugee populations of eastern Algonkian tribesmen, had settlements in the Ohio country at least dating from the mid-eighteenth century. These Indians were largely independent of Iroquois League control. From 1807 onward, Cayugas from the Buffalo Creek Reservation in New York joined these Ohio Iroquois. By 1819, two separate reservations had been established by treaty in Ohio, one composed of Indians referred to in the literature as the Senecas of Sandusky, the other a mixed band of Senecas and Shawnees around Lewiston, Ohio. The Senecas of Sandusky concluded a treaty with the United States government on February 28, 1831, whereby they ceded all claims to their Ohio lands, totaling forty thousand acres. In return, they were to receive approximately sixty-seven thousand fertile

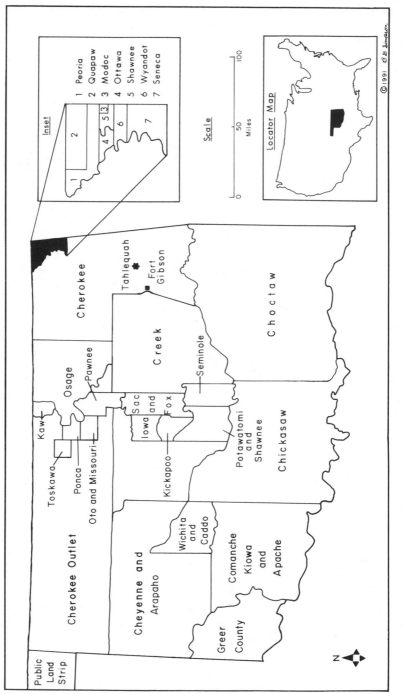

8. Indian Territory, 1860–1888, based on a map by Francis Paul Prucha.

9. The Civil War in the Trans-Mississippi West,
based on a map by L. Philip Denoyer.

acres in Indian Territory north of the Cherokee Nation adjoining the Missouri border. In late 1831, four hundred Sandusky Senecas began the eight-month journey from Dayton, Ohio, to their new lands along the Cowskin River in northeastern Indian Territory. Delayed by floods, winter storms, and deaths of their kinsmen en route, they arrived at their new home on July 4, 1832, only to find that part of their land west of the Neosho River had already been assigned to the Cherokees.

A second mixed band composed of 300 Senecas and Shawnees also set out for Indian Territory. Only 258 of these Indians arrived along the Cowskin River on December 13, 1832, the remainder having succumbed to cholera and other illnesses during the journey. Upon their arrival, they also discovered that their lands had been assigned to the Cherokees. Eventually, on December 29, 1832, 13 Sandusky Senecas and 11 Seneca and Shawnee leaders signed another treaty with federal officials along the Cowskin River Indian Territory, after adjudication by a presidential commission. The tribes ceded all their lands west of the Neosho or Grand River in exchange for an equal amount east of the Neosho, north of the Cherokee border and east of Missouri in present-day Ottawa County, Oklahoma.[1]

These Iroquois people never lost contact with their mother culture at Onondaga and at Brantford, Ontario. They carried their Iroquois religious traditions west with them. Eastern and western Iroquois interacted at times. These Indians were joined in the period 1846–52 by New York Iroquois, including 44 Cayugas, who had agreed in the nefarious Treaty of Buffalo Creek of 1838 to exchange their claims in the East for Kansas lands. Although most of these Indians died of cholera, exposure, or starvation during the removal process or returned to New York, some remained in Indian Territory; by 1862, 145 people identified as Cayugas were residing in the West.[2]

Iroquois in Indian Territory found themselves engulfed in the sectional crisis, the lawless activity of bleeding Kansas in the 1850s, and the intense fighting between Union and Confederate forces after 1861. Although only one major military engagement was fought in the heart of Iroquois country — Cowskin Prairie on June 1, 1862 — stories about the war are still part of the Indian oral tradition. The exploits of Colonel William C. Quantrill and other "border ruffians" fill the folklore of Indian country in present-day northeastern Oklahoma. Quantrill and his marauders, who served themselves as much if not more than the Confederacy, used the Iroquois's wooded hill country region for their hideouts and staging areas for raids. From there, Quantrill trained and sent out bushwackers and guerrilla fighters, destroying property, stealing livestock, and butchering civilian populations until he was killed in 1865. As a nineteenth-century terrorist,

Quantrill had few peers in spreading violence and destruction. Although commissioned by the Confederates to harass Union border settlements in Kansas and Missouri and to counter Jayhawkers, private bands of raiders from Kansas, Quantrill at times attacked Confederate settlements as well, and his operations ranged from northern Texas to Lawrence, Kansas.[3]

Confederate leaders were keenly interested in the vast trans-Mississippi West, where most Indians resided. They consciously set about winning Indian leaders to their cause in 1861. By April, Federal troops had withdrawn from Indian Territory because they were needed in the East. The area soon came under the control of Confederate forces. By September 1861, P. P. Elder, the Neosho Indian agent, reported that he was unable to pay annuities to the Indians, who were "cut off from loyal citizens" and surrounded by rebels. Soon after, Elder shifted the agency's operations to Kansas.[4] The Union abandonment of posts in Indian Territory violated treaties with the Indian nations guaranteeing them military protection.[5]

Despite repeated federal assurances, the Indian Territory had shrunk considerably since the time of the Iroquois removals in the early 1830s. In 1853, the commissioner of Indian affairs indicated that the Indians in the region signed "without enthusiasm" treaties accepting the further reduction of Indian Territory. These treaties were followed the next year by the Kansas-Nebraska Act in which the existing Indian Territory was partitioned and the northern half was organized as Kansas and Nebraska territories. By 1856, the Indians were major victims of the mini–Civil War in Kansas. The sectional conflict masked motives of land sharks and politicians who lusted after the nearly ten million acres of Indian lands in the eastern part of Kansas.[6]

Even during the Civil War, Kansas whites attempted to obtain the large Indian land base — nearly one-fifth of the entire area of the state. Both federal and Sunflower State politicians determined to acquire the Indians' valuable lands. The Kansas state legislature resolved that all Indian land titles be extinguished and asked President Lincoln to negotiate treaties to remove them from the state. Commissioner Dole wrote in his annual report for 1862: "The people of Kansas are very earnest in the expression of their wishes for the transfer of the Indian tribes within that state to the Indian country on the south." He insisted that the move would benefit the Indians by protecting them from whites who wanted their money and property. He explained another important motive — that removal "would result in benefit to the government by diminishing the expenses now annually incurred" by eliminating the number of Indian agencies and agents involved in their supervision. Although Commissioner Dole went to Kansas and drew up treaties with five Indian groups, including the Shawnee and New

York Indians, these agreements did not go into effect. Only after the war did the general removal of Indians from Kansas begin, and it was to have serious results for Iroquois in Indian Territory.[7]

At the time of the outbreak of the Civil War, the Iroquois in Indian Territory were mostly subsistence farmers and ranchers, owning no slaves; they supplemented their livelihood by fishing in the Neosho and Elk rivers or the Grand Lake (Lake of the Cherokees) and hunting in the well-wooded Ozark country of today's Arkansas, Oklahoma, and Missouri. They had no interest in states' rights issues except as they bore on their lands or their relationship with the government. In the first months of 1861, most were neutral on the issues that led to war between North and South.

On March 1, 1861, Robert Toombs, secretary of state for the Confederacy, proposed a resolution which was quickly submitted and passed in the Confederate Senate, authorizing President Jefferson Davis to appoint and send a special emissary to the Indian nations of Indian Territory. Albert Pike, a New Englander by birth, who had lived in Arkansas for many years, was selected to negotiate with the Indians. A military veteran of the Mexican War, Pike had served with Robert E. Lee in that conflict. He was well versed in Greek, Latin, French, Spanish, and Sanskrit, as well as several Indian languages. In Arkansas, he had become a well-known writer and attorney. Pike was soon given the title of commissioner of Indian affairs in the new Confederate Bureau of Indian Affairs. His primary responsibility was to negotiate treaties with the tribes west of Arkansas to keep them neutral and acquire their friendship for the Confederacy.[8]

On August 10, 1861, a motley Southern army headed by Generals Sterling Price and Ben McCulloch faced a surprise attack initiated by General Nathaniel Lyon, an aggressive and impetuous Union commander, at Wilson's Creek, near Springfield, Missouri, less than two hundred miles from Iroquois country. Dividing his army of six thousand men, Lyon attacked the much larger Confederate forces at dawn. The Confederates, some of whom were wearing blue uniforms, confused Union General Franz Sigel, who ordered his men to hold fire. The Southerners cut down and routed Sigel's men while Lyon's badly outnumbered command ran out of ammunition. Lyon was killed. The Union army, led by a major, the top-ranking Federal officer who was not a casualty, then retreated one hundred miles to Rolla, Missouri.

Soon after, Pike, in cooperation with Chief John Ross of the Cherokee Nation, began to negotiate with the Indian nations of the Indian Territory. In September, Ross sent letters out to the Osages, Shawnees, Senecas, Senecas and Shawnees, and Quapaws notifying them "that a highly distinguished officer [Pike] of the Confederate States of America" had "been commissioned by his Government to enter into treaties with the Indian Nations west of Arkansas" and that the Creeks, Choctaws, Seminoles "and other remnants of tribes up the red river, have already entered into Treaties of Alliance, offensive and defensive with the said States." Despite past tensions between Cherokees and these smaller Indian nations, Ross cordially invited them to council on September 25 to meet General Pike "that, a Conference might be had with you upon matters of the greatest importance to the peace and prosperity of your respective Nations. And that the United Brotherhood of the Indian Nations might be preserved and perpetuated. Hoping that you will not fail to meet us around our great council fire, to smoke the pipe of Peace and shake the right hand of Brotherly love! Thy friend and Brother."[9]

Ross, in a letter to the Creeks on September 19, clearly explained his motives: "Brothers — My advice and desire, under the present extraordinary crisis is, for all the red Brethren to be united among themselves in the support of our common rights and interest by forming an alliance of peace and friendship with the Confederate States of America."[10] Later in the war, Ross abandoned his support of the Confederacy. His own nation was badly split in the war. Confederate Cherokees were led by Ross's nemesis, Chief Stand Watie, a leading military strategist in the war in the trans-Mississippi West.

According to one of Pike's biographers, the general took the small Indian groups such as the Seneca and the Seneca and Shawnee "for granted, for there were too few of them to do any damage and they would have to take whatever was offered them."[11] Nevertheless, the Senecas, unlike the Five Civilized Tribes, did not agree to come into the war as Confederate military allies. Little Town Spicer, the principal chief of the Seneca tribe, Lewis Davis, principal chief of the Senecas and Shawnees, as well as councillors and warriors of the two communities, met, negotiated, and signed a lengthy forty-three-article treaty with General Pike on October 4, 1861, at Park Hill, Ross's residence, in the Cherokee Nation.[12]

Under the provisions of the treaty, the Indians agreed "to place themselves under the laws and protection of the Confederate States of America, in peace and war forever, and agree to be true and loyal to them under all circumstances." The Confederacy agreed to be "friends and protectors" of the Indians and "to defend them in the enjoyment of all their rights, possessions, and property" and to protect them from being molested by any power, people, or state. The Confederate government promised them "undisturbed use, occupancy, and enjoyment of their lands 'as long as grass shall grow and water run'" on the lands guaranteed in United States treaties with the Indians "so long as the said tribes or bands desire the same." These lands could be sold or ceded only to the Confederate States of America; "in case the said tribes or bands respectively become extinct," the lands would revert to the Confederacy. The Confederate States assumed federal and state annuity payments to the Indians and agreed to pay $2,400 for a twenty-year period beginning in 1862 "for the benefit of the Seneca tribe, including the Cayugas and Mohawks," who resided with these Indians. Pike promised that a physician, blacksmith, teacher, wagonmaker, and wheelwright would be hired for the Indians' benefit, a Confederate Indian agent and interpreter appointed, a school and gristmill built, and a "good rifle" and sufficient ammunition provided for Indian warriors.[13]

The Confederates, nevertheless, were given wide latitude. They secured the right-of-way to build roads, erect railroads, and construct military outposts "as they deem necessary" in the Indians' territory. The Confederacy in turn promised the Indians that their lands "shall never be included within the bounds of any State or Territory," nor would any of the laws of any state or territory ever be extended over them. The president of the Confederate States would serve with the "same care and superintendence over them as was heretofore had by the President of the United States." Nevertheless, the Indian nations would retain their hunting rights. The treaty also reaffirmed "peace and brotherhood" with the other nations of Indian Territory. Although assuring equal justice under law, the Confederates in Article XIII extended their criminal jurisdiction to both Indians and non-Indians. Equally disturbing to the Indians was Article XX, which interfered with tribal enrollment. Even though the Confederacy recognized the right of the Indians to set membership and receive and incorporate new members on an equal basis, the article required these Indian communities to accept the widow or widower of a tribal member "to be a member of the tribe in which he marries or has married."[14]

The treaty reflected the Southern mind-set about slavery and the exigencies of 1861. Article XII provided for "perpetual peace and friendship," maintaining that the chiefs and headmen "shall do all in their power to take and *restore any negroes,* horses, or other property stolen from white men or from persons belonging to either of said five nations, and to catch and give up any person among them who may kill or steal or do any other evil act" (emphasis added). Article XVII forbade the Senecas and others to have "talks or councils with any white men or Indians without the knowledge and consent of the agent of the Confederate States." Thus, from the terms of the agreement, it is clear that Pike's treaty with the Senecas in 1861 was not an agreement among equals but a treaty imposed by the Confederacy, an occupying force in Indian Territory.[15] Despite later pronouncements by Washington officials after the war, the Iroquois were in no position to refuse the Confederate or even Cherokee demands in October 1861.

On October 8, Chief John Ross of the Cherokee Nation wrote from Tahlequah about the negotiations with General Pike, indicating the dilemma facing the smaller Indian nations of northeastern Indian Territory. He claimed that the Senecas, Shawnees, Quapaws, and Osages were "well satisfied and in fine spirits" after the conclusion of their treaties with General Pike and were "not expected to furnish any warriors for the [Confederate] service — except the Osages who have agreed to furnish 500 warriors." These nations had "friends and relatives in Kansas," which was a Union-held state, and they were determined to be flexible. Ross suggested that "it was thought best, to leave our *doors open* for the reception [of these Indians] as soon as they can see their way clear to travel along the *White Path,* that leads into *our Houses!*"[16] These Indian communities had been dominated by their more populous and stronger Cherokee neighbors to the south since the 1830s, and Ross appeared to suggest that they would follow the Cherokee lead if they were not coerced or forced into a corner. The reference to a "White Path" may not mean assimilation into the white man's culture but is perhaps a cryptic reference to White Path, one of the leaders of the Cherokee antiremoval party headed by Ross.[17]

The Confederate Congress followed up on General Pike's series of treaties with the Indians by attempting to organize a judicial system, establishing courts in Indian Country in the winter of 1862. One of the two districts was Cha-la-ki, which included the Senecas as well as the Cherokees, Creeks, Osages, Quapaws, Shawnees, and Seminoles. This judicial system never functioned, however, because of the exigencies of war and the constant bloodletting in Indian Territory.[18]

Union military success was also to thwart these ambitious plans. On November 19, 1861, Union General James G. Blunt turned back Confederate forces attempting to capture Fort Gibson in Indian Territory. A change in Confederate fortunes was also to occur in the Arkansas Ozarks, within a hundred miles of Iroquois Country, in March 1862. On March 7, Confederate General Earl Van Dorn's army of sixteen thousand men attacked Union forces at Elkhorn Tavern or Pea Ridge. Van Dorn had linked up with Generals McCulloch and Price and then tried to outflank Union General Samuel R. Curtis's twelve-thousand-man force. Curtis had been warned of the Confederate maneuver and was ready for the attack. His artillery dispersed Stand Watie's Confederate Cherokee regiments, his lines held against Confederate assaults, and one of his soldiers shot and killed

General McCulloch. When Van Dorn started running out of ammunition, Curtis routed the rebel forces and defeated the Confederacy in this major battle.[19]

On June 6, 1862, war erupted in Iroquois country, at Cowskin Prairie, near the present site of the Seneca-Cayuga Green Corn Stomp Grounds in the vicinity of Grove, Oklahoma. Colonel Charles Doubleday, commanding the Union Indian expedition of one thousand men, after crossing the Kansas line, came on General Stand Watie's Confederate Cherokees. Doubleday sent one battalion across the Grand River to occupy a position behind the Confederate forces. The remainder of his force formed a skirmish line, crossed the river, and prepared to assault the Confederate position. The Union artillery commenced firing just after sundown at 9:00 P.M. and continued well into the morning of June 7. Watie and his men escaped the Union trap, marching in retreat to Fort Smith, but leaving behind five to six hundred horses and cattle. Although Watie had abandoned his position, the engagement was indecisive, in part because Doubleday, on strict orders, refused to pursue the retreating Cherokee chief.[20]

War continued all around Iroquois country in 1862. On July 3, 1862, the Confederates were routed in a brief but decisive engagement at Locust Grove, north of Tahlequah on the east side of the Neosho River. The Neosho-Granby area of eastern Missouri was the site of fighting on September 30, 1862, and again on October 28, 1864, at the two battles of Newtonia.

By the spring of 1862, the Senecas and the Senecas and Shawnees, after accepting one payment of annuities from their Confederate agent, asked for Union protection. Agent Elder, now temporarily in exile at Fort Scott, Kansas, reported that the Indians under his administration were "all loyal." When Elder returned to Seneca and Shawnee country in July 1862, he found it "ruthlessly plundered of horses and cattle." The majority of the Indians had fled to the interior of Kansas, where their "hogs and cattles have fallen a sacrifice to tender mercies of our own and rebel soldiers."[21]

The Iroquois were among the fifteen to seventeen thousand Indian war refugees in Kansas in 1862. By the fall of 1862, 10 percent of these refugees were to die as a result of unfit or inadequate diet and the lack of clothing and shelter. Besides frostbite, Indians suffered from measles, mumps, diphtheria, and pneumonia. Later, smallpox raged among the Indians of the Neosho Agency.[22] In September, John Melton, a Seneca chief, pleaded for assistance from Commissioner Dole, describing the disaster that had befallen his people in the Civil War. On behalf of war refugees from their temporary home in Wyandotte City, Melton poignantly wrote:

I wish to state to you our grievances and if it is in your power to have some assistance rendered to us. I am representing part of the Seneca Nation of loyal Indians who have been driven away from our homes in the Indian Territory by the secessionists and rebels to our government and been compelled to come North for safety. There are about one hundred and twenty-three of us here at present mostly women and children. What we could manage to bring with us we did and it has all been exhausted in supporting us and we are now very destitute and we are almost [in] starving condition, having no money, provisions or the comforts of life. All our clothing, blankets and care[?] are worn out and we are nearly naked. There are two payments of annuities still back which are due and unpaid from the Government and it is that which leaves [us] in such a destitute condition. These being unpaid compels us to call upon the Government for aid for us in our dark hour. We request going to call upon our Great Father and induce him to send us his obedient children social aid and assistance. We send him our best compliments.[23]

By the end of 1862 and the beginning of 1863, Commissioner Dole indicated that the Iroquois had "repented their digression" and had thrown "off the authority of the rebels and returned to their [U.S.] allegiance." Dole concluded that he had "no doubts" as "to their fidelity and future loyalty." These comments were made not simply as a result of the Iroquois's return to the Union fold. Some Iroquois of Indian Territory had by this time joined the Union army as members of the Kansas Home Guard and cavalry units. Cayuga refugees in the vicinity of Kansas City provided "every able-bodied man of serviceable age" to the Union military effort; Senecas of Neosho "furnished more soldiers for the Union forces in the Civil War" than their immediate neighbors the Quapaws as well as the "Mixed Band of Senecas and Shawnees."[24]

The deteriorating situation led the Iroquois to turn more and more to the Union for help. The Senecas and Shawnees, assigned to lands with "Black Bob's Band" adjoining the Kansas-Missouri border, were robbed of practically all of their possessions by Quantrill's marauders in September 1862. Quantrill crossed over the Missouri-Kansas line and attacked Black Bob lands, "robbing the Indians of practically everything they possessed, their clothing, their household goods, their saddles, their ponies, their provisions, and driving the original owners quite away. They fired upon them as they fled and committed atrocities upon the helpless ones who lagged behind."[25]

Quantrill's actions pushed the Indians further into Union arms. On January 12, 1863, S. S. Scott, the Confederate Indian commissioner, in a report to James A. Seddon, Confederate secretary of war, described the return of certain Confederate allied Indians to the Union fold. "In reference to the condition and feelings of the small tribes located in the northeastern corner of the Indian country — the Osages, Quapaws, Senecas, and Senecas and Shawnees — but little is known. Their country, exposed as it is to invasion by Kansas desperadoes, has been completely under the control of the North almost from the very day of their having entered into treaties with this Government."[26]

On July 2, 1863, the Union cavalry broke through Stand Watie's line and scattered the Southern forces at the Battle of Cabin Creek after the Cherokee chief and his men surprised a Federal column protecting a supply wagon train en route to Fort Gibson. On July 17, Union and Confederate forces met at the Battle of Honey Springs in the eastern part of the Creek Nation. The battle, the major one in Indian Territory during the Civil War, was a devastating defeat for the Confederacy. General James G. Blunt moved across the Arkansas River and marched on the Confederate forces at Elk Creek. The Battle of Honey Springs also resulted in Blunt's capture of the key Confederate outpost of Fort Smith in September 1863.

In retaliation, Quantrill's activities in the summer of 1863 were even more ghoulish than before. After General Blunt and his Union forces won the Battle of Honey Springs, Quantrill decided to strike back with a vengeance. In August, Major Henry Z. Curtis, Samuel Curtis's son and General Blunt's chief of staff, had established a military outpost at Baxter Springs, Kansas, less than fifty miles from Seneca lands, to protect and facilitate communications between Fort Scott, fifty-eight miles to the north, and Fort Gibson in Indian Territory. On October 8, 1863, Quantrill's bushwackers attacked the Union cooking camp at Baxter Spring. They then dressed in Federal uniforms and attacked Blunt's small group of wagons protected by Federal cavalry. Quantrill's guerrillas overwhelmed the panic-stricken Union forces, killing seventy out of one hundred of Blunt's army, including Major Curtis. The Union forces were shot, killed, stripped, robbed of their possessions, then mutilated.

In early 1864, the commissioner of Indian affairs praised the six hundred Quapaw, Seneca, and Shawnee Indians residing in Kansas for the near-universal military service of their men and their wartime sacrifices. He added that "they have proven themselves to be good and efficient soldiers" despite the "general feeling of discontent prevailing among them because of the destitution of their families." The commissioner condemned the rebels for stealing cattle from "these defenders, unfortunate, and truly loyal people."[27] In that same report, agent Elder said it would be safer for these Indians to remain on the Ottawa Reservation in Kansas rather than return to their farms in Indian Territory. Because Iroquois lands were halfway between the well-fortified Union-held positions at Fort Scott and Fort Gibson, Elder warned that they would be unprotected if they returned on the "traveled route and beat of guerrillas and bushwackers, in their passage south to Missouri and *vice versa*, with the strong probability for a considerable time, that it will be infested by those thieves, robbers, and assassins, both life and property are in no small degree endangered." Elder, near Ohio City, Kansas, further reported that the Indians of his agency were "exhausted physically" and that many of their young men "were in the service of the United States," leaving their older men, women, and children without protection if they returned to their reservations. Elder recommended that the Indians temporarily remain at the Ottawa Reservation, where they had already commenced their farming for the year.[28]

The agent's recommendation was reasonable because Stand Watie's Confederate forces had made a comeback. At Pleasant Bluff in June 1864, Stand Watie's soldiers ambushed and captured a Union supply ship on the Grand River. More importantly, the Cherokee general and his men surprised and defeated a large Union army at Cabin Creek on the Fort Scott–Fort Gibson military road in September, capturing three hundred supply wagons.

Only in April 1865 did the Indians of the Neosho Agency begin returning to their homes in Indian Territory. They once again initiated truck farming and attempted to pick up the pieces of their lives. Many returned from the Ottawa Reservation eighty miles to the north only to find their community laid waste as a result of the war. Although fighting continued in Indian Territory even after Lee's surrender at Appomattox, it was only a matter of time before Confederate recalcitrants abandoned the Lost Cause. Andrew Johnson, the new president of the United States, began to think about reestablishing federal authority over Indian Territory.

In September 1865, Johnson appointed a commissioner to meet with the Indians of Indian Territory. Among the members of the commission were Dennis N. Cooley, commissioner of Indian affairs; Elijah Sells, superintendent of the Southern Superintendency; Thomas Wistar, a leading member of the Seocity of Friends; and military representatives W. S. Harney and Ely S. Parker. Charles Mix of the Bureau of Indian Affairs served as one of the recording secretaries at the meetings. Major George C. Snow, the United States Indian agent for the Osages, Quapaws, Senecas, and Shawnees, was also in attendance. These men were to congregate at Fort Smith with Cherokee, Chickasaw, Choctaw, Creek, Osage, Seminole, Seneca, Seneca and Shawnee, and Wyandot Indian delegates.

The council was called to order on September 8 by Commissioner Cooley after a benediction in the Cherokee language. Cooley informed the Indians that they had violated their treaties with the United States by making treaties with the Confederacy and thereby "forfeited all *rights*" under treaties with the United States "and must be considered at the mercy of the government." Although Cooley added that "there was every disposition to treat them leniently," his message was clear. The United States government planned to make new treaties, demanding new concessions, from each of these nations.[29]

On the second day of the conference, the commissioner informed the Indian delegates that he was empowered by Washington to secure the following terms from them:

1st. That each tribe must enter into a treaty for permanent peace and amity among themselves, each other as tribes, and with the United States.

2d. [That each] tribe settled in the "Indian country" bind themselves, at the call of the United States authorities, to assist in compelling the wild tribes of the plain to keep the peace.

3d. [That] slavery [was] to be abolished, and [that] measures . . . be taken to incorporate the slaves into the tribes, with their rights guaranteed.

4th. [That] a general stipulation . . . [be made as to the] final abolition of slavery.

5th. [That] a part of the Indian country to be set apart, to be purchased for the use of such Indians from Kansas or elsewhere, as the government may desire to colonize therein.

6th. That the policy of the government to unite all the Indian tribes of this region into one consolidated government should be accepted.

7th. That no white persons, except government employees, or officers or employees of internal improvement companies authorized by government, will be permitted to reside in the country, unless incorporated with the several nations.[30]

The fifth point — securing the resettlement of Indians "from Kansas or elsewhere" — was to have a great bearing on the future direction of Iroquois history in Indian Territory and later in Oklahoma.

On the third day of the conference, the Senecas and several other Indian nations replied to the commissioners, "partly to express a willingness to accept those propositions, with some modifications." Apparently annoyed at accusations of disloyalty and breaking treaties, however, the Indian leaders attempted to explain "the manner in which their nations" had become "involved with the late confederacy." They insisted that they had "never showed any sympathy with the rebellion, but came north, abandoning their homes." They maintained that they were innocent victims.

Chief Isaac Warrior, a "Cowskin Seneca," on behalf of the Senecas, Senecas and Shawnees, and Quapaws, insisted "that the old treaties made between you and us many years back have been lived up to." After agreeing to new treaties, the Indians pleaded for compensation from the United States "government for which they suffered the loss of everything" except their lands.[31]

Despite their protest and the attendance of Ely Parker, the Iroquois in Indian Territory were treated as if they were Stand Watie's Confederate Cherokees—as losers of the Civil War. The humiliating "agreement with the Cherokee and Other Tribes in the Indian Territory" was concluded on September 13, 1865, at Fort Smith. After being forced to admit to their "transgressions," Chief Warrior, Chief Lewis Davis, A. McDonald, Goodhunt, James Tallchief, and Lewis Denny of the Senecas and Shawnees and representatives from seven other Indian nations were forced to "acknowledge themselves to be under the protection of the United States of America, and covenant and agree that hereafter they will in all things recognize the government of the United States as exercising exclusive jurisdiction over them" and that they will "not enter into any allegiance or conventional agreement with any state, nation, power or sovereign whatsoever."[32]

The impact of the Civil War on the Iroquois of Indian Territory was more serious than these words of condemnation or the severe physical and economic devastation and dislocation brought by the conflict. Under the guise of aiding the Indians who had suffered during the Civil War, federal officials, on February 23, 1867, signed a treaty with the Seneca, Mixed Seneca and Shawnee, Quapaw, Confederated Peoria, Kaskaskia, Wea and Piankeshaw, Miami, Ottawa, and Wyandot tribes at a meeting held in Washington, D.C. George Spicer and John Mash were delegates of the Senecas, and John Whitetree, John Young, and Lewis Davis were delegates of the Mixed Senecas and Shawnees. Lewis V. Bogy, commissioner of Indian affairs, W. H. Watson, special commissioner, Thomas Murphy, superintendent, and George C. Snow and G. A. Colton, Indian agents, represented the United States government.[33]

Under the treaty, the Senecas, who had been confederated with the Shawnees as the Senecas and Shawnees or Mixed Senecas and Shawnees, agreed to "dissolve their connection with the said Shawnees and to unite with the Senecas." The Senecas ceded twenty thousand acres of their Neosho lands on the north side of their reservation, established in the 1830s, to the federal government for $20,000. The Mixed Senecas and Shawnees ceded two parcels of their lands totaling forty-two thousand acres, guaranteed since the 1830s, to the federal government for $36,000. The treaty, which was ratified by the Senate and promulgated by the president in 1868, insisted that this was a "means of rebuilding their [Seneca, Mixed Seneca and Shawnee, and Quapaw] homes, re-opening their farms, and supporting their families" because they had been "driven from their reservations early in the late war, and suffered greatly for several years." Article 12 masked the real motivation behind the treaty. Because these Indians "were driven from their homes during the late war and their property destroyed," the article provided for "a commission of not to exceed two persons to be appointed by the Secretary of the Interior, who shall proceed to the country and make careful investigation of their claims for losses."[34]

Other provisions of the Treaty of 1867 reveal a more sordid motive — the continued lobbying of Kansas interests to rid that state of Indians by relocating them. The treaty provided precisely that objective by removing the Peoria, Kaskaskia, Wea, Piankeshaw, Miami, Ottawa, and Wyandot tribes from Kansas to the lands ceded by the Senecas, Senecas and Shawnees, and Quapaws in Articles 1 through 4. Eight years later, the Modocs, a recently conquered Indian community from the area near the California-Oregon border, were removed because of their alleged transgressions to the remaining "vacated" lands of the Senecas, Senecas and Shawnees, and Quapaws.[35]

Although the treaty reaffirmed Seneca possession of approximately sixty-five thousand acres of land, the underlying federal message to the Indians was clear: Indians would be removed at will and the Indian Territory would continue to shrink to satisfy the immediate political and economic needs of the dominant society. The opening up of Indian Territory in 1889 and the Dawes Commission were several decades off, but the road to these federal policies was already being built in the Civil War and Reconstruction.

Peter Wilson. A Cayuga Indian, Wilson was a physician at Versailles, New York, who at times served as United States government interpreter. He urged Iroquois participation in the Civil War and fought against exclusion of Indian troops from the conflict. Photograph from Arthur C. Parker, *An Analytical History of the Seneca Indians.* Rochester, 1926; reprint, Port Washington, N.Y.: Ira J. Friedman, 1967.

Cornelius C. Cusick. Lieutenant Cusick commanded the Iroquois troops of Company D, 132d New York State Volunteer Infantry during the Civil War. A Tuscarora sachem, Cusick later served as a commissioned officer on the trans-Mississippi frontier from 1866 to 1891. Photograph from Cusick's Appointments/Commissions/Promotions File. Courtesy of the National Archives.

VOLUNTEER ENLISTMENT.

(Copy)   June 18, 1862

STATE OF New York.   City TOWN OF Buffalo

I, I. Newton Parker born in the Town of Pembroke in the State of New York aged Twenty nine years, and by occupation a Farmer Do HEREBY ACKNOWLEDGE to have volunteered this Eighteenth day of June 1862 to serve as a **Soldier** in the Army of the United States of America, for the period of THREE YEARS, unless sooner discharged by proper authority: Do also agree to accept such bounty, pay, rations and clothing, as are, or may be, established by the law for volunteers. And I, I. Newton Parker do solemnly swear, that I will bear true faith and allegiance to the **United States of America**, and that I will serve them honestly and faithfully against all their enemies or opposers whomsoever; and that I will observe and obey the orders of the President of the United States, and the orders of the officers appointed over me, according to the Rules and Articles of War.

Sworn and subscribed to, at the city of Buffalo   Sheldon Sturgeon this 18th day of June 1862   1st Lieut 1st Inftry BEFORE C. C. Cusick, 1st Lieut   Mustering & Disbursing Officer Co H. 53d Reg. N. Y. S. Vols.

I CERTIFY, ON HONOR, That I have carefully examined the above named Volunteer, agreeably to the General Regulations of the Army, and that, in my opinion, he is free from all bodily defects and mental infirmity which would, in any way, disqualify him from performing the duties of a soldier.

EXAMINING SURGEON.

I CERTIFY, ON HONOR, That I have minutely inspected the Volunteer, I. N. Parker previously to his enlistment, and that he was entirely sober when enlisted; that, to the best of my judgment and belief, he is of lawful age; and that, in accepting him as duly qualified to perform the duties of an able-bodied soldier, I have strictly observed the Regulations which govern the recruiting service.

This soldier has dark eyes, black hair, dark complexion, is 5 feet, 8¾ inches high. and was attached the 53d Regt N. Y. V. Company H and afterwards transferred to the 132nd Regiment of New York State Volunteers His la Empire Brigade — Co. D. Capt Wm Van De Bosch. Lieut C. C. Cusick

RECRUITING OFFICER.

Isaac Newton Parker's Volunteer Enlistment Papers, June 18, 1862. Sergeant Parker, a Tonawanda Seneca, chronicled his activities and those of his fellow Iroquois troops of Company D, 132d New York State Volunteer Infantry. Courtesy of the Buffalo and Erie County Historical Society.

Ely S. Parker as he appeared when he became Grant's Military Secretary. Courtesy of the Buffalo and Erie County Historical Society.

U.S. Grant and staff, 1864. *Far right:* Ely S. Parker. Courtesy of the Buffalo and Erie County Historical Society.

Samuel George about 1860. Painting by Sanford Thayer. The medallion is probably a peace medal. Courtesy of the Onondaga Historical Association.

Samuel George, about 1860, wearing silver earrings. Courtesy of the Buffalo and Erie County Historical Society.

Seneca Nation Political Leaders in the post-Civil War period. Casler Redeye (*left, above*), Harrison Halftown (*right, above*), and Andrew John, Jr. (*left*) were all presidents of the Seneca Nation of Indians. Samuel Jimerson, John, and Redeye signed the February 3, 1874, Seneca protest against the allotment and long-term leasing of the Allegany Indian reservation. Courtesy of the Smithsonian Institution National Anthropological Archives.

Left to right: Samuel Jimerson, Casler Redeye, and Harrison Halftown. Courtesy of the Smithsonian Institution National Anthropological Archives.

Oneida Civil War veterans. Henry Webster (*left, above*), Cedelous Peters (*right, above*), and Jemison Skenandore (*left*). Courtesy of the Oneida Nation Museum.

Lewis Henry Morgan. Courtesy of the Buffalo and Erie County Historical Society.

Asher Wright, missionary to the Senecas, 1831–75. Wright was a major force in Seneca life for over four decades. He influenced the direction of Seneca Christianity, education, governmental relations with the United States, politics, and social welfare. Courtesy of the Buffalo and Erie County Historical Society.

Thomas Asylum for Orphans and Destitute Indians. The Thomas Asylum, later renamed the Thomas Indian School, founded by Philip Thomas in 1856, housed orphans of Indian soldiers killed in the war. It was a major educational and social welfare institution for one hundred years. Courtesy of the U.S. Government Printing Office.

Grand Army of the Republic veterans' gathering at Gowanda, N.Y., Water Street, ca. 1907. *Back row, fourth from left:* Jimmy Cornplanter, a Seneca Indian, who died in 1919. Courtesy of the Seneca-Iroquois National Museum.

PART TWO

THE OTHER WAR: THE HOME FRONT

8

Chief Samuel George,
Iroquois Confederacy Spokesman

The Civil War dramatically affected the home front of the Iroquois in Indian Territory; however, other Iroquois communities were also affected, albeit less directly and with fewer personal and property losses. The Civil War broke down the traditional separation of Indian and non-Indian worlds. From enlistment to combat to mustering out, Iroquois soldiers and sailors were exposed to new situations far from the rural isolation of their reservations. Equally important, because of the war, leaders on the home front were also less isolated, having to contend with a variety of issues, most notably the problems engendered by Indian enlistment in the Union army. Iroquois leaders had to contend with the long-standing issues that had affected their communities. Land claims, a perennial issue in Iroquoia, burst to the surface during the Civil War and affected tribal politics as well as Indian-white relations in the early 1860s. Hence in New York, Iroquois leaders developed new tactics and refined older strategies of cultural survival. By examining the life of Samuel George, perhaps the consummate Onondaga Indian conservative of the nineteenth century and principal spokesman of the Iroquois Confederacy during the Civil War era, one can appreciate the flexible adaptation of Iroquoian culture in the nineteenth century.

F. D. Huntington, the Episcopal bishop of central New York in 1889, labeled George the "ablest pagan chief of this generation."[1] Despite a certain cultural myopia, Huntington's appraisal was accurate. George was among the most influential Onondaga "traditionals" of the century. Unlike other Onondaga leaders of the same period such as Chief Albert Cusick, who converted to Christianity, George held steadfastly to his native beliefs.[2] He did not reject change outright and did permit Western education

103

among his people, but he was also a strong advocate of Indian sovereignty and treaty rights. Like Onondaga conservatives then and now, he urged a separate course for the Iroquois and opposed amalgamation into the American body politic.

George was born into the Wolf Clan of the Onondagas on the Buffalo Creek Reservation in 1795. This level and well-wooded tract of 83,555 fertile acres along Cayuga, Cazenovia, and Buffalo creeks, which included much of the present-day city of Buffalo, was the central site of Indian life in New York in the sixty years that followed the American Revolution. It attracted a substantial number of Iroquois refugees from all of the Six Nations. Although the Senecas were the most numerous and politically influential on the reservation, the Onondagas were well represented. In 1816, out of a total of 450 Onondagas in New York, 210 were residing at the Buffalo Creek Reservation. As late as 1837, there were 197 Onondagas on the reservation — approximately 40 percent of all Onondagas in New York State. They occupied a square-mile tract on the southerly side of the reservation along Cazenovia Creek.[3]

The Seneca prophet Handsome Lake, at times a resident of the Buffalo Creek Reservation, received his first vision in 1799, when George was still a small boy. The word of the prophet spread quickly. He spoke against the use of alcohol and against witchcraft and urged the Iroquois to return to traditional ceremonies. At the same time, he urged the Indians to learn to farm in the white manner, and he gave religious sanction to a male role in agriculture. He also preached the transformation of the Indian family structure from the traditional extended family or clan to the nuclear family structure of Europeans. And he urged his people not to give any more land to the white man and to take no part in the wars of the whites. Although innovative in some respects, Handsome Lake's movement was basically conservative in that it called for the restoration of Iroquois beliefs and ceremonies that had fallen into disuse. He accepted the old gods and myths, the ancient dream rites, and the old annual calendar.[4]

It is not surprising that Samuel George's nation, the Onondaga, was receptive to the prophet's conservative preaching. The Onondagas had not prospered under white domination. The millions of acres they had held in 1776 were gone. By the 1820s they were reduced to a reservation of 6,100 acres at Onondaga and to living with other members of the Six Nations at Buffalo Creek and along the Grand River near Brantford, Ontario. Divided by the events of the American Revolution, by the proselytizing of white missionaries, and by the power plays of their own leaders, they were impressed by Handsome Lake's call for solidarity and temperance. Many

Onondagas converted to his teachings. The prophet died while visiting the Onondaga Reservation in 1815 and was buried beneath the floor of the old Onondaga longhouse, a site marked today by a monument in the center of the reservation.[5]

Samuel George was twenty when the prophet died. The historical record gives no hint of contact between the two, and George, like many Iroquois, ignored Handsome Lake's proscription against Indian participation in the white man's wars. The Iroquois, including a sizable detachment of Onondagas, served on the American side in the War of 1812. They viewed themselves as citizens of their separate nations and as allies of the United States under the direct command of their own chiefs, especially the Seneca leader Farmer's Brother. Onondagas, including Samuel George, followed the leadership of their chiefs, Captains Cold (Cole) and LaFort. Ironically, in the war the Onondagas were fighting against British-allied Iroquois, including Onondagas, from the Six Nations Reserve in Ontario.[6]

The Iroquois, including the Onondagas, derived little benefit from the war. They suffered casualties in battle and endured smallpox epidemics, and several of the fiercest engagements of the war took place on their lands along the Niagara River. But for Samuel George, the war was a theater in which he displayed courage, endurance, and physical prowess, all of which play a role in the making of a leader among the Iroquois. Serving along the Buffalo-to-Albany corridor during the conflict, George excelled as a runner. He was a thin, sinewy man with strong features, whose physical appearance was frequently mentioned in the records. He was viewed by one observer as "a noble specimen of a man" for his athletic prowess and presence. George's greatest achievement during the War of 1812 was to run from American headquarters at Buffalo to the arsenal at Canandaigua and back, a distance of 150 miles, in two days.[7]

George's running ability was legendary. Orlando Allen, who later helped cheat the Iroquois out of their lands, wrote that George was virtually unbeatable in foot races. The only challenge to his string of victories came from John Titus, a Seneca Indian from the Allegany Reservation. According to Allen, Titus defeated George only once:

> On one occasion Titus achieved by strategy, what he could not by speed, and that was by keeping close up to George until within a few steps of the goal, and then just before crossing the line, putting forth all of his powers, slipped by leaving George no time to recover the lost race, as he probably could have done in ten strides. George was exceedingly mortified at the result and was careful not to be thus outwitted again. I think he was on no other occasion beaten in these races.[8]

The importance of runners in Iroquois history should not be underestimated. They were not merely gifted athletes. Iroquois runners summoned councils, conveyed intelligence from nation to nation, and warned of impending danger. George's contemporary Lewis Henry Morgan, in his classic *League of the Ho-de-no-sau-nee, or Iroquois,* observed: "Swiftness of foot was an acquirement, among the Iroquois, which brought the individual into high repute."[9] George's rise to power and influence in the Iroquois councils was a direct result of his physical prowess.[10]

George later received a pension of $120 for his participation in the War of 1812. In his pension request for three years of service in the defense of the Niagara frontier he asked to be compensated for the following: one hat ($5.00), ordinary (nonuniform) coat ($25.00), one vest ($3.50), one pair of "leggins" ($3.50), two blankets ($10.00), one knapsack ($3.00), one canteen ($.25), "use" of one rifle ($10.00), one canoe ($6.00), two vests ($7.00), two pairs of stockings ($1.00), two shirts ($4.00), two pairs of moccasins ($2.00), one neckerchief ($1.50), and one "scalping knife" ($.50).[11] He also requested $2.00 compensation for his transportation expenses between Buffalo Creek and Fort Niagara (eighty miles round trip).

From the end of the War of 1812 until 1838, George virtually disappears from the historical record; it is, nevertheless, possible to reconstruct a part of this period of his life. George and his people nearly met destruction in the three decades after the War of 1812. Following the opening of the Erie Canal in 1825, population rapidly increased in central and western New York. The city of Buffalo was formally incorporated in 1831 and soon became a major Great Lakes port, creating further pressure for expansion; however, the Buffalo Creek Reservation blocked the city's expansion to the southeast. Land speculators soon took advantage of the Iroquois, who were bitterly divided by matters such as land sales, methods of selecting chiefs, education, and religion that separated the Indians into different camps and made them susceptible to manipulation. Land speculators and corrupt federal officials took advantage of the situation, employed bribery and coercion, and induced some of the chiefs to sign the Treaty of Buffalo Creek in 1838, by which the Indians lost the Buffalo Creek Reservation. Among the Iroquois signatories to the treaty were two Onondaga warriors, William John and Noah Silversmith, who acted without authority from the chiefs and received $2,000 for their "cooperation." George led the opposition to the treaty and signed petitions to that effect.

The Onondagas were the most resistant to change of all the New York Iroquois. One article of the treaty offered them cash compensation totaling $4,500 to move west.[12] Few of them moved, in sharp contrast to the substantial number of Cayugas and Oneidas who left New York after the signing. The Onondaga and Tonawanda chiefs vociferously opposed the Seneca political revolution of 1848 that had overturned the old chieftain system of government and had established a republic, the Seneca Nation of Indians, an elected political system apart from the Iroquois Confederacy. For more than two decades, they tried to restore the old chieftain system of government on the Allegany and Cattaraugus reservations. Samuel George was one of the Onondaga leaders who supported the Senecas in their attempt to restore the traditional government. Writing in 1850, he praised the Old Chiefs party at Cattaraugus and urged them "to defend the rights of the system of our old Indian government . . . so highly important to us all to maintain."[13]

Onondaga conservatism was also reflected in other ways, Jabez Hyde, a missionary at Buffalo Creek from 1811 to 1820, commented in his journal that the Onondagas were strongly opposed to conversion. Despite the frequent visits of Episcopal, Methodist, Presbyterian, and Quaker missionaries and the building of a Methodist and Episcopal church, as well as an Episcopal school at Onondaga in the nineteenth century, a minority of the Onondagas were converted. Although the Onondaga chiefs permitted these sects on the reservation, the missionaries' Christian message was not universally accepted. As late as 1890, there were only 68 Christians at Onondaga out of a population of 494 residents (including 86 Oneidas); nevertheless, the Council of Chiefs permitted these sects, as well as the New York superintendent of public instruction, to operate schools on the reservation.[14]

To preserve their identity, Onondagas retained their separate existence, spoke their own languages, performed their ceremonies, continued to observe their native religion, did not push for state or federal suffrage, and viewed themselves as citizens of sovereign nation-states. Most importantly, they protested every effort to undermine their tribal land base after the loss of the Buffalo Creek Reservation and their return to the homeland in central New York. After the death of the Onondaga chief Captain Cold (Ut-ha-wah), the confederacy's council fire, which had burned at Buffalo Creek, was rekindled at Onondaga. The sacred wampum was returned to the Onondaga longhouse in 1847. After a brief residence at the Cattaraugus Reservation in the mid-1840s, Samuel George moved his wife nd five children to Onondaga. It was there in 1850 that he became a chief, taking the name Hononwirehdonh, the Great Wolf, the hereditary keeper of the wampum held by a member of the Wolf Clan of the Onondaga Nation.[15]

The attainment of this title, which he held until his death in 1873, was the culmination of four decades of apprenticeship for leadership.

Hononwirehdonh was no ordinary title. As anthropologist Annemarie Shimony states: "He is arbiter of disputes and the tie-breaker in voting. To him are left decisions of referral back to the individual phratries [tribal social subdivisions], and to him accrues the task of 'cooling down the fire' when arguments break out." He is also "the wampum keeper of the League, and the only chief to constitute a phratry all by himself."[16] Thus at a time of bitter dissension caused by the Buffalo Creek Treaty and its aftermath and continued talk by federal and state officials of Iroquois removal from New York, the Hononwirehdonh, with his responsibility to help create consensus and pacify diverse elements, held a strategic position in the struggle for Iroquois survival.

In the early 1850s, a bill to survey the Onondaga Reservation was introduced and passed in the New York State Assembly without the prior approval or knowledge of the Onondaga Council of Chiefs. When the chiefs learned of this bill, they protested, insisting that surveying was the first step in the division of the reservation into individual allotments and ultimate Indian land loss, "thereby destroying that bond of common interest which unites and holds Indian communities together."[17] The bill failed to pass the New York State Senate, but these efforts continued through the late nineteenth and early twentieth centuries. The movement to survey and allot the reservation was supported by disgruntled Onondagas, some of whom were Christian converts, who objected to the power of the traditional Council of Chiefs. They accused the chiefs of personally profiting from their position by allowing whites to strip timber on the reservation. There is also evidence that some Onondagas did not welcome Indian refugees from the Buffalo Creek Reservation with open arms.[18]

During the Civil War, Samuel George was the leading spokesman of the Iroquois Confederacy in dealing with Washington officials. By 1863, he was given the honorary rank of brevet general by the U.S. government and was acknowledged to be the principal chief of the Six Nations. Although the Iroquois were generally eager to enlist in the conflict despite religious proscriptions, they reacted strongly to certain abuses in the recruitment process. Much of the Iroquois criticism centered on the military conscription system. The Enrollment Act of 1863, which set categories of priority for conscription of all able-bodied male citizens, allowed many reasons for exemptions. The act exempted anyone who could pay a $300 exemption fee or provide a substitute.[19] Though no Iroquois were drafted during the Civil War, in sharp contrast to World War II and Vietnam, they were affected by the Enrollment Act.[20] Because most of the Indians in New York were poor, some were attracted by the bounty, as were their brethren in Wisconsin. Non-Indian bounty brokers actively recruited Indians as replacements. But the Indians were also victims of unscrupulous brokers. By 1863, forty-three Iroquois, mostly Senecas, serving in the 24th New York Cavalry, 86th, 97th, and 100th New York Volunteers, and 13th and 14th New York Heavy Artillery, asked to be released from service, claiming that they had never received all or part of their promised bounties or that they were underage recruits, some being only fifteen or sixteen years old.

These forty-three Indians became a cause célèbre in Iroquoia. News of their plight eventually reached the Tuscarora Company in North Carolina. On February 26, 1863, Newt Parker spelled out his company's concern about their fellow tribesmen:

> The friends of the boys here are in quite a stew aint they? They have written to Washington to the President asking for discharge of the Indians here. They (the boys here) say that their district attorney and Isaac Halftown [president of the Seneca Nation] and others have come to Washington, says they had council, the councillors did. Do you hear anything about it? I have written a great long letter to the relations of the boys here through Mr. Asher Wright. You may hear of it — by Sister [sister-in-law] Martha.[21]

Although most of the soldiers involved were Senecas, Samuel George led the protest. In November 1863, he met with President Lincoln to discuss the matter. As a designated official of the Six Nations, George followed the traditional course established by earlier chiefs, who held that negotiations affecting the Iroquois must be made directly with the president of the United States on a basis of equal nations.[22] In his talk with Lincoln, George undoubtedly reaffirmed the federal-Indian treaty relationship and questioned the right of Congress to pass legislation such as the Enrollment Act without prior deliberation and approval of the Iroquois League Council.

George convinced Lincoln to intervene on behalf of the Indian recruits. On November 20, 1863, Lincoln wrote Secretary of War Edwin Stanton: "Please see and hear the Sec. of Interior and Comm. of Indian Affairs with Genl. George, Indian Chief and discharge such of the men as the chief applies for and who have not received bounties." Seventeen days later, the assistant adjutant general's office issued Special Order No. 542, which allowed for the discharge of thirteen Iroquois Indians serving in the 13th New York Heavy Artillery and one in the 86th New York Volunteers. On December 23, thirteen of the fourteen Indians were released from military service. The order read: "Discharged by direction of the President at the request of the Chief of the Six Nations Indians."[23]

George was less successful in securing the discharge of the other Indians, though he and the Senecas frequently petitioned for their release. In June 1864, Seneca leaders insisted that they had "authorized Samuel George head chief among the Onondagas and representative of the Six Nations to present our supplication." The Senecas repeated George's arguments to Lincoln, maintaining that there was no law allowing for the drafting or enlistment of Indian minor children and objecting to conscription of Indians into military service without prior tribal consent, which went against historic precedent and treaties. A month later, George wrote the commissioner of Indian affairs. Recalling his official visit to Washington and interviews with politicians nine months earlier, George repeated his stand about discharging the Indians. "We agreed [that] those who have not received Bounty from the Government shall be discharged from the service, notwithstanding many [of] our young men taken away . . . I hope that you will discharge them without further delay."[24]

After substantial negotiations, the remaining Indians won the right to be discharged but only after they were required to pay back whatever bounty they had received. Unfortunately, most of them had already spent the money, and though at least three repaid the bounty and were discharged, the majority stayed in military service to the end of the Civil War. At least two of these Indians, Privates Ira Pierce and John B. Williams, died in the conflict — Pierce at Petersburg and Williams as a prisoner of war at Andersonville Prison.[25]

Despite his limited victory, George's efforts helped reinforce the Iroquois's traditional belief in their sovereignty. Reaffirming treaty rights, meeting with the Great Father in Washington, and rejecting conscription without tribal consent are as strongly established in the conservative agenda of the Onondagas today as they were during the Civil War. Although success is important, symbolism, form, and style are equally important in the Iroquois traditional mind.[26]

George next displayed his leadership as a consensus builder in the Iroquois's pursuit of their so-called Kansas claim. William Dole, the commissioner of Indian affairs in 1862, recognized that "these Indians have very considerable unadjusted claims against the United States, arising under the provisions and stipulations of the Buffalo Creek Treaty of January 15, 1838." Under this fraudulent treaty the "entire body of these Indians" was scheduled to emigrate to Kansas, then part of Indian Territory, where 1,824,000 acres were set aside for them; in return the Indians "agreed" to cede 500,000 acres of land in Wisconsin to the United States government. Many of those Indians who left New York for the West perished as a result of disease, exposure, and starvation or were "compelled to subsist mainly by the charities of the tribes there residing." Those who survived or returned to New York later claimed that they failed to receive their proper due under the treaty. Dole agreed: "Very many complaints have been received at this office upon this subject, and it is believed that in some instances they are founded in justice." The commissioner urged congressional legislation to make a "final adjustment of all the claims of the New York Indians," including both those "still residing in New York" and "those who emigrated to Kansas under the treaty of 1838."[27]

The Kansas claim, which was settled in a per capita cash award by the United States Court of Claims in the 1890s, led to a major brouhaha in 1864. At a time when Iroquois soldiers and sailors were fighting and dying for the Union cause, Iroquois leaders were in a serious confrontation with the Interior Department. In May 1864, Secretary of the Interior J. P. Usher sent Charles Mix as his "special commissioner" to meet with the Iroquois leaders. Mix was no mere lowly functionary in the Bureau of Indian Affairs. He was the chief clerk, serving as commissioner of Indian affairs in 1858 and as acting commissioner during the frequent absences of commissioners from the capital. According to his biographer, "Mix seems to have written most of the annual reports for the bureau, or at least to have compiled the basic reports which the commissioners could revise slightly and sign."[28] Equally important, Mix had long been involved with negotiating with the Indians of New York and was one of the signatories to the Tonawanda Treaty of 1857; nevertheless, he made major mistakes in 1864 that were to sabotage any hope of resolving the Kansas claim.[29]

Because of poor weather, Mix arrived several days late to the negotiating session at the Cattaraugus Indian Reservation. George opened the council at the Newtown Longhouse "by taking off the ashes from the embers" and delivering "the speech of salutation and welcome." He then informed the representatives of each of the Iroquois communities present that the meeting had been called to discuss the Kansas claim and that the proceedings had the blessing of the Grand Council. The Indian delegates then caucused and elected a president—Henry Silverheels, president of the Seneca Nation—and two secretaries—A. Sim Logan, a Seneca, and Dr. Peter Wilson, a Cayuga—to preside and take minutes at the meeting, which was soon adjourned to the council chambers of the Seneca Nation. Nervously, Mix viewed the Indians as somehow conspiring against him. After Silverheels arrived and spoke, Mix requested that the "chiefs and delegates furnish evidence to show that they have been appointed and authorized to act for their tribes in the premises." When Peter Wilson responded by asking the commissioner to present his own credentials to the council, Mix became enraged.[30]

Wilson had been a long-standing advocate of the Kansas claim. His Indian community, mostly residents of the Senecas' Cattaraugus Indian Reservation, had been dispossessed of all their tribal lands in the years after the American Revolution. Many had gone west after the conclusion of the Buffalo Creek Treaty. Wilson was a graduate of Hamilton College and Geneva Medical College. Even though he was a Cayuga, he had served as interpreter for the Senecas in dealings with the government. He had worked with Quaker philanthropist Philip Thomas on charitable and educational matters since the 1840s. He had helped secure military pensions from the federal government for Iroquois veterans of the War of 1812. One of these pensioners was Samuel George. Despite these credentials, Wilson was viewed by some in Iroquoia as a political opportunist and a self-promoter. His penchant for political turmoil as well as his heavy alcohol use also engendered criticism. Thus, by the time of Mix's meeting with the Iroquois over the Kansas claim, some of the Iroquois were uneasy about Wilson.[31]

Commissioner Mix foolishly refused to present his credentials, although it was standard practice for federal officials to do so when negotiating with the Iroquois. Mix retorted: "It is the custom and practice of the government, in its dealings with the Indians, to require credentials. It is the right of the superior power to require of the inferior power. This requirement is in accordance with the practice of the government."[32]

Thus Mix insulted the majority of Indians present and made it impossible for the meeting to continue. Despite Indian resentment of Wilson, few defended Mix. Iroquois conservatives believed that negotiations should be approached in a reciprocal fashion, despite the power Washington commanded. Wilson responded to Mix that the Indian nations "are equal with the President of the United States and the commissioner is nothing but a servant." Therefore, Mix could not dictate to them. Although the commissioner later reported that there was some opposition to Wilson on the part of two Senecas and one Cayuga Indian, the vast majority of Iroquois clearly were not interested in hearing any more from Mix. Further aggravating matters, Mix later insisted that Wilson's and the council's actions were an insult to President Lincoln.[33]

Secretary Usher then dispatched John Manley as "special U.S. Indian Agent within the New York Agency." Manley, who remained an important figure in administering policy directives in New York for the next decade, reported to the Indians that the Interior Department "will not again consent to a convention in relation to your Kansas land claims." He informed the Indians that Mix's conduct met the approval of President Lincoln, that American officials were annoyed by the insults directed at them, and that the United States "does not accept insult or wrong against its authority from any source or power, great or small."[34] This delay in the claim's resolution was to have far-reaching consequences.

After this fiasco, Iroquois unity over the claim temporarily came apart, and individual communities asked Washington for separate negotiations.[35] Negotiations between the Six Nations and the federal government finally resumed again at the Cattaraugus Reservation in December 1868 after a semblance of Indian unity was restored. A treaty was drafted and signed by all parties compensating the Indians one dollar per acre for 1,824,000 acres of land. Because of opposition in the United States Senate, the death of a key senator, and the end of treaty making between the government and the Indians after 1871, the Kansas claim remained unresolved. Two decades after Samuel George's death, the United States Court of Claims finally adjudicated the controversy, providing an award of $1,998,744.46 to the "New York Indians" in the 1890s.[36]

George's failure to maintain consensus in the resolution of the Kansas claim surely was a bitter pill. Nevertheless, his stewardship is revealing. He presided over two negotiations with federal authorities at the Cattaraugus Indian Reservation, not at Onondaga, the Iroquois Confederacy's present location for the Grand Council. Even after the Senecas' loss of the Buffalo Creek Reservation and the creation of the Seneca Nation of Indians that deposed the old chief system, the political focus of Iroquoian traditional life in the mid-nineteenth century was with the Senecas, not the Onondagas. Wampum had been returned to Onondaga in 1847. The ritual cycle had led Seaman William Jones to go immediately to Onondaga on his return home from the Civil War. Nevertheless, important political issues such as the Kansas claim led Onondaga chiefs such as George to journey to Seneca country. The tensions between the Iroquois Confederacy and individual Iroquois councils, which have existed over the years at different levels of combustion, apparently were somewhat mitigated during the Civil War, leading to George's role as Iroquois spokesman on behalf of underage Seneca recruits.

Following the war, George continued to serve as Iroquois spokesman. In March 1870, as head chief, he wrote to Governor John Hoffman of New York to complain about whites stripping timber on the Onondaga Reservation, to inquire about the status of an Indian agent, and to raise questions about leasing. In June 1870, he asked Hoffman for information about money owed to the Indians by New York State.[37]

From 1869 to 1873, George was formally licensed to practice medicine and was appointed government physician to the Onondagas after a petition was signed by thirty-three leading Indians and non-Indians in the environs of Syracuse. His long involvement as a traditional medicine man is clear from the historic record. R. H. Gardner, the Indian agent at that time, formally endorsed George's appointment: "I believe Captain George can doctor the Indians as well as a white man. After considerable experience on the subject, I believed that the Indians lived under his treatment and are as healthful as when treated by any other physician."[38]

During the last two decades of George's life, his gift for oratory was noted by observers of the Indian world. According to William Beauchamp, the prominent missionary and keen observer of the Onondaga world in the nineteenth and early twentieth centuries, George "was both shrewd and eloquent" and "full of official dignity and seldom condescending to speak English." Although "thin and rather fun-looking," George was frequently a featured speaker at public events. His speeches were translated from Onondaga into English. His fame as a storyteller was widespread and undoubtedly added to his prestige and power among his own people and outsiders in the non-Indian environs of Syracuse. Beauchamp added: "I have heard him speak, and he was fond of story-telling, having a good stock to draw upon. He remembered when the Onondagas moved up the valley to their present reservation village, many building bark houses at that time."[39]

Oratory was the path to leadership among the Iroquois. Lewis Henry Morgan observed in 1851: "By the cultivation and exercise of this capacity, was opened the pathway to distinction; and the chief or warrior gifted with its magical power could elevate himself as rapidly, as he who gained renown upon the warpath." George's speaking abilities, in combination with his diplomatic and medical skills and his physical prowess, gave him a position of particular influence at the council fires of the Iroquois Confederacy.[40]

Until his death on September 24, 1873, George lived in a small frame, single-story house just northeast of the Onondaga Council House, about a quarter of a mile from the center of the reservation. He remained a traditional to the end, never converting to Christianity. Although a Christian sermon was presented at his funeral by Bishop Huntington and other Episcopal leaders, George was buried with Indian rites as prescribed by the Great Binding Law of his Iroquois people.[41]

Samuel George witnessed striking changes in the status of the Iroquois during his lifetime. He was directly involved in two wars—in the War of 1812 as a combatant and in the Civil War as an Iroquois spokesman. He undoubtedly observed and was affected by the Iroquois revitalization movement inspired by Handsome Lake's visions, which stimulated changes in the agriculture, the basic family patterns, and the religion of the Iroquois.

He lived through a period of explosive growth in the white population of central and western New York during which his people lost substantial amounts of land and suffered environmental deterioration and social circumscription. He endured a failed Indian leadership that was incapable of stemming the tide of land speculators and missionaries, as he endured the increased dependence of the Indian on the white man caused by the economic and political changes brought about by American industrialization in combination with a shrinking Indian land base.

Despite these revolutionary changes, George remained an Iroquois conservative to the end. His rise to influence among his people had been along the traditional paths to authority. His brand of conservatism allowed him to accept but modify the teachings of Handsome Lake. Although he faithfully ascribed to the ceremonials, kept his Iroquoian language alive, and rejected alienation of Indian lands, he served the American cause in two major wars. He also permitted missionaries and schools to be maintained on the Onondaga Reservation and was a well-known and admired personality off the reservation. While dealing with the likes of Bishop Huntington, Commissioner Mix, Governor Hoffman, or President Lincoln, George attempted in a practical but mostly traditional way to serve his people and to express Indian concerns despite the often debilitating internal discord that was reflected in the Iroquois policy and the incredible pressures from the non-Indian world. George's steadfastness in maintaining tradition, however flexible in approach, makes him worthy of study and explains much about Iroquois survival well over a century after his death.

9

Railroading

Non-Indian settlement patterns in New York State changed Iroquois life in the second half of the nineteenth century. From 1850 to 1870, the population of surrounding non-Indian communities grew rapidly. In these two decades, Buffalo's population rose from 42,261 to 117,714, while that of Syracuse increased from 22,271 to 43,051. Even in the sparsely populated North Country, inhabited by Mohawks, the city of Malone increased in population from 4,545 to 7,186.[1]

Between 1850 and 1870, the Native American population in New York State increased only slightly, and on some reservations it declined sharply. Iroquois communities periodically suffered major health crises resulting in high mortality rates. The New York Yearly Meeting of Friends reported 135 cases of smallpox raging among the Seneca Nation in 1862, largely because the disease was misdiagnosed and public health measures were delayed. The population of the Tonawanda Reservation declined from 602 persons in 1855 to 509 a decade later, more than a 15 percent drop. Forty-four Tonawanda Senecas died of smallpox, which caused nearly a 7 percent decrease in the community's population.[2]

One of the greatest demographic changes affected the Seneca Nation in this period. The town of Salamanca, now a largely non-Indian city 85 percent of which is on the Senecas' Allegany Indian Reservation, as well as five other surrounding non-Indian communities — Carrolton, Great Valley, Red House, Vandalia, and West Salamanca — were settled by non-Indians between 1850 and 1875.[3] On June 28, 1850, the newly created Seneca Nation of Indians, still in political turmoil as a result of the Seneca revolution of 1848, leased a 145-acre right-of-way for $3,000 to the New York and Erie Railroad, later the Erie Railroad, for 11.66 miles of track through the Allegany Reservation. Although leasing of Indian lands re-

117

quired formal federal approval, this 1850 agreement was confirmed by the action of the New York State legislature. The Erie Railroad, which had been chartered by the legislature in 1832, was to shape southwestern New York as well as state and Seneca politics well into the twentieth century. In April 1851, the Erie's last spike was driven into the track near Cuba, and the railroad was officially opened on May 14, 1851.[4] On August 20, 1863, while many Senecas were away fighting for the Union cause, the Erie Railroad leased an additional 23.85 acres for $2,385 for the "construction, occupancy and maintenance" of its rail activities. According to one Salamanca historian, it "was this second deal which initiated the junction of the Erie Railroad and the Atlantic and Great Western Railroad at Salamanca, also laying the foundations for the other villages which served as railroad depots."[5]

The railroad shaped Indian policy within the state of New York from 1850 to 1875. The railroad also transported significant numbers of people and resources and stimulated further entrepreneurial activities. During the Civil War, James McHenry, an English iron magnate, and his friend and business associate the Marquis of Salamanca, a Spanish royalist who had made a fortune in investing and constructing railways throughout France, Italy, and Spain, extended the Atlantic and Great Western Railroad 369 miles from Salamanca, named after the marquis, to Dayton, Ohio. Between 1864 and 1866, the Atlantic and Great Western built a spur line south to Oil City, Pennsylvania, to take advantage of newly found petroleum fields. The Seneca Nation later approved a lease to the Buffalo and Pittsburgh Railroad. In each of these instances, the railroads were to control their leased rights-of-way as long as they continued to operate.[6] Four days after the surrender at Appomattox, Thomas Wistar of the Society of Friends reported that the railroads, which were now crisscrossing the Allegany Reservation, had six stations on Seneca lands and that fifty acres of tribal lands were being used by the railroads for depots, machine shops, and other buildings.[7]

Seneca tribal records reveal that whites were soon illegally squatting on tribal lands. Railroad construction crews and rail service were followed by other whites, including farmers and persons in service occupations for the railroad. Moreover, Edwin L. Drake's successful drilling of the first oil well in nearby Titusville, Pennsylvania, in 1859 stimulated non-Indian population growth in northwestern Pennsylvania and southwestern New York. The discovery of oil also spurred outside investment and rail development. In 1861, the Atlantic and Great Western Railroad transported 50,000 gallons of oil in a five-month period. By the late 1870s and until the first decade of the twentieth century, the area in and around the Allegany Reservation was one of the major oil-exporting regions of the United States. In 1899 alone, 75,695 barrels of oil were produced by the Seneca Oil Company, a non-Indian venture operating on the reservation; the next year the company was absorbed by the South Penn Oil Company, a subsidiary of Standard Oil, for $2 million. The railways also transported other rich resources of the area such as leather hides, lumber, hemlock bark, coal, and natural gas.[8]

Thus the town of Salamanca, which was incorporated with the village of Bucktooth in 1861, achieved virtually overnight a population of 1,881 non-Indians by 1870. Going against federal, state, and tribal laws, these non-Indian squatters subsequently leased reservation lands at low rentals from individual Senecas. Federal census records for 1860 and 1870 indicate that the white population on the Allegany Indian Reservation grew significantly in that decade, perhaps suggesting that leasing was a means for individual Seneca families to survive when numerous Indian men were away serving in the Union army and navy.[9]

In 1866, the Philadelphia Yearly Meeting of Friends reported on this phenomenon and warned of its consequences: "Their [Senecas'] attention was also called to the large number of white people who occupy their lands, partly attracted thither by the two Rail Roads which run through them, and the depots erected there, and the danger of their ultimately losing the control or being dispossessed of them." The report described the large white population in less than complimentary terms: "many of whom are of low moral character and expose them [the Senecas] to corrupting examples and associations and present temptations which they have not firmness to resist." The Friends added: "The Rail Roads and stations on the Allegheny [sic] Reservation greatly increase the evils which proceed from this cause; and it must continue to operate so long as the Indians are located around and near the villages." By 1875, some of the whites had already made sizable profits by subleasing Indian land; 420 leasing arrangements had been made, and the total white investment on the Allegany Reservation had reached $1,359,775. Approximately one-third of the reservation was leased to non-Indians.[10]

The rapid, uncontrolled white settlement of the Allegany Indian Reservation was accomplished at a time when the government of the Seneca Nation was weak. It had little power to rid the reservation of squatters or control the action of individual tribesmen. The Seneca Nation had a severely divided polity between 1850 and 1880, which limited its ability to control outside encroachment by whites or entrepreneurial activity by individual Senecas going against tribal custom. In addition, federal officials failed to carry out their primary trust responsibility to protect tribal interests from unscrupulous white predators seeking unfair advantage.[11]

As a result of the Buffalo Creek Treaty of 1838, the Seneca polity, which had always been multidimensional and diverse, further splintered. Senecas began accusing their chiefs of assenting to the nefarious treaty. Out of the politics of blame came a political revolution and a new political entity, the Seneca Nation of Indians, a republican form of government outside the purview of the Iroquois Confederacy. In 1848, the Senecas at the Allegany, Cattaraugus, and Oil Spring reservations overturned the old chief system of government and formally created an elected system of tribal government chartered under the laws of New York State. Yet a significant number of Senecas, as well as their allies such as Samuel George, drawn from the other Iroquois communities, resisted this revolution well after its apparent success.[12] Even as late as the Civil War era, determined efforts were being made to overturn it.

In 1864, Commissioner Dole reported the efforts of certain Seneca councillors at the Allegany and Cattaraugus reservations "to subvert and overturn the constitution and republican form of government adopted by the Senecas some years since." Accusing them of undermining the "tranquillity, welfare and best interest of their people," the commissioner insisted that their intention was "to foist upon them their old barbarian and irresponsible mode of government by chiefs."[13]

Dole apparently misread the complex battles being fought within the Seneca polity in 1864. By the time of his report, Seneca divisions had led to the formation of political parties. After the Seneca revolution of 1848, the New Government party opposed the Old Chiefs party. Each came to power in the two decades after 1848. Even though the Old Chiefs party was initially committed to overthrowing the changes wrought by the revolution and frequently called for annulling the new form of government, the party's members generally participated in the Seneca electoral process in the period. By the late 1850s and 1860s, although some individual former chiefs still refused to participate, others were candidates on both parties' tickets.[14]

In the fall of 1864, the political battling reached a new height. In that year, Henry Silverheels was elected president of the Seneca Nation. On October 4, the Seneca constitution was amended, vesting legislative authority "in a council of Sachems and Chiefs to be chosen, elected and inaugurated according to the rules, regulations, and customs of the ancient Confederacy of the Iroquois." In November, a Six Nations Council, at the urging of a majority of the Seneca Nation's elected council, created thirty-five Seneca sachems and chiefs, declared the Seneca constitution null and void, and attempted to remove President Silverheels from office. Silverheels rejected these actions and successfully appealed to Commissioner Dole to intervene in the controversy. Thus, by the end of 1864, the Seneca polity was in crisis, just at the time leasing became a factor in Seneca life. Disputed Seneca elections in 1876 and 1878 occurred precisely when oil and other mineral leasing became major tribal concerns.[15]

Individual Seneca entrepreneurs took advantage of the confusion in the tribal polity for their own profit. Senecas Lyman Shongo and Charles Halftown leased land on the eastern end of Allegany to the Vandalia Chemical Works, which purchased large quantities of hemlock bark and processed it into an extract for use in the leather tanning industry. Another Seneca, John Lewis, made sixty-seven leases involving sixty-nine acres of tribal property and collected $1,325.50 per annum. Other large Seneca entrepreneurs included Charles Kennedy, who consummated twenty-six leases, and Lucy Hoag, who arranged twenty-one leases. Many of the leases made between whites and individual Senecas were subsequently subleased by the whites at great profit to themselves.[16]

By 1874, Salamanca was a well-established city of over two thousand non-Indians. The thriving community, dotted by railroad buildings, bridges, and tracks, also had three churches, four schools, four physicians, two attorneys, a pharmacist, a butcher, a cabinetmaker, a policeman, three teamsters, twelve merchants, seven hotel keepers, a grocer, a shoemaker, two carpenters, a clerk, and a wagon shop owner. One of the more extensive of these white enterprises was a barrel-making factory.[17]

The largely non-Indian community of Salamanca had much in common with other frontier towns of the day. Like white settlements in the trans-Mississippi West, the community was largely an outgrowth of a land rush stimulated by the railroad, followed by development of mineral resources but with one major difference — Salamanca was located almost entirely on Indian land without the sanction of a treaty or congressional legislation. Thus it was no coincidence that the non-Indian lessees, encouraged by railroad officials, began to try to secure a legal basis for their illegal occupation of Seneca lands. Although attempts before the Civil War at getting at Indian lands had failed, largely because of the preemptive claim of the Ogden Land Company to the Allegany and Cattaraugus Indian reservations, railroad politics in the post–Civil War era added a powerful new dimension to this effort at dispossessing the Indians.[18]

Taking advantage of divisions among the Senecas, the non-Indian lessees and their political representatives at the local, state, and national levels began agitating to secure validity for their illegal arrangements, longer-term leasing agreements, or even title to their leased lands. Salamancans sent memorials to the New York State legislature in hope of validating their leasing arrangements with individual Senecas. In 1865, the legislature passed private bills confirming illegal leasing arrangements made between non-Indians and Senecas.[19] When efforts at confirming all leases at the state level failed, the lessees and their representatives began to seek a solution at the federal level.

In January 1871, both houses of the New York State legislature passed a concurrent resolution asking Congress to grant legal title to the lessees at Allegany. The resolution described the white settlement as the result of "the natural business location" of Salamanca and the previous confirmation of leases by the legislature. To strengthen the resolution, the legislators insisted that the federal agent had recommended the "sale of this Reservation" as early as 1868.[20]

In 1871, the Salamancans received a setback when Judge George Baker of the New York Supreme Court declared all the leases null and void because they violated the federal Indian Trade and Intercourse Act of 1834, which gave the United States exclusive jurisdiction over Indian affairs. The Seneca Nation then began ejectment proceedings against some of the lessees. In response, Hudson Ansley, town supervisor of Salamanca, wrote a letter of protest to the commissioner of Indian affairs contending that the court decision was a "great injustice" and claiming that the whites had been "invited and encouraged to settle upon" the reservation. Ansley and the Board of Supervisors of Cattaraugus County further elaborated on their grievances and requested that the secretary of the interior appoint a commission to examine "the matters at issue between white settlers and the Seneca Nation of Indians with a view to legislation which will tend to prevent further misunderstanding." Contending that the Indians had sufficient land — "300 acres to each man, woman and child of said nation" — Ansley's and his cohorts' message was clear: the federal government must allow and facilitate allotment of the Allegany Reservation.[21]

The movement to get Congress to confirm the leases or allot reservation lands retroactively gained impetus when Judge William Daniels in 1873 in a decision in Cattaraugus County upheld the Seneca Nation's contentions that the legislature had no legal authority to make laws regulating the use of Seneca lands. As long as the United States recognized the existence of the Seneca Nation and because of existing federal-Indian treaties, Daniels argued that the state had no jurisdiction. The implications of this decision were significant because the railroads as well as the non-Indian lessees had no federal authorization to lease lands on Allegany. With millions of dollars worth of railroad money invested in Salamanca in the balance and two thousand non-Indian voters up in arms, Congress was faced with powerful lobbying interests.[22] Ansley, now chairman of the local "committee of citizens," wrote to the secretary of the interior on July 10, 1873, in support of Congressman Walter Sessions's efforts to "quiet title to the lands of the Seneca Nation of Indians" and to protect "white settlers on the Reservations from wrong or injury which might be attempted by reason of the insufficiency of their title."[23]

In January 1874, Congressman Sessions, an attorney from Harmony, New York, who practiced law in the southwestern part of the state near Seneca country, introduced a bill into the House of Representatives. The bill was aimed at confirming existing leases, extinguishing the claims of the Ogden Land Company, and "allowing" the Senecas to allot their lands.[24] The Salamancans were also aided in their efforts by the actions of the Interior Department, especially Daniel Sherman, the United States Indian agent in New York State in the 1870s. Sherman, a non-Indian who had served as attorney for the Seneca Nation from 1855 to 1868 as well as for the town of Salamanca, had failed to report to his supervisors in Washington that the Allegany Indian Reservation had become overrun by squatters and illegal lessees. Suddenly in 1874 and 1875, Sherman began pushing for "relief" for the non-Indian residents of the town. In an 1875 letter to the commissioner of Indian affairs that was quoted during congressional debate, Sherman described the numerous ways the lessees had improved Salamanca, including bringing more than a million dollars of financial investment to the city. He insisted that they were now "entitled to some relief by the legislation of Congress."[25]

On June 3, 1874, a united Seneca Nation tribal council meeting at the Cattaraugus Reservation passed a resolution condemning congressional efforts to confirm these illegal leases retroactively and sent a formal protest to Washington. President William Nephew, fifteen councillors, and the tribal clerk signed the protest. The signatories, who also included two future presidents of the Seneca Nation — Casler Redeye and Andrew John, Jr.— argued against House Bill No. 3080, the so-called Sessions bill. They insisted that confirmation of illegal leases violated federal treaties with the Senecas, the federal Trade and Intercourse Act of 1834, New York State laws of 1813, 1821, and 1843, as well as "laws, customs, and usages of the Seneca tribe and Nation." The petitioners added

that the Seneca Nation holds all of said lands in tribal or national capacity; that their lands have not been allotted or divided; all the right any individual Indian has therein is confined to possession; that to confer the right of leasing upon individuals would work injustice among our people. That such an act would compel Indians to go into the courts of the United States, or the State of New York, to obtain possession of their

lands if a white man disputed it, as those tribunals would have sole jurisdiction to try all questions of right to your petitioners' land, and thus
our courts would be legislated out of jurisdiction to try actions concerning the possession of their lands.[26]

The Senecas were not saved from allotment and land loss, the fate
of many western Indians, by a well-meaning Congress but by savvy Seneca
leaders and their attorneys. The irony is that the Seneca Nation ironically
used the so-called Ogden Land Company preemptive right to Seneca lands
to its advantage. On September 12, 1810, David A. Ogden of New York
City had purchased for himself and his associates the Holland Land Company's interests in Seneca lands in New York. The Ogden Land Company,
not a corporation but consisting of the heirs of Ogden and his partners,
contributed to Seneca suspicions of the motives of white people. Tempered
only by the activities of well-meaning Friends missionaries, the Ogden Land
Company continually interfered in Seneca politics throughout the first half
of the nineteenth century. As a land speculator, the company sought to
remove the Indians from New York State so it could profit from the sale
of their lands. It pursued this objective through bribery, whiskey, the threat
of force, and deliberate misrepresentation of facts. The company was in-
strumental in one of the most flagrant land swindles in New York history,
the Treaty of Buffalo Creek of 1838, in which some Iroquois chiefs in New
York were prevailed upon to sell the remainder of their reservations in the
state to the company. Only after considerable agitation by many of the
Indians and their white friends were the Senecas able to sign a second
treaty in 1842, the so-called compromise treaty, which returned to the Indians the Allegany and Cattaraugus reservations. The results of these events
caused the political upheaval of 1848 that led to the formation of the Seneca Nation of Indians.[27]

Bitter memories of the actions of the Ogdens and other land speculators lingered in Iroquois country throughout the nineteenth century.
Nevertheless (and ironically), the Ogden Land Company's preemptive claim
had helped to cloud the issue of allotment and let the Senecas keep their
land. The question was raised about how Congress or the state of New
York could partition Seneca land and allow for its sale to whites other than
the Ogden Land Company. During the second half of the nineteenth and
well into the twentieth century, both Washington and Albany, pressured
by the white lessees and their political representatives, grappled with the
issue of buying out the company's preemptive right. Congressmen and as-
semblymen repeatedly introduced legislation to extinguish the claim.
Despite the government's recognition of the legality of the claim, the In-

dians questioned whether the Ogden Land Company had any right to sell their land. At the same time, the Senecas resisted government efforts to extinguish the claim because they believed that would be the first step in separating them from their land. Meanwhile, the Ogden Land Company held out for more settlement money, demanding more than Congress believed it deserved. The impasse helped the Senecas hold onto their land base, resist the threat of allotment, and survive as a people. Yet by 1875, despite warding off allotment, the Seneca Nation could not prevent Congress from forcing long-term leasing at Allegany.[28]

In the mid-1870s Congress had been shaken by the Credit Mobilier railroad scandal. Because of this climate of corruption, the Sessions bill was hotly debated in 1874 and 1875. Predictably, congressional supporters of railroad legislation pushed the lease legislation. Lewis V. Bogy, senator from Missouri, former commissioner of Indian affairs, and a major railroad executive, spoke in defense of the bill. He insisted falsely that the "tribe [Seneca Nation] as a tribe is in favor of the bill." He added:

> These Indians now are neither hunters nor farmers. They are living from hand to mouth upon an immense domain producing very little, doing very little, and are in a very inferior condition. It is for their benefit that these towns should spring up on their reservation, for they will advance in a higher civilization. It would be for their benefit if the tribal organization was taken away from them as soon as possible. There is no question about that.[29]

In debate, Bogy's advocacy of the bill was supported by Senators John J. Ingalls of Kansas and Reuben V. Fenton of New York. Ingalls, whose state had removed most of its Indian population during the previous decade, reiterated Bogy's arguments in Social Darwinist fashion. Fenton, who was from Jamestown, within thirty miles of the Allegany Indian Reservation, and who had served as governor of New York from 1865 to 1868, defended congressional action to confirm the leases, although he admitted their illegality: "The leases made with some of the individual Indians were not taken before the council for confirmation." He continued: "According to the laws and customs of the Seneca Nation and in some cases the leases entered into with the white people by individual Indians are invalid."[30]

The opposition to the leasing bill was led by Thomas F. Bayard, Sr., of Delaware, Morgan C. Hamilton of Texas, Thomas Clay McCreery of Kentucky, and John P. Stockton of New Jersey. Bayard, who later served as secretary of state in the first Cleveland administration, was the most eloquent of the four men:

> This people [Seneca] have a tribal organization. That organization gives
> to them a certain polity of their own. They have tribunals of justice and
> equity, according to their own rights. . . . The customs and their laws
> are not idle forms; they are practical and efficient for their purposes. The
> question is whether, when they come in collision with the greater power
> that surrounds them, might shall be right; whether justice shall be sus-
> tained between the strong and the weak.

Hamilton, an opponent of the railroad interests, insisted that leasing would
be the first step toward loss of land: "I believe if this bill passes, these Indians will be deprived of the last acre of land that they own in that territory." He accused New York State officials, Interior Department personnel,
and railroad interests of conspiring for "public plunder" and overthrowing
the sanctity of "solemn treaties." McCreery emphasized that the federal
government had trust responsibilities as "guardian of the red man." He
blasted the proponents of the bill who had introduced the piece of legislation "in utter disregard" of those who were most deeply affected. Stockton
insisted that the Senecas' "title is as sacred as your title" and urged his colleagues to vote down the bill.[31] Despite the accuracy of the four men's
arguments, they failed to convince their colleagues.

On February 19, 1875, President Grant signed "An Act to Authorize
the Seneca Nation of New York Indians to Lease Lands Within the Cattaraugus and Allegany Reservations, and to Confirm Existing Leases" after
the Senate passed the bill on the same day by a two-to-one margin.[32] In
the first section of the legislation, apparently not coincidentally, Congress
confirmed the existing railroad leases with the Seneca Nation. The law also
created a commission of three members to "survey, locate, and establish
proper boundaries and limits of the villages of Vandalia, Carrolton, Great
Valley, Salamanca, West Salamanca, and Red House, within the said
Allegany Reservation." These so-called congressional villages were subject to state legal jurisdiction. All existing individual leases with the "Indians or said Seneca Nation" were made valid and binding for a five-year
period, after which they could be renewed for twelve years.[33]

Congress extended these original leases, totaling more than three thousand, on September 30, 1890. This time the leases were extended for
ninety-nine years effective on February 19, 1892.[34] All of these leases were
undervalued and none had accelerator clauses attached to them. These two
acts also gave white Salamancans, numbering nearly eight thousand by
1900, the hope that someday Congress would respond to their lobbying
efforts by giving them fee simple title to Seneca lands. Despite the repeated
attempts by the non-Indian lessees of the congressional villages to secure

title from 1892 to 1985, their efforts failed repeatedly, in part because of concerns over the Ogden preemptive claim, changing directions of Indian policies, waning power of southwestern New York interests, and the actions of Seneca leaders themselves.[35]

Not until 1990 did Congress attempt to redress past wrongdoings. The Seneca Nation Settlement Act, passed unanimously by both houses of Congress, was signed into law by President George Bush on November 3, 1990. The act provides federal monetary compensation to the Seneca Nation for failures of the federal government to carry out its trust responsibilities and protect Seneca interests by properly supervising the leases from 1850 onward.[36] This compensation came at the time when the Seneca Nation had renegotiated two new consecutive forty-year leases with Salamanca and the other five congressional villages. This time the lease agreements contain accelerator clauses.[37]

Thus the Seneca Nation faced a war on the home front that had a longer-lasting legacy than the Civil War itself. The Seneca Nation's "lost cause" was not defeat on the battlefields of Virginia but legislative railroading in the halls of Congress in 1875.

10

Women at War

The Civil War had a devastating effect on women as well as men. The war brought widowhood and economic destitution to mothers, daughters, and wives, as well as bureaucratic red tape that plagued family members seeking federal pensions. For several generations, women were affected by the legacies of the Civil War, and their lives were forever shaped by it.

The dearth of information on Iroquois women in the Civil War era stands in marked contrast to the records of the American Revolution and the War of 1812. In both of these earlier conflicts, women followed their men to war but were largely restricted from battle. They served in a support role in each war, although they were apparently armed and stood ready for combat. At least five Iroquois women received military pensions for service in the War of 1812: Julia John (Seneca), [Aunt] Dinah John (Onondaga), Susan Jacob (Onondaga), Polly Cooper (Oneida), and Dolly Skanandoah (Oneida). Despite this tradition of military service, Iroquois women did not accompany their men to war in 1861.[1]

Much has been written about Iroquois women's roles, largely emphasizing the position of power they held in traditional society. From the earliest, observers have commented about the so-called Iroquois matriarchate.[2] In 1724, Father Joseph Lafitau, a prominent Jesuit missionary, wrote:

> Nothing is more real, however, than the women's superiority. It is they who really maintain the tribe, the nobility of blood, the genealogical tree, the order of generations and conservation of the families. In them resides all the real authority: the lands, fields and all their harvest belong to them; they are the soul of the councils, the arbiters of peace and war; they hold the taxes and the public treasure; it is to them that the slaves are en-

trusted; they arrange the marriages; the children are under their authority; and the order of succession is found on their blood.[3]

Nearly 250 years later, anthropologist Judith Brown insisted that "Iroquois matrons enjoyed unusual authority in their society, perhaps more than women have ever enjoyed anywhere at any time." Brown emphasized that the "authority over the household resided in the matron and not in one of her male relatives." The household, the longhouse, was the "analogy on which the League was built," thus helping "to consolidate the considerable power of the Iroquois matrons."[4]

More recently anthropologist Elisabeth Tooker emphasized the balance of male-female roles in Iroquoian society, maintaining that men and women occupied different but equally important domains — the forest and the clearing. The latter was the province of the women, who maintained the village while men were at war, on the hunt, or trading. In the clearing, women did "all the agricultural work of planting, tending, and harvesting of crops," maintaining the constancy of Iroquoian society. To Tooker, the reciprocal obligations of men and women to maintain these two domains was a major basis and reason for success of Iroquoian social and economic organization.[5]

Iroquois women's roles had noticeably changed by the first half of the nineteenth century. The missionaries and the Seneca prophet Handsome Lake changed Iroquoian sex roles. Both white clerics and the Seneca prophet emphasized the nuclear family in place of extended families and the acceptance of men's roles in the traditional world of horticulture. The clearing was no longer the unique domain of women. New Western values and new concepts of women's work were introduced. Despite Iroquois women's resistance to outsiders' efforts to change them, missionaries discouraged women's work in the fields and emphasized household duties, which they insisted was women's proper sphere. Through schooling, the missionaries attempted to transform Indian society from the bottom up, using children to educate their parents.[6]

At the Friends school at Tunesassa, the older girls were employed to "assist in the daily business of the house," while the boys were employed in work, mostly of agricultural nature, "adapted to their strength."[7] One Friends educator noted in May 1863 that the Indians had "generally discarded their former Indian costumes," adopting the clothing of the whites. In somewhat exaggerated fashion, she insisted that "their women have been mostly withdrawn from outdoor or field labor, and are employed in their appropriate household duties."[8] One goal of educating Indian women was described in a Friends report issued at the end of the Civil

War: "We believe also that the training in household duties, received by the female scholars [at Tunesassa] . . . may have a very useful influence upon their parents when they return to their homes, as it, no doubt, will upon themselves when they become housekeepers."[9] A similar goal was frequently expressed by the superintendents of state-run public schools on the reservations.[10]

Census records indicate that these efforts to transform Indian women's roles were not altogether successful. Women filled the labor void caused by enlistment of their menfolk during the Civil War. From 1855 to 1865, agricultural acreage of improved reservation land increased from 14,197.25 to 15,398.25 acres. An analysis of census records also indicates that the war moved the Iroquois away from subsistence and toward a market-generated economy. Despite serious flooding in western New York in 1862 and two smallpox epidemics during the war, the production of apples, buckwheat, and oats increased dramatically while the harvest of barley, beans, corn, and wheat declined. The number of horses, the size of cattle heads used for beef production, not dairy, and the shearing of lambs' wool all increased before dropping in 1865. The increased output of livestock feed—apples, buckwheat, and oats—and the number of livestock animals that could be used for military purposes and wool production for military uniforms suggest that the needs of the Union army drove the reservation economy.[11] Despite the importance of women to the wartime economy, the return of husbands, sons, fathers, and brothers in 1865 displaced most Indian women in the agricultural work force. In 1875, 37 women, 51.4 percent polled, identified themselves in the New York State census as farmers. In marked contrast, 557 men, 66 percent polled, identified themselves as farmers. By 1900, only 3 percent of all Seneca women listed in the census were farmers or farm laborers.[12]

The impact of the war on Iroquois women is most evident in Civil War pension records. As early as 1862, Congress passed legislation that provided benefits for injured and disabled veterans as well as widows, children, and other dependent relatives of soldiers who had died either in Civil War service for the Union or of causes that could be directly traced to military service. On June 27, 1890, Congress widened the number of persons eligible to receive a pension. After that date, the federal government provided a pension to a widow of any honorably discharged Union soldier or sailor who had served ninety days or more, regardless of the cause of the soldier's death, provided she had married the soldier or sailor before June 27, 1890.[13] As historian Amy E. Holmes has written, this act "amounted to an old-age pension for veterans' widows that affected not only those women who had been married during the Civil War but women who had

CHART 5

Iroquois Widowhood, 1855 and 1865

Reservation	1855	1865
Cattaraugus	46	64
Allegany	24	35
Oneida	3	9
Onondaga	8	17
St. Regis (Akwesasne)	10	16
Tonawanda	32	41
Tuscarora	14	13
TOTAL	137	195

Source: Derived from New York State, *Census of the State of New York for 1865,* comp. Franklin B. Hough (Albany: Charles Van Benthuysen & Son, 1867).

married Union veterans up to twenty-five years after the war had ended."[14]

Wisconsin Oneidas, took greater advantage of the Civil War pension system than did their counterparts in the New York homeland. Thomas Donaldson, who collected the 1890 census information on the Iroquois, attributed the small number of pension applications in New York to the "loss of papers, absence of papers with pension agents, lapse of time since the war, [and] with absolute ignorance for years that any benefits would flow from service."[15]

Most Wisconsin Oneidas overcame bureaucratic mine fields to secure pensions. As early as 1865, Evelina King, whose husband was killed at the battle for Atlanta, and Christine Doxtator, whose husband, Paul Doxtator of Company G, died of dysentery in service in 1864, swiftly secured their $8 per month pensions. Susan Antoin (Antoine), whose son Abraham died of chronic diarrhea while in the Union army, received a pension because her husband was infirm and Abraham was her sole source of support. Over a half-century after the Civil War, Sarah Bread, mother of twelve children, received a widow's pension after her husband, Peter, died in 1918.[16] In a more unusual case, Mary Doxtator, the mother of eleven children and wife of Paul C. Doxtator of Company F, applied for a widow's pension after her husband's death in 1921. Although Private Doxtator had earlier received a pension as an invalid, he had been absent without leave from the Union army from November 23, 1864, to May 9, 1865. Doxtator's name was removed from the company's list of deserters when he returned after Lee's surrender. Despite his spotty military record, both Doxtator and his widow received pensions.[17]

The process was not without obstacles, major setbacks, and permanent disappointments. Before Mary Fletcher Baird could secure her $8 per month after the death of her husband, Thomas, from typhoid fever in 1864, she was a victim of the smallpox epidemic that raged within her Wisconsin Oneida community.[18] Sallie Anthony, the daughter of Thomas Antone (Anthony), failed in her efforts to secure a survivor's pension. Because of the misspellings of Thomas's last name in the Company G muster rolls, her application was rejected despite documentation from the local Episcopal minister and other Oneida members of G Company who had served with her father. Disturbingly, Sallie was informed by the military that the cause of her father's death in service was "by whiskey."[19]

The insensitive, bureaucratic nature of the process was compounded by Victorian standards of morality. One such case was that of Celinda Danforth, the widow of Cobus, who had died at war in 1864. For twenty years, Celinda received a pension, but in 1885 she was dropped from the rolls. In suspending her payment, the Pension Board stated that the "pensioner has been living in open and notorious adulterous cohabitation with other men — since soldier's death. Had 6 illegitimate children." Thus late nineteenth-century standards of morality apparently affected Indian as well as non-Indian.[20]

The pension records of the 132d New York State Volunteer Infantry reveal other important information about Iroquois women in the Civil War era. William Kennedy, the young soldier killed at Batchelder's Creek, left a mother behind. Under the act of 1890, she received his $8-a-month pension. Because she was a Longhouse follower, she had no Christian name. In the records, she is referred to by her Seneca Indian name, Go-non-ce-tok, or more frequently as "the widow Kennedy" because her husband had died before the war.[21]

Sergeant Foster J. Hudson's mother, Louisa, had less success convincing the Pension Board of the merits of her application. Despite sworn statements by military personnel and prominent Senecas and the efforts of missionary Asher Wright, Louisa Hudson failed to obtain her pension. The widow, who lived in a hemlock board shanty and owned "one cow and nothing else," had insisted that her son was her sole provider. Foster had sent his army pay home to his destitute mother because "he was unwilling that his mother should labor in the cornfield as had been her custom." Louisa had sent her son to be educated at an academy to learn the "ideas of white people," suggesting that his ideas about his mother's labor had been transformed by his schooling in the white man's world.

Unfortunately, because of a discrepancy in the date of her husband's death, Louisa Hudson never received a pension; she died before the error could be corrected.[22]

In sharp contrast, Lizzie Cusick, Captain Cornelius C. Cusick's widow, succeeded in her efforts to secure a pension. She had married Captain Cusick in Cleveland in 1879. Because of Cusick's fame and political connections, Lizzie, who was the sole support of their son Alton, was able to secure passage of a private congressional bill in 1906, increasing her widow's pension from a meager $8 to $20 per month.[23]

The ways the war touched and transformed women's as well as men's lives is particularly clear in the case of Peter Bread, a respected Oneida family man active in the local Holy Apostles Episcopal Church. Bread died in 1918; however, the local mailman never delivered his last pension check. His relatives frequently attempted to secure this payment for Bread's widow, who was in desperate need of money to pay for nursing expenses. Their attempts finally ended in failure in 1936, when they were informed that the one-year statute of limitations on claims had run out.[24]

Although there is little evidence to measure their loss, psychological pain, and economic destitution from the American Civil War, Iroquois women were affected by the conflict for generations. Affidavits and letters found in pension records reveal that many of the soldiers came back severely disabled and needed extensive care from their families. Mary King recounted her husband's great pain from his head to his hips. In her deposition of September 22, 1896, she swore that he "always complained of pains" in one of his legs. Wooster King, a raftsman by occupation, who had been shot through both hips at the Battle of Fair Oaks while serving in Company K of the 57th Pennsylvania Volunteer Infantry, suffered from partial numbness in his right leg, a stiff right foot, and severe rheumatism. Even after receiving a disability discharge in 1863, he was, according to Philip Fatty, a Civil War veteran, "always lame in his right leg after that and always used a cane to aid him in walking." Unable to return to rafting, King was often confined to bed. With the aid of powerful Seneca politicians such as Willie C. Hoag, as well as powerful white Salamanca benefactors, Mary King was eventually awarded her widow's pension in 1896 and continued to receive it until her death in 1925.[25]

The desperate economic conditions facing widows and mothers of deceased soldiers in the post–Civil War era is made poignantly clear in pension applications. In 1888, Sally Plummer, the mother of Cornelius Plummer of K Company of the 57th Pennsylvania Volunteer Infantry, who was killed in action, revealed in her deposition that her only income was a $4 annuity payment and "10–12 yards of 'factory' or calico treaty cloth," which she received under the terms of the Pickering Treaty; consequently, she was awarded a $12-per-month pension under the law of 1890. To receive a pension, Achsah Halftown Shongo, the widow of Thomas Shongo of K Company of the 57th Pennsylvania Volunteer Infantry, had to prove that her husband had drowned in the Ohio River, falling overboard from a steamboat in the late 1860s. She also had to produce documentation to prove that she was married at age fourteen, "according to Indian custom," by William Redeye. Furthermore, she had to swear that she had not lived with any man since her husband's death. Achsah could not read or write and none of her wedding guests were still alive. The processing of her widow's pension was delayed for almost twelve years because she was not able to prove her case until 1903.[26] Thus, long after the last shot was fired, the Civil War dramatically affected women's lives in Iroquoia.

11

Children at War

Despite the distance from the battle-field, Iroquois children were not immune from the horrors of the Civil War. The sons and daughters of combatants killed in war applied for Civil War pensions well into the twentieth century. For example, Thomas Baird of the 14th Wisconsin Infantry left a widow and six children when he died of typhoid fever at Big Shanty, Georgia, in the summer of 1864. Although five of his children later received minors' pensions, a sixth, William Baird, was turned down for financial assistance right down to 1910.[1]

The scars of the war were visible for decades following the war. In 1888, Peter Garrow, whose father was a St. Regis Mohawk killed in Civil War combat and whose mother was French Canadian, described his family's plight before a New York State Assembly committee in 1888. Garrow stated that "his father died when we were young" and that he and his three brothers struggled to survive. Even though he continued to live on the St. Regis Mohawk (Akwesasne) Reservation, Garrow and his brothers were seen as outcasts because his connection to Mohawk society was severed at the death of his father.[2]

Much about children's lives during the Civil War is revealed in the educational records of the era. These records also provide information about a wide range of subjects — public health; the economy of reservations; men's and women's roles; Iroquois conservatism in the face of change; federal, state, and religious society policies toward the Indians; and the overall impact of the war on Iroquois communities.[3]

In schools run by religious groups and the state, educational policies in mid-nineteenth-century America were culturally myopic and often coercive in nature, aimed at assimilating Indian children into mainstream America. The overall design had a four-pronged formula: the christianiz-

137

ing activities of missionaries on reservations to stamp out "paganism"; the exposure of the Indians to white Americans' ways through New York State–supported schools established from the mid-1840s onward; the division of tribal lands among individual Indians to instill personal initiative, allegedly required by the free enterprise system; and finally, in return for accepting land in severalty, the "rewarding" of Indians with United States citizenship. The New York State superintendent of common schools wrote in 1849: "Is it not obvious that the practical *communism* imposed by our laws upon the Indians, obstructs their advance in knowledge and civilization, and deprives them of the chief stimulus to industry and frugality. . . . If the Indian is to be civilized and educated, he must cease to be a savage. We must allow him to partition and cultivate his land, if we would not have all our efforts to educate and enlighten him prove illusive."[4]

Fifteen years later, this assimilationist message was elaborated on by Jonathan Kneeland, the superintendent of the Onondaga Indian School. In his report in 1864, he advocated making Onondagas "tax-paying, arms-bearing citizens." Comparing the education of American Indians to that of the mentally retarded, he added, "The great state of New York cannot, in honor of justice, refuse to aid the feeblest and dullest of her dependent children." Kneeland blamed the Onondaga Reservation's proximity to "knavish whites" in the nearby city of Syracuse for the Onondaga school's failures. He recommended that non-Indians be hired as teachers and that the state support the overthrow of the existing Indian political system, the Onondaga Council of Chiefs, which he also blamed for the lack of success in educating Indians. In his report in 1865, Kneeland argued for the state's abandonment of "the letter of old treaties" to save the Indians "from extinction." He maintained that the course of citizenship and state jurisdiction worked on Indian lives in the same manner that it worked to fuse "the lower type of emigrants from foreign lands" into American society. The next year, Kneeland promoted outright coercive methods: "No class of men ever learned, or is likely to learn, the duties of citizenship, except by being thrown into the onward flowing tide of rights, duties and progress."[5]

Iroquois leaders such as Samuel George recognized the importance of learning the white man's ways and allowed schools to operate, although they resented the more aggressive and outspoken white proponents of change. In fact, each of the Iroquois communities supported these educational efforts. The Seneca Nation contributed its own money for the maintenance of schools. It also provided a grant of land for the creation of the Thomas Asylum for Orphans and Destitute Indians and imposed a timber tax to support the operations of the institution. In 1866, the Senecas provided $600 of tribal funds for the improvement of schoolhouses. In the same year, they provided $1,000 from their Watson oil lease for the maintenance of the Thomas Asylum. Nor was this generosity associated only with the Senecas. Each Iroquois community provided land for school use and raised funds to support the schools.[6]

The education of Iroquois in the period was often characterized by noble rhetoric and less than noble results. In 1846, the New York State legislature had enacted a law providing for school buildings and annual appropriations for the education of American Indians on four of the reservations: Allegany, Cattaraugus, Onondaga, and St. Regis (Akwesasne). State-administered schools were established at Tonawanda and Tuscarora in 1855 and at Oneida in 1857. In 1856, New York State legally assumed responsibility for "providing the means of education for all the Indian children in the state."[7] By 1862, twenty-two state schools were operating on Iroquois reservations with a total enrollment of well over eight hundred pupils. By 1865–66, twenty-five state schools were operating, and approximately one thousand Iroquois pupils were enrolled. Yet the average rate of attendance on any one day was approximately 48 percent.[8]

The schools were underfunded from the start. Teachers' salaries were scandalous. Although they were raised in 1864, teachers still received only between $5 and $6 per month during the school year 1865–66. The teachers, mostly non-Indian women, received substantially lower wages than their counterparts off reservations.[9] During the Civil War, one annual report of the state superintendent of public instruction indicated that these teachers were willing to serve the Indians under difficult, less financially rewarding circumstances because they were working for humanitarian reasons to "uplift" the downtrodden Indian.[10]

Despite resistance by superintendents such as Kneeland to the hiring of Indian teachers, by the time the Civil War ended, at least five Iroquois held teaching positions in the Indian schools: Daniel and Harriet [Hattie] Two Guns, A. S. Logan, and D. W. Pierce at Cattaraugus and Mary Mt. Pleasant at Tuscarora.[11] The superintendent of the two Tuscarora schools hailed Mt. Pleasant's hiring and lauded her work in 1866. "Miss Mt. Pleasant is an Indian lady, and has succeeded far beyond my expectations. She has proved herself an apt teacher and good disciplinarian. Heretofore the school under her charge has been badly managed, a new teacher having been employed almost every term." Despite the superintendent's high praise, Mt. Pleasant had no better success than her white colleagues. Only one-third of her Tuscarora pupils attended her classes on any given day.[12]

The high level of truancy had many causes. One superintendent complained that the school textbooks "in use are in a language that the pupils do not understand; consequently none but teachers of unusual patience

and tact can succeed in making even moderate progress in these schools."
Although new texts emphasizing "object teaching" and new maps were
adopted for classroom use in 1864, truancy continued to be a major problem.[13] School administrators and teachers were concerned with securing
more state money and better facilities and had little understanding of Iroquois mores. At their best, they were paternalistic; at their worst, they
were openly hostile and racist toward the pupils and their parents.

Without doubt, one reason for truancy and other symptoms of educational failure was that many Indians were opposed to the philosophy of
the schools, which emphasized foisting values of the dominant white culture on Indian communities. In his 1862 report, the superintendent of public instruction indicated that active opposition by the Iroquois Longhouse
people had subsided, "yet many of the parents feel so little interest in the
education of their children, that teachers still find it impossible to secure
a prompt attendance of the scholars."[14]

Perhaps the clearest reason for truancy and limited educational success was presented by William Gillis, the superintendent at the St. Regis
Mohawk School at Fort Covington. Gillis preceded his reasons for student truancy by praising Mohawk tribal economic successes in farming
and in raising dairy cattle. Then he said that he believed the limited educational success among Mohawks was attributable to the excessive mobil-
ity of students and their families:

> The roving propensity of the tribe is on the increase, if possible. Nearly
> one-half of them are now absent from the reservation, some of them spend-
> ing their time in the cities and villages of the United States and Canada,
> vending their trinkets, while others go far into the western and northern
> forests, in pursuit of game for manufacturing baskets and trinkets. Were
> it not for this roaming disposition, much more might be done in forward-
> ing the educational and moral interest of this unfortunate tribe.[15]

Gillis, who was more perceptive and more culturally sensitive than the
average state Indian school administrator of the era, accurately explained
that an overwhelming number of Mohawk pupils were not attending school
because a significant percentage of the Indian families were in dire economic straits, requiring their children to work on the farms or leave for
more distant parts to sell baskets, fish, hunt, or pursue other laboring activities. On all reservations, Indian youth, as well as women and elders,
apparently filled the void in the farm labor work force caused by the enlistment of Indian fathers and other family members into military service.[16]
Thus it can be argued that Indian schools, already tenuously accepted by

the Iroquois, were perceived by the Indians as unimportant in the overall picture of family and community economic survival during the Civil War.

The Indian schools at times faced even greater crises than truant students and obdurate parents. In 1862, the school year was considerably shortened at the Allegany school because smallpox "prevailed these many weeks." A similar situation occurred at the Tonawanda Reservation in 1864.[17]

Available school records show that the Civil War had a dramatic impact on school life. E. M. Pettit, the superintendent of the Seneca schools, wrote in November 1863 that many of his former students, "some of whom have learned to read and write in the schools," had enlisted in the army. He indicated that these battle-hardened veterans wrote back to their friends "thrilling accounts of battles and amusing accounts of camp life."[18] In the past, Iroquois villagers waited for runners to return from the warpath with news of faraway battles ranging from Huronia to Cherokee country. Now they waited for mail deliveries for news about battles at Chattanooga, Petersburg, and Spotsylvania.

Besides state efforts in the educational realm, religious societies, on a smaller scale, provided schools and teachers for instructing the Iroquois. Although there were Baptist and Roman Catholic Indian schools, one of the more famous of these endeavors was the Friends' school at Tunesassa, founded by Joseph Elkinton and his wife, Mary Nutt, of Philadelphia in the 1820s. Originally two separate day schools operated — one each for boys and girls. In 1852, the Tunesassa Boarding School was established; it continued in operation until 1938. The boarding school, which also included a farm, had no more than twenty-five children at any one time during the Civil War. Between 60 and 80 percent of the students were girls who ranged in age from ten to fifteen. It was largely a trade school, with boys "employed in work adopted to their strength" while the "large girls assist[ed] in the daily business of the home." The New Testament was read to the Indian children every morning and was employed by the teachers "as a reading book." In opposition to Iroquoian traditions, women were discouraged from agricultural pursuits. Much of the focus of the girls' education centered around instructing them in "household duties" because, according to Thomas Wistar of Philadelphia, the Elkintons believed that "female scholars" would "have a very useful influence upon their parents when they return to their homes, as it, no doubt, will upon themselves when they become housekeepers."[19] After the Civil War, a similar Friends educational endeavor, the Seneca Indian School, was established in Indian Territory.[20]

Missionaries also provided education for the Wisconsin Oneidas. On an average winter day, only fourteen of the thirty-five enrolled students attended the combined Methodist Episcopal school; in spring and summer terms, only twenty of forty-nine students attended. The teacher later explained that the poor attendance in winter was caused in part by the "severity" of the climate "and the great depth of the snow." Although William McGuffey's *Readers* and other standard mid-nineteenth-century schoolbooks were used, the frustrated teacher observed that there were too many obstacles to succeed, including the lack of a proper school building and the dire poverty of the children. "My schoolhouse is quite small, and in arranging the seats and desks the comfort of the children could not have been taken into account. Many of the children at this mission are destitute of suitable clothing to enable them to attend school. If the government would appropriate a small amount for this purpose, I have no doubt it would secure a much larger attendance." The teacher added that those children who attended regularly made "good progress in their studies." Unfortunately, when the "children become large enough to be any service at home they are taken out of school, and the consequence is that nearly all they have learned is soon forgotten."[21]

Because of the devastating effects of the Civil War, orphanages played an unusually important role in American society in the last decades of the nineteenth century. In this era, the Thomas Asylum for Orphans and Destitute Indians, primarily a manual trades school founded on the Cattaraugus Reservation in 1856 by Asher Wright and Philip Thomas, became one of the more important educational institutions among the Iroquois.[22] The asylum housed Seneca, Cayuga, and Oneida children, including orphans of fathers killed in military service during the bloody conflict. Wright occasionally sought financial assistance for these Civil War orphans from the federal government.[23] The asylum's annual report for 1866 reveals the institution's role in providing services for these unfortunate children:

> Several of the children are orphans of Indian soldiers who perished in the army. The father of one boy was shot through the head in the battle of Fair Oaks; the father of a boy and a girl was killed near Petersburg; two others each of whom leaves a little girl, have not been heard from, and are supposed to have died on the battlefield or in rebel prisons. The wife of one of the soldiers died while he was in the army, and two of his children were received into the asylum, where they are still retained because he has not been able since his return to provide for them.[24]

The Thomas Asylum, whose name was changed to the Thomas School in the early twentieth century, continued in operation until 1957, housing children from all the Six Nations communities in New York as well as from two Algonkian reservations on Long Island. A year before it opened, the Seneca Nation of Indians had given its three officers fifteen acres of tribal lands to fund and operate the institution. From 1856 to 1875, the Thomas Asylum was subject to the regulations of the New York State Department of Public Instruction. Although not affiliated with any denomination, it received donations from religious societies, a token amount of federal dollars from the Bureau of Indian Affairs, and New York State funds for construction, maintenance of buildings, and per capita student aid, all of which proved inadequate. The Civil War undermined the institution's financial base. According to Asher Wright, the Thomas Asylum "suffered somewhat seriously from the diversion of the charities of the community consequent upon the war." The war led to cutbacks from the state and the federal governments as well because of the need for the "strictest economy."[25]

In contrast to most institutions educating Native Americans at the time, the Thomas Asylum had an Indian Board of Managers, established in 1862, which was elected by districts and supported by an Indian tax on timber. In 1875, Lewis Seneca, an Indian and president of the Board of Managers, reported that the staff at the asylum, who often doubled as teachers, was composed of a superintendent, matron, assistant matron, seamstress, housekeeper, assistant laundress, and general assistant. Indians were employed on staff after the first decade of operation, although no Indian ever served as superintendent in the one-hundred-year history of the institution.[26]

The staff provided a simple elementary education for boys and girls. Inculcating self-reliance was emphasized most. The children were "plainly clad" and received "wholesome food." Girls were trained in home economics, boys in the rudiments of agriculture. To assure "habits of industry," both the boys and the girls at the age of sixteen were placed with white families as part of an early version of the "outing system," a policy later employed at Carlisle and Hampton institutes. One report of the time observed: "Lads are taught to get their living from the cultivation of the soil; and the girls how to perform the duties pertaining to a civilized household."[27] Most of the work of the school was done by child labor — running the laundry, cleaning, cooking, making brooms, raising crops, chopping wood, pulling out stumps, milking the cows, and so on. Wright described the goals and progress of the asylum in 1864:

> The children are taught habits of industry. The boys acquire a much better knowledge of agricultural pursuits than any others on the reservation and more dexterity in the use of tools. The idea that Indians have an innate aversion to labor proves entirely unfounded in the case of these chil-

dren. On the contrary they appear to find pleasure in industrial pursuits to a greater degree than is usual with white children. Those girls who have been placed in white families to perfect their knowledge of housekeeping have surprised their employees by their capability and energy in the performance of domestic duties.

Wright added that some of the boys who had left the institution joined the Union military, thus, in his opinion, not "shirking their responsibilities." They frequently wrote back to their "friends at home; and their letters are often quite interesting and always abound in expressions of loyalty and patriotism."[28]

A series of devastating epidemics swept through the asylum during the Civil War years. Twelve of the fifty-six resident children died in 1864 alone — eight from dysentery, three from measles, and one from consumption.[29] On September 30, 1864, Wright was forced to explain the high death rate; he wrote to the Bureau of Indian Affairs subagent in New York, defending the administration of the institution. Wright insisted that these diseases were as rampant outside the institution as in, proving "just as fatal among others as it has been there." Defensively, Wright observed that, since the institution's founding in 1856, the death rate at the asylum was lower than in the population at large. Besides, he insisted, the "children were sadly diseased before they were taken under care."[30] Despite Wright's exhortations, the asylum's reputation had been damaged, requiring many years to repair.

Because of constant funding crises, New York State formally assumed total administrative responsibility for the Thomas Asylum in 1875 and placed it under the supervision of the State Board of Charities, which classified American Indians in the same category with youthful offenders and lunatics, a fact not lost on the Indians. The Thomas Asylum as well as the renamed Thomas School had a prisonlike institutional quality and an assimilationist focus not allowing students to speak their Iroquois languages throughout much of its history. Although it produced some of the most outstanding Iroquois community leaders, the Thomas School reflected the cultural insensitivity, paternalistic charity, and overall neglect characteristic of white educational administrative dealings with Native Americans.[31]

12

Two Wars

The Iroquois Indians faced two wars between 1861 and 1865. At times the war on the home front was as intense as that on Southern battlefields. In Indian Territory, the home front merged with the battlefield, resulting in massive destruction not found in other Iroquois communities.

The fighting of the Civil War resulted in changes that affected the Iroquois for generations. The loss of Indian lives, especially at Oneida, Wisconsin, severely weakened communities, just at the time when pressures for tribal dissolution were increasing. Moreover, the physical and emotional scars of the war had long-lasting effects on every Iroquois community. Although it is difficult to measure the psychological damage the war wrought on veterans, the records reveal much about the impact of war on their wives, mothers, daughters, and sons. They faced a more difficult path of survival after the death or infirmity of their menfolk. They also had to contend with many bureaucratic obstacles in securing Civil War pensions well into the twentieth century.

Participation in this great armed struggle was no passing event in Iroquois history. Iroquois communities, according to the subagent of the New York Agency in 1864, expressed true commitment to the armed struggle against the South as well as "sympathy towards our people, and of veneration and confidence in the President."[1] Admiration for Lincoln's leadership of the Union was reflected to the end of the war. The Powless-Archiquette Diary, which focuses almost exclusively on Oneida community history of the mid-nineteenth century, noted Lincoln's tragic assassination: "Abraham Lincoln, President of the United States for four years, and one month and ten days, shot in Ford's Theatre on Good Friday night about 10:00 o'clock April 14, 1865."[2] Despite the actions of the Lincoln administration with respect to other American Indian communities such as the execution of thirty-eight Santee Sioux leaders in 1862 and the Navajo Long Walk of 1864, the Iroquois had few objections to the Great Father's leadership during the Civil War. The generally favorable impression of Lincoln was reinforced by the chief executive's meeting with Chief Samuel George and the president's quick response to Iroquois appeals that led to several individual Indian military discharges from Union service.

The war had other important results. As part of the ritual of national commemoration and mourning, Iroquois veterans of the war, as numerous photographs attest, proudly donned their Union uniforms and participated in solemn ceremonies in honor of their fallen white, black, and Indian colleagues.[3] With the formal designation in 1868 of May 30 as Decoration Day, now Memorial Day, to honor Union soldiers and sailors, Grand Army of the Republic (GAR) posts throughout the nation celebrated with parades, speeches, and decoration of graves., The GAR, which admitted Iroquois Indians to its ranks, had well over four hundred thousand members by 1890. Its influence was all-encompassing, including much more than sponsoring picnics and pageants, as a fraternal organization, or as a lobbyist on Capitol Hill.[4] According to one historian:

[The GAR] was a standard Victorian fraternal order, complete with ceremonial ranks and a secret, semireligious ritual. It was an arena for business clientage and deal cutting. It was a provider of local charity in an age without significant public relief. And it was the purveyor of a preservationist, socially conservative version of the war that had ramifications beyond the ranks of veterans. Among members of the G.A.R., Union veteranhood embraced all of these behaviors, not just the pension lobbying for which the order is usually remembered.[5]

Much of the 1890 census information about Iroquois veterans was provided by GAR posts.[6]

At Ely S. Parker's funeral at Fairfield, Connecticut, in 1895, honorary pallbearers included representatives from the GAR as well as from Iroquois communities. Eighteen months later, Parker was reinterred beside the graves of other Indians, including his ancestor Red Jacket, at Forest Lawn Cemetery in Buffalo. On Decoration Day in 1905, Samuel H. Beckwith, who was General Grant's cipher telegraph operator, unveiled a headstone marking Parker's grave in a commemoration sponsored by the GAR and the Buffalo Historical Society. The GAR participated on a smaller scale in the funeral of Cornelius C. Cusick, who was buried with military honors at Old Fort Niagara in 1904. Through the 1920s, mourners paid respect at both Indian and GAR funerary rites for Iroquois Civil War veterans.[7]

The ritual of war affected not only those who had fought in the bloody conflict. The post–Civil War generation also participated in the pageantry. Linas S. Pierce, an Iroquois student at Carlisle Institute, proudly wrote his uncle in early May 1901 that the school's band, of which he was a member, was scheduled to play at the Memorial Day commemoration at Gettysburg.[8]

Historian Reid Mitchell has written that "volunteers did become soldiers. But the transformation from civilian to soldier was rarely completed. One reason for this is that in some ways the company — the basic military unit — functioned as an extension of the soldier's home community." Mitchell added that unlike the French Foreign Legion, the soldiers in the Union army did not "join in order 'to forget'" but were constantly reminded of their civilian life by association with other soldiers and officers from their home communities.[9] As was true of the 14th Wisconsin Volunteer Infantry, many Iroquois soldiers were recruited by the same officers, enlisted on the same day, and returned home together. These Oneidas saw going to war as a way to escape impoverishment, and most joined the action in the last half of the Civil War as bounty replacements. And although most Iroquois soldiers had common bonds, as seen in the 132d New York State Volunteers, they joined the Union effort to satisfy certain aspects of their Iroquois identity, namely to use the war, as others had before them, to gain status and prestige within their communities. The Civil War provided them with status and helped them join the ranks of elders who had waged war on the Niagara frontier during the War of 1812. These new warrior-volunteers were against the proscription enunciated by Handsome Lake as well as the teachings of their Quaker missionaries.[10]

Isaac Newton Parker's letters reveal that events on the Indian reservation during the war were not far from his mind when he was eight hundred miles away on North Carolina battlefields. While worrying about his parents' and his wife's health, his physical separation from his wife, and fears of combat and death, Parker also described the war, the South, camp life, and his fellow Indians in the Tuscarora Company. Parker was one of the few educated Indians in his regiment, and his letters suggest that his detailed descriptions were not intended solely for his wife, his sister, or his sister-in-law but were passed around or read aloud at Tonawanda and other Iroquois communities. He and other Indian members of his company hoped that his family members, the most educated of reservation residents, would write back to him with information about conditions and doings at home. As a result of the intensity of the fighting in 1863, Parker, in his letters, questioned further Iroquois enlistment. Later, he was especially concerned about recruitment frauds at home and the enlistment of underage Senecas in the war effort.

To Parker and to the average Iroquois soldier, the war was not about any great social issue such as the abolition of slavery. Iroquois rarely mentioned blacks in their correspondence or diaries, except in passing. Iroquois reservations in western New York and southern Ontario were in or adjacent to areas through which abolitionists had conveyed slaves to freedom on the underground railroad. As early as the mid-1820s, the town of Olean in Cattaraugus County, only a short distance from the Allegany Indian Reservation, was involved in underground railroad activity. Niagara Falls near the Tuscarora Reservation was a main terminus of this route, and the Six Nations Reserve, Iroquois lands along the Grand River, provided safe haven for fugitive slaves. Moreover, some of the earliest antislavery societies were founded in areas adjacent to Iroquois reservations, including one at Ellicottville, New York, in 1839.[11] Yet the Iroquois in New York, Wisconsin, and Indian Territory had different agendas than slavery when they enlisted in the Civil War. The pursuit of the Kansas and other claims, maintenance of tribal sovereignty, and preservation of Iroquois identity were more important to most Native Americans than the Thirteenth, Fourteenth, and Fifteenth Amendments to the United States Constitution. Despite this generalization, there were, however, some exceptions.

Some Iroquois were apparently influenced by the idealism of the Civil War era. Most Iroquois in New York, but not all, do not vote to this day, claiming that this preserves their separate Indian national existence. Yet in 1876, Abraham [Abram] Elm, an Oneida Indian who was one of the founders of the Society of American Indians in 1911, attempted to vote for his choice as congressman. He was arrested, indicted for illegal voting, tried, and convicted. Elm, born at Oneida, New York, in 1842, was a Civil War veteran who had been a member of Company B of the 5th Vermont Volunteer Infantry. Upon appeal, the United States District Court for the Northern District of New York heard Elm's arguments and concluded that he was a United States citizen and therefore had the right to vote in the election.[12]

Despite winning his freedom, Elm and his Oneida people actually lost the case. The United States District Court held that the New York State legislature allotted the Oneida Indian Reservation in 1843 after "the main body of the Oneidas were removed to Wisconsin in the 1820s and 1830s." The remaining "twenty families which constituted the remnant of the Oneidas reside in the vicinity of their original reservation." Blinded by racism and ignorance about Oneida life, the court added that, because non-Indian dwellings were now interspersed with those of the Indians and the

Indians were no longer set apart by "custom, language and color" from the surrounding population, a distinct Oneida community no longer existed in New York. Consequently, Elm, although born an Indian, allegedly no longer had a "tribe." The recently ratified Fourteenth Amendment to the Constitution had excluded "Indians not taxed" from citizenship and suffrage; however, because of Elm's alleged lack of tribal status, he did not fall into the category of "Indians not taxed." Because the majority of Oneidas had been allotted and removed from New York, the remaining families had no separate tribal status. The court added: "They are native; they owe no allegiance other than to the government of the United States, and they have been placed by the State upon an equality with its citizens respecting important rights denied to [a]liens." The court then found for Elm and his constitutional right to vote.[13]

Much to Elm's regret, this case was later cited as evidence of "Indian willingness" to assimilate by the New York State Assembly Special Committee to Investigate the Indian Problem in 1888–89, more commonly known as the Whipple Committee for its chairman, Assemblyman J. S. Whipple of Salamanca. This special committee and its report of 1889 caused resentment among the Iroquois toward New York State government that lasts to the present day.[14] Iroquois family life, customs, land claims, life-style, and religious practices and traditions were held in contempt by the assembly committee and given as the reason for the "need for the changes in landed patterns and tribal governments." The report concluded that the "Indian problem" could be solved only by ending the Indians' separate status, giving them full citizenship, and absorbing them "into the great mass of the American people." The committee's findings cited disgruntled or deposed Indian leaders or so-called Indian experts such as C. N. Sims, chancellor of Syracuse University, to back up its case.

The report was harshest toward the Onondagas because both missionaries and state officials apparently were most frustrated in dealing with their conservatism and resistance to change. With no understanding of cultural relativism, the report condemned the traditional governmental leadership on the reservation as "corrupt and vicious," characterized the religious practices as "depraved, immoral, and superstitious," and described the social and industrial state as one of "chronic barbarism." It insisted: "Their present condition is infamously vile and detestable, and just so long will there remain upon the fair name of the Empire State a stain of no small magnitude." The Whipple Report maintained that reservation lands, especially Onondaga, Allegany, and Cattaraugus, be allotted in severalty among tribal members with suitable restrictions as to alienation of lands to whites and protection from judgments and debts. It urged the extension of state laws and jurisdiction over Indians and their absorption into citizenship. The report concluded: "These Indian people have been kept as 'wards' or children long enough. They should now be educated to be men, not Indians, in order to finally and once and for all solve the 'Indian problem.'"[15]

In 1882, Sims had headed an official commission to examine conditions at the Onondaga Reservation, which led to a report blaming the Indians' "general indolence" for their "lack of progress." Before a meeting of the Whipple Committee held at Onondaga on July 9, 1888, Sims recommended that the Indians in New York "be detribalized, and made citizens" because "they don't deserve exemption any more than the colored people of the south, and the best of them would survive the shock, and the rest of them better go down."[16] Thus for the Indians, progress was equated with that of the black freedman, however different their circumstances. In each case, paternalistic white reformers with little knowledge of either race were making decisions that were to affect nonwhite communities. In this thinking, "race progress" required Indians as well as blacks to be sent to boarding schools, such as Hampton Institute in Virginia, to receive discipline and an industrial education to uplift them from their own communities' alleged failings.[17]

For the next twenty-five years, Iroquois communities in New York fought efforts to allot their lands. Unlike their more successful kin in New York, Wisconsin Oneida and Oklahoma Seneca-Cayugas, weakened by the Civil War, could not stem the tide, and their lands were allotted from the 1890s onward. By 1934, the Oneidas had less than ninety acres left of their original sixty-five-thousand-acre Wisconsin land base. The Seneca-Cayugas suffered a similar fate, being dispossessed of most of their sixty-five-thousand-acre Oklahoma land base.[18]

The war years had other far-reaching effects that undermined Iroquois life. The expansion of the Atlantic and Great Western Railroad from 1851 to 1864 helped make Salamanca a major rail terminus, bringing a sizable white population, industry, and agriculture to the city and its environs. It also laid the foundations for illegal leasing arrangements that were retroactively ratified by Congress in 1875 and 1890. The significant demographic changes in the Southern Tier before, during, and immediately after the Civil War became the basis of a major contemporary Indian-white controversy.

From the early 1840s to the mid-1870s, New York State increasingly assumed legislative authority over the Iroquois. Much of this action, but not all, was done unilaterally and some of it ran counter to federal-Iroquois treaty arrangements. Although this movement began as early as 1813, it picked up momentum in the 1840s. From 1846 onward, the New York State legislature provided money for Indian schools. Within three decades, more than twenty-six schools were in operation from Niagara Falls to Southampton, Long Island, regulated by the New York State Department of Public Instruction. The legislature chartered the Thomas Asylum in 1855 and twenty years later placed it under the supervision of the New York State Board of Charities.

More threatening to Indian existence were state intrusions in other areas. In 1843, New York State allotted Oneida lands. In 1845, the legislature passed a law laying out and establishing highways through Indian reservations. In 1850, Albany legislators ratified a leasing arrangement between the Senecas and the New York and Erie Railroad. A similar lease was ratified between the Senecas and the Atlantic and Great Western Railroad during the Civil War. All of these actions went against congressional statutes or federal-Iroquois treaties. It is little wonder that New York State officials continued to chip away at the Indian land base after the Civil War. They tried by state enactments to confirm illegal leasing agreements made by Salamancans in the 1860s and early 1870s and continued to push for allotment of Iroquois lands until the second decade of the twentieth century. Despite losing the battle against leasing in 1875 and 1890, the Iroquois and their white allies successfully fought back further alienation of their tribal land bases until the 1950s.[19]

The impact of the Civil War on the Iroquois did not end at Appomattox but continued throughout the nineteenth and twentieth centuries. The war itself was one of the most destructive events for the Iroquois in the nineteenth century, ranking just behind the War of 1812 and the disaster of Indian removal caused by the fraudulent Treaty of Buffalo Creek of 1838. The war brought population decline while white settlement constantly increased. To the Iroquois, the Civil War years brought rapid changes and permanent intrusions into their communities. They were becoming less and less separated from the white world. Iroquois communities increasingly became dependent as a result of growing state services and were pulled into the market economy by the building of highways and railways through their reservations. Despite the efforts of Iroquois conservatives such as Samuel George to adapt to change, the Iroquois communities witnessed "future shock" in the rapid speedup of outside forces in the war and its aftermath.

NOTES
BIBLIOGRAPHY
INDEX

Notes

APS   American Philosophical Society, Philadelphia, Pa.

BECHS   Buffalo and Erie County Historical Society, Buffalo, N.Y.

CP   Cornelius Plummer

CWPR   Civil War Pension Records, National Archives, Washington, D.C.

ESP   Ely S. Parker

FHL, SC   Friends Historical Library, Swarthmore College, Swarthmore, Pa.

INP   Isaac Newton Parker

MR   Microfilm Reel

NA   National Archives, Washington, D.C.

NAA   National Anthropological Archives, Smithsonian Institution, Washington, D.C.

NYSA   New York State Archives, Albany, N.Y.

NYSL   New York State Library, Manuscript Division, Albany, N.Y.

NYS, SPI   New York State, Superintendent of Public Instruction

NYYM, HRR New York Yearly Meeting Records, Religious Society of Friends, Haviland Records Room, New York City

OHA   Onondaga Historical Association, Syracuse, N.Y.

OIA, M234 Office of Indian Affairs (Central Office), Correspondence and Related Records. Letters Received, 1824–80, Microfilm Publication 234

OR   U.S. War Department, *The War of the Rebellion: A Compilation of the Official Records of the Union and Confederate Armies.* 128 vols. Washington, D.C., U.S. Government Printing Office, 1880–1901.

PYM   Philadelphia Yearly Meeting

QC, HC   Quaker Collection, Haverford College, Haverford, Pa.

RG   Record Group

RMSC   Rochester Museum and Science Center, Rochester, N.Y.

SHSW   State Historical Society of Wisconsin, Madison, Wisc.

SINM   Seneca-Iroquois National Museum, Salamanca, N.Y.

SPI   Superintendent of Public Instruction

USCIA   United States Commissioner of Indian Affairs

Whipple Report   New York State Legislature. Assembly. *Report of the Special Committee to Investigate the Indian Problem of the State of New York . . .* 2 vols. Albany, 1889.

INTRODUCTION

1. The African-American and the Native American experiences in the Civil War were generally quite different. One exception occurred during the Civil War Draft Riots of July 1863. Peter Heuston, a sixty-three-year-old Mohawk Indian, a veteran of the Mexican War, "was brutally attacked and shockingly beaten, on the 13th of July [1863], by a gang of ruffians, who thought him to be of the African race because of his dark complexion. He died within four days, at Bellevue Hospital, from his injuries" (David M. Barnes, *The Draft Riots in New York: July, 1863. The Metropolitan Police: Their Services During Riot Week. Their Honorable Record* [New York: Baker & Goodwin, 1863], pp. 113–16; Barnes was a reporter for the *New York Times* during the Draft Riots).

2. Bruce Catton, *Reflections on the Civil War*, ed. John Leekley (1981; paperback rpt. New York: Berkley, 1982), p. 40.

3. James C. Fitzpatrick, "The Ninth Corps," *New York Herald*, June 30, 1864, p. 1.

4. "Chief Silverheels' Capture," *Warren* (Pa.) *Mail*, Aug. 23, 1887, p. 1.

5. Phillip S. Paludan, *"A People's Contest": The Union and Civil War, 1861–1865* (New York: Harper & Row, 1988), p. 20; Maris A. Vinovskis, ed., *Toward a Social History of the American Civil War: Exploratory Essays* (Cambridge: Cambridge Univ. Press, 1990), p. 10.

6. Interview of George Heron, July 3, 1990, Allegany Indian Reservation. Mr. Heron, the former president of the Seneca Nation and a highly decorated veteran of World War II, remembered these funerals as major but solemn reservation events of the 1920s. See chaps. 10–12 for an extensive discussion of pensions.

7. See Laurence M. Hauptman, *Formulating American Indian Policy in New York State, 1970–1986* (Albany: State Univ. of New York Press, 1988), pp. 3–17; Barbara Graymont, "New York State Indian Policy after the Revolution," *New York History* 57 (Oct. 1976): 440–74; Henry S. Manley, "Buying Buffalo from the Indians," *New York History* 28 (July 1947): 313–29; Jack Campisi, "The Oneida Treaty Period, 1783–1838," in Campisi and Laurence M. Hauptman, eds., *The Oneida Indian Experience: Two Perspectives* (Syracuse: Syracuse Univ. Press, 1988), pp. 48–64; and Campisi, "From Stanwix to Canandaigua: National Policy, States' Rights, and Indian Land," in Christopher Vecsey and William A. Starna, eds., *Iroquois Land Claims* (Syracuse: Syracuse Univ. Press, 1988), pp. 49–66.

1. THE CALL TO ARMS: IROQUOIS WARRIORS/VOLUNTEERS

1. Catton, *Reflections on the Civil War*, pp. 49–50.

2. See chart 1. For estimates of Iroquois populations in this period, see United States Bureau of the Census, *Population of the United States in 1870: Ninth Census* (Washington, D.C.: 1872), p. xii; Franklin B. Hough, comp., *Census of the State of New York for 1855*

(Albany, N.Y.: Charles Van Benthuysen & Sons, 1857), pp. 500–519; Franklin B. Hough, comp., *Census of the State of New York for 1865* (Albany, N.Y.: Charles Van Benthuysen & Sons, 1867), pp. 600–607; C. W. Seaton, comp., *Census of the State of New York for 1875* (Albany, N.Y.: Weed, Parsons & Co., 1877), pp. 196, 397–403; United States Commissioner of Indian Affairs, *Annual Reports, 1860–1865* (Washington, D.C.: U.S. Government Printing Office, 1861–1866). For problems in using Indian census data in New York State, see Robert E. Bieder and Christopher Plant, "Annuity Census as a Source for Historical Research: The 1858 and 1869 Tonawanda Seneca Annuity Censuses," *American Indian Culture and Research Journal* 5, no. 1 (1981), pp. 33–46; and "Census [1990] on Reservation: 2 Indians, 759 Whites," *New York Times*, Feb. 24, 1991. Valuable population information can also be found in nongovernmental sources. See Society of Friends, *A Brief Sketch of the Efforts of [the] Philadelphia Yearly Meeting of the Religious Society of Friends to Promote the Civilization and Improvement of the Indians; also of the Present Conditions of the Tribes in the State of New York* (Philadelphia: Indian Committee of the Philadelphia Yearly Meeting of Friends, 1866).

3. Manley, "Buying Buffalo from the Indians," pp. 313–29; Jack Campisi, "Consequences of the Kansas Claims to Oneida Tribal Identity," in *Proceedings of the First Congress, Canadian Ethnology Society*, ed. Jerome H. Barkow, [Canada] National Museum of Man Ethnology Division, *Mercury Series Paper* 17 (Ottawa, 1974), pp. 35–47; Thomas S. Abler, "Factional Dispute and Party Conflict in the Political System of the Seneca Nation (1845–1895): An Ethnohistorical Analysis" (Ph.D. diss., Univ. of Toronto, 1969), pp. 91–104; Abler, "Friends, Factions, and the Seneca Revolution of 1848," *Niagara Frontier* 21 (Winter 1974): 74–79; George H. J. Abrams, *The Seneca People* (Phoenix: Indian Tribal Series, 1976), pp. 56–90.

4. For the text of the treaty, see Charles J. Kappler, comp., *Indian Affairs: Laws and Treaties* (Washington, D.C.: U.S. Government Printing Office, 1903–41), 2:502–16.

5. Philip E. Thomas to George W. Manypenny, June 6, 1855, Marcus H. Johnson to George Manypenny, Nov. 25, 1856, with attached notice of a sale of land for taxes, Oct. 10, 1856, signed by Harvey Baldwin, New York Agency Records, OIA, M234, MR588, RG75, NA; Nathaniel Starbuck to "Respected Friend," Mar. 12, 1856, and Philip E. Thomas to George T. Trimble, Amos Willetts, and William C. White, Nov. 20, 1856, Papers and Letters Relating to the Work of the Joint Indian Committee of Four Yearly Meetings, 1835–63, File 21, 1856–57, NYYM, HRR.

6. Petition of the Councillors of the Seneca Nation to the President of the United States, June 2, 1858, New York Agency Records, OIA, M234, MR589, RG75, NA.

7. Fragment of a letter written by Philip E. Thomas, 1858 or 1859, New York Agency Records, OIA, M234, MR589 (plate 0089), RG75, NA.

8. Nicholson Parker to ESP, May 17, 1860, ESP MSS, APS.

9. George S. Snyderman, "Behind the Tree of Peace: A Sociological Analysis of Iroquois Warfare," *Pennsylvania Archaeologist* 38 (Fall 1948): 3–93.

10. NYS, SPI, *9th Annual Report* (Albany, 1862), app. D.

11. NYS, SPI, *11th Annual Report* (Albany, 1864), p. 88.

12. INP to Sara Jemison Parker, Aug. 17, 1862, INP MSS, BECHS.

13. Laurence M. Hauptman, Iroquois Field Notes, 1971–91. See the photograph of Iroquois veterans in Hauptman, *Formulating American Indian Policy in New York State*, p. 122.

14. Reginald Horsman, "The Wisconsin Oneidas in the Preallotment Years," in Campisi and Hauptman, eds., *Oneida Indian Experience*, p. 14. This feeling is especially noticeable among the Oneidas and Tuscaroras, as gleaned from interviews with Ray Elm (Oneida) and Edison Mt. Pleasant, Oct. 21–22, 1984, Fort Stanwix National Historic Site, Rome, N.Y., and Loretta Metoxen (Oneida), June 22, 1983, Oneida, Wisc. Elm and Chief Mt. Pleasant are tribal historians, and Metoxen spent two decades in military service.

15. Peter Wilson to General Scroggs, Nov. 11, 1861, Letters Concerning Indian Volunteers, Wilkeson Family MSS, box 11, BECHS.

16. Charles M. Snyder, ed., *Red and White on the New York Frontier: Insights from the Papers of Erastus Granger, Indian Agent, 1807–1819* (Harrison, N.Y.: Harbor Hill Books, 1978), p. 56.

17. Barbara Graymont, *The Iroquois in the American Revolution* (Syracuse: Syracuse Univ. Press, 1972), pp. 20–21, 23. The scholarly literature on Iroquois warfare is extensive. Besides Graymont's excellent book, see Snyderman, "Behind the Tree of Peace"; Anthony F. C. Wallace, *The Death and Rebirth of the Seneca* (New York: Knopf, 1970), pp. 30–50; and Daniel Richter, "War and Culture: The Iroquois Experience," *William and Mary Quarterly* 3d ser. 40, no. 4 (1983): 537–44.

18. Laurence M. Hauptman, "Samuel George (1795–1873): A Study of Onondaga Conservatism," *New York History* 70 (Jan. 1989): 4–22. See chap. 8.

19. William N. Fenton, "The Iroquois in History," in Eleanor B. Leacock and Nancy O. Lurie, eds., *North American Indians in Historical Perspective* (New York: Random House, 1971), pp. 160–61.

20. During the Civil War, Iroquois leaders asked officials in Washington to nominate Martindale to negotiate and resolve their Kansas claims (Peter Wilson, Maris Pierce et al. to William P. Dole, Apr. 28, 1864, New York Agency Records, OIA, M234, MR590, RG75, NA). For Martindale, see William H. Armstrong, *Warrior in Two Camps:* Ely S. Parker, *Union General and Seneca Chief* (Syracuse: Syracuse Univ. Press, 1978), pp. 64–67, 77–78.

21. Armstrong, *Warrior in Two Camps*, pp. 78–83.

22. INP to Sara Jemison Parker, Oct. 9, 1861, INP MSS, BECHS.

23. C. [Chauncey] C. Jemison [Jamieson] to INP, Aug. 5, 1862, NYSL; INP to Sara Jemison Parker, Nov. 12, 1961, INP MSS, BECHS.

24. Peter Wilson to General Scroggs, Nov. 11, 1861.

25. For Allen, see Manley, "Buying Buffalo from the Indians," pp. 313–29.

26. C. C. Jemison to Orlando Allen, Nov. 12, 1861, Letters Concerning Indian Volunteers, Wilkeson Family MSS, Box 11, BECHS. For a contrast with the raising of African-American troops, see William Seraile, "The Struggle to Raise Black Regiments in New York State, 1861–1864," *New-York Historical Society Quarterly* 58 (July 1974): 215–33.

27. Orlando Allen to William Wilkeson, Nov. 13, 1861, Letters Concerning Indian Volunteers, Wilkeson Family MSS, box 11, BECHS.

28. *OR*, ser. 3, vol. 1, p. 161.

29. N. T. Strong to William P. Dole, Nov. 21, 1861, New York Agency Records, OIA, M234, MR589, RG75, NA.

30. Colonel John Fisk to ESP Apr. 4, 1862, ESP MSS, APS; ESP to William P. Dole, Mar. 5, 1862, Dole to ESP, Mar. 12, 1862, New York Agency Records, OIA, M234, MR590, RG75, NA.

31. C. C. Jemison to INP, Aug. 5, 1862; INP to Sara Jemison Parker, Nov. 12, 1861.

32. Gerald E. Wheeler and A. Stuart Pitt, "The 53rd New York: A Zoo-Zoo Tale," *New York History* 37 (Oct. 1956): 415–20.

33. Wooster King to "My Dear friend," Dec. 11, 1861, #87.0009.003, SINM. For the 57th Pennsylvania Volunteer Infantry, see *OR*, ser. 3, 1:161 and Samuel P. Bates, comp., *History of the Pennsylvania Volunteers* 2 vols. (Harrisburg, Pa.: B. Singerly, 1869), 2:246–84. Company K also had the following Iroquois Indians on its muster rolls: Ira Bucktooth, Chauncey Jemison (Jimison), Thompson Jemison (Jimison), Wilson Pierce, Martin Redeye, Thomas Shongo, Jonas Snow, and Joseph White. "Commencement List," Regimental Books, Com-

pany K, 57th Pennsylvania Volunteer Infantry, Records of the Adjutant General's Office, RG94, NA.

34. Cornelius Plummer to Nathaniel Plummer, Dec. 11, 1861, #87.0009.0004, SINM.

35. CP to Jesse Plummer, Feb. 20, 1862, #87.009.009, SINM.

36. CP to Wilson Pierce, Apr. 1, 1862, #87.0009.0014, SINM.

37. Levi T. Williams to father of CP, June 1, 1862, #87.009.0015, SINM.

38. Ibid.

39. Willet Pierce to his father, June 5, 1862, #87.009.0015, SINM.

40. Regimental Books, Company K, 57th Pennsylvania Volunteer Infantry, Records of the Adjutant General's Office, RG94, NA.

41. Report of Six Nations Council, Newtown, Nov. 29, 1862, J. N. B. Hewitt MSS, 3550, NAA.

42. Benjamin A. Gould, *Investigations in the Military and Anthropological Statistics of American Soldiers* (Cambridge, Mass.: Hurd and Houghton for the United States Sanitary Commission, 1869).

43. John S. Haller, Jr., *Outcasts from Evolution: Scientific Attitudes of Racial Inferiority, 1859–1900* (Urbana: Univ. of Illinois Press, 1971), pp. 22–30, 58, 62–63, 86–87, 94; and Haller, "Civil War Anthropometry: The Making of a Racial Ideology," *Civil War History* 16 (Dec. 1970): 309–24.

44. Marshall T. Newman, "The Physique of the Seneca Indians of Western New York State," *Journal of the Washington Academy of Sciences* 17 (Nov. 1957): 357–62.

45. Gould, *Investigations*, pp. 45, 127, 150, 152, 211, 238, 462–67. According to George Bird Grinnell, the Iroquois soldiers during the American Civil War excelled all others as a group in "physical strength and vigor" (*The Story of the Indian* [New York: Macmillan, 1911], p. 262).

46. Dudley A. Beekman to Col. Hugh Hastings, Mar. 21, 1897; A. Luersen to Col. Hugh Hastings, May 23, 1897, Grand Army of the Republic MSS, 132d New York State Volunteer Infantry, Package 14, NYSL.

2. THE TUSCARORA COMPANY: THROUGH THE EYES OF ISAAC NEWTON PARKER

1. For a portrait of this regiment, see Laurence M. Hauptman, "The Tuscarora Company: An Iroquois Unit in the American Civil War," *Turtle Quarterly* (Spring 1988): 10–12.

2. Armstrong, *Warrior in Two Camps*, pp. 7–17. INP Enlistment Papers, June 18, 1862, and "Description of Isaac Newton Parker, 'Third Sergeant of Co. D. 132nd Reg't N.Y.S.V.' Taken From the: Descriptive Roll Book of Co. D 132 Regiment N.Y. Vol. Infantry, P. J. Claussen, Col. Commanding," Sept. 15, 1862, INP MSS, BECHS; M. Stagers and Co. to INP, Jan. 8, 1857, ESP to Caroline Parker, July 19, 1850, INP to ESP, Dec. 16, 1850, June 31, 1851, Oct. 15, 30, 1852, Caroline Parker to ESP, May 29, 1850, ESP MSS, APS.

3. Lewis Henry Morgan, *The League of the Ho-de-no-sau-nee, or Iroquois* (1851; paperback rpt. New York: Corinth Books, 1962). Lewis Henry Morgan to INP, Dec. 19, 1849, Nov. 4, 1851, Caroline Parker to ESP, July 5, 1853, ESP MSS, APS.

4. Arthur C. Parker, *The Life of General Ely S. Parker, Last Grand Sachem of the Iroquois and General Grant's Military Secretary*, Publications of the Buffalo Historical Society, 23 (Buffalo, 1919), pp. 100, 189; Grant Foreman, *The Last Trek of the Indians* (1946; rpt. New York: Russell & Russell, 1972), p. 33n. 50. For Newt Parker's escapades, see Armstrong, *Warrior in Two Camps*, pp. 56–57, 139; INP to Caroline Parker, Aug. 7, 1853, Caro-

line Parker to ESP, Feb. 15, 1855, Apr. 5, 1859, Chauncey C. Jemison to Caroline Parker, Nov. 30, 1854, Theron Seymour to ESP, Dec. 11, 1854, ESP MSS, APS.

5. INP to Martha Hoyt Parker, Aug. 15, 1863, ESP MSS, APS. For a recent analysis of German regiments, see William L. Burton, *Melting Pot Soldiers: The Union's Ethnic Soldiers* (Ames: Iowa State Univ. Press, 1989), pp. 72–111.

6. INP to Sara Jemison Parker, Aug. 17, 1862, INP MSS, BECHS.

7. INP Compiled Service Record, Records of the Adjutant General's Office, RG94, NA; INP to Sara Jemison Parker, Feb. 3, Dec. 27, 1863, INP MSS, BECHS; INP to Caroline Parker, June 26, 1864, ESP MSS, APS.

8. Armstrong, *Warrior in Two Camps*, pp. 82, 104–5.

9. INP to Sara Jemison Parker, Dec. 1, 1862, Feb. 3, 1863, INP MSS, BECHS.

10. INP to Sara Jemison Parker, Dec. 24, 25, 1862, Jan. 15, 1863, INP MSS, BECHS.

11. Fragment of letter (written by INP), Jan. 15, 1863, INP MSS, BECHS.

12. INP to Sara Jemison Parker, Jan. 15, 1863, INP MSS, BECHS; INP, fragment of letter, Jan. 15, 1863, INP to Sara Jemison Parker, Aug. 17, 1862, Feb. 3, 26, Apr. 3, May 17, 1863, INP MSS, BECHS.

13. INP to Sara Jemison Parker, Oct. 5, 1863, INP MSS, BECHS.

14. Morning Reports, Feb. 1863; Feb., Mar., Aug. 1864 (Monthly Summaries), Co. D., 132 NYS Volunteer Infantry, Records of the Adjutant General's Office, RG94, NA. For more on Isaacs, see New York State Historian, *2nd Annual Report* (Albany, 1897), pp. 129–30.

15. New York State Historian, *2nd Annual Report* (Albany, 1897), pp. 126–27.

16. INP to Sara Jemison Parker, Feb. 3, 26, Oct. 5, 18, 1863, INP MSS, BECHS. Whiskey rations, an "army gallon," were dispensed to the troops on this and other occasions.

17. Morning Reports, Mar., May, Nov. 1863; July 1864 (Monthly Summaries), Records of the Adjutant General's Office, RG94, NA.

18. INP to Martha Hoyt Parker, Aug. 15, 1863, ESP MSS, APS.

19. Descriptive Muster Rolls, Regimental Books, D Company, 132d NYS Volunteer Infantry, Records of the Adjutant General's Office, RG94, NA.

20. INP to Martha Hoyt Parker, Aug. 15, 1863, ESP MSS, APS.

21. INP to Martha Hoyt Parker, Apr. 1, 1864, ibid.

22. INP to Sara Jemison Parker, Dec. 1, 1862, INP, fragment of letter, Jan. 15, 1863; undated letter and other INP letters to Sara Jemison Parker, early 1863, Feb. 3, 26, Apr. 3, May 17, Oct. 5, 18, Nov. 4, Dec. 27, 1863; Jan. 3, 1864, INP MSS, BECHS.

23. H. Craig Miner, *The Corporation and the Indian: Tribal Sovereignty and Industrial Civilization in Indian Territory* (Columbia: Univ. of Missouri Press, 1976), pp. 27–28; Foreman, *Last Trek of the Indians*, p. 339n. 50.

24. INP to Sara Jemison Parker, June 21, 1863, INP MSS, BECHS.

25. INP to Sara Jemison Parker, Oct. 18, Dec. 20, 1863, ibid.

26. Lewis Henry Morgan to General Benjamin Butler, Dec. 14, 1863, in Military Service Record of INP, Records of the Adjutant General's Office, RG94, NA.

27. INP to Martha Hoyt Parker, Apr. 1, 1864, ESP MSS, APS.

28. INP to Caroline Parker, June 26, 1864, ibid.

29. *OR*, ser. 1, vol. 33, p. 62. For the Battle of Bachelder's (Batchelor's) Creek, see ibid., pp. 62–76, and chap. 3 below.

30. Ibid., p. 67.

31. Map of Union forces at New Bern and Notes of Battle of Bachelder's Creek, Feb. 1, 1864, and other notes, May 10, 1864, Sergeant Isaac Newton Parker, "Color Bearer," 132d N.Y.V Infantry, ESP MSS, APS.

32. Descriptive Muster Roll, Regimental Books, D Company, 132d NYS Volunteer Infantry, Records of the Adjutant General's Office, RG94, NA; Pension Record of William Kennedy, certificate 308,776, application 519187, "Widow Kennedy, mother of William Kennedy," CWPR, NA.

33. Daniel G. Kelley, *What I Saw and Suffered in Rebel Prisons* (Buffalo, N.Y.: Thomas, Howard & Johnson, 1868), pp. 16–41. I identified John Williams of the 24th New York Cavalry as an Iroquois Indian because his name appears with other Senecas in Special Order No. 126, Mar. 24, 1864, New York Agency Records, OIA, M234, MR590, RG75, NA. The order called for his discharge on refunding his local bounty. He was captured before he did so.

34. INP to Asher Wright, Apr. 1, 1865, Foster John Hudson Pension Records, mother's application (Louisa Johnnyjohn Hudson), CWPR, NA.

35. Ibid.

36. Order Books, Regimental Books, D Company, 132d NYS Volunteer Infantry, Records of the Adjutant General's Office, RG94, NA.

37. Armstrong, *Warrior in Two Camps*, p. 139; Miner, *The Corporation and the Indian*, pp. 27–28; Foreman, *Last Trek of the Indians*, p. 339n. 50; Arthur C. Parker, *Life of General Ely S. Parker*, p. 189; "An Indian Officer," newsclipping (undated), Lewis Henry Morgan MSS, Box 27, Folder 8, Rush Rhees Library, University of Rochester. The author acknowledges the help of Professor Elisabeth Tooker in calling this newsclipping to my attention.

3. "WAR EAGLE": LIEUTENANT CORNELIUS C. CUSICK

1. New York State Historian, *2nd Annual Report*, Appendix F; Elias Johnson, *Legends, Traditions and Laws, of the Iroquois or Six Nations, and History of the Tuscarora Indians* (Lockport, N.Y.: Union Printing and Publishing, 1881), pp. 171–72; E. Roy Johnson, *The Tuscaroras: History—Traditions—Culture* (Murfreesboro, N.C.: Johnson Publishing Co., 1968), 2:228–29. I thank Professor Barbara Graymont for sharing with me her knowledge about the Cusick-Rickard family and Tuscarora history.

2. Cornelius C. Cusick to Adjutant General, U.S. Army, Apr. 2, 1883, ACP Branch Document File, 1888, Box 1168, Records of the Adjutant General's Office, RG94, NA; Cornelius C. Cusick's death certificate, Jan. 2, 1904, in widow's [Lizzie B. Cusick] pension application 800,281, certificate 587,550, CWPR, NA; E. Roy Johnson, *Tuscaroras*, p. 220; Graymont, *Iroquois in the American Revolution*, p. 197; Elias Johnson, *Legends, Traditions and Laws*, pp. 165–66; David Cusick, *Sketches of Ancient History of the Six Nations*. 2d ed. (Lockport, N.Y., 1827); Barbara Graymont, "The Tuscarora New Year Festival," *New York History* 50 (Apr. 1969): 149–52. In approximately 1825, Nicholas and James Cusick prepared a vocabulary of the Tuscarora language at the behest of the War Department (MSS 3803, APS). Nicholas Cusick and his son James supported the Buffalo Creek Treaty. See Nicholas Cusick to Ransom H. Gillet, Jan. 1838 and Cusick et al. to the United States Senate and House of Representatives, Oct. 3, 1838, Special Case File 29, RG75, NA. James Cusick's activities concerning removal are documented in New York Agency Records, OIA, M234, MR586, RG75, NA. The Cusicks' stance in favor of removal tarnished the family's reputation among the Tuscaroras well into the twentieth century (interview with Chief Edison Mt. Pleasant, Nov. 30, 1984, Tuscarora Indian Reservation).

3. Barbara Graymont, ed., *Fighting Tuscarora: The Autobiography of Chief Clinton Rickard* (Syracuse: Syracuse Univ. Press, 1973); Laurence M. Hauptman, *The Iroquois Struggle for Survival: World War II to Red Power* (Syracuse: Syracuse Univ. Press, 1986), pp. 151–78.

4. Graymont, ed., *Fighting Tuscarora*, p. 14.

5. Peter J. Claassen to Whom It May Concern, Jan. 14, 1865, ACP Branch Document File 1888, Box 1168, Records of the Adjutant General's Office, RG94, NA; E. Roy Johnson, *Tuscaroras*, 2:228–29.

6. E. Roy Johnson, *The Tuscaroras*, 2:228–29. Cusick was frequently referred to as chief of the Tuscaroras. See, for example, Claassen to Whom It May Concern, Jan. 14, 1865.

7. Cornelius C. Cusick to Abraham Lincoln, Jan. 23, 1865, ACP Branch Document File 1888, Box 1168, Records of the Office of the Adjutant General, RG94, NA.

8. Approximately thirty-five Tuscaroras served with the United States military in the War of 1812; twenty-three Tuscaroras volunteered to serve in the Union army during the Civil War. Five were assigned to the Tuscarora Company in 1862: Cusick, George Garlow, Hulett Jacobs, Jeremiah Peters, and John Peters (Elias Johnson, *Legends, Traditions and Laws*, pp. 167–72). Seventeen Tuscaroras received pensions from the United States government for service in the War of 1812 (New York State Adjutant General's Office, *Index of Awards: Soldiers of the War of 1812* [Baltimore: Genealogical Publishing Co., 1969], p. 573).

9. See chart 2. For Cusick's enlistment efforts, see chap. 2 and also New York State Historian, *2nd Annual Report*, app. F.

10. Cornelius C. Cusick, Military Service Record; Descriptive Muster Rolls of D Company, 132d NYS Volunteer Infantry, Records of the Adjutant General's Office, RG94, NA. For the removal of the Tuscaroras from the Carolinas in the early eighteenth century, see Douglas W. Boyce, "Tuscarora Political Organization, Ethnic Identity and Sociohistorical Demography, 1711–1825" (Ph.D. diss., Univ. of North Carolina, 1973); David Landy, "Tuscarora Among the Iroquois," in *Handbook of North American Indians*, vol. 15, *Northeast*, ed. Bruce G. Trigger (Washington, D.C.: Smithsonian Institution, 1978), pp. 518–24; and Landy, "Tuscarora Tribalism and National Identity," *Ethnohistory* 5 (1958): 250–84.

11. Quoted in John G. Barrett, *The Civil War in North Carolina* (Chapel Hill: Univ. of North Carolina Press, 1963), p. 202.

12. Ibid., pp. 203–12.

13. Ibid.

14. Ibid. The battle can be traced in *OR*, ser. 1, vol. 33, pp. 60–76.

15. *OR*, ser. 1, vol. 33, p. 76.

16. R. Emmett Fiske to Whom It May Concern, Jan. 13, 1865, ACP Branch Document, File 1888, Box 1168, Records of the Adjutant General's Office, RG94, NA.

17. New York State Historian, *2nd Annual Report*, app. F.

18. Fiske to Whom It May Concern, Jan. 13, 1865; *OR*, ser. 1, vol. 40, pt. 1, p. 814.

19. New York State Historian, *2nd Annual Report*, app. F.

20. Cusick to Lincoln, Jan. 23, 1865.

21. Claassen to Whom It May Concern, Jan. 14, 1865.

22. E. L. Porter to E. D. Morgan, May 28, 1866, ACP Branch Document, File 1888, Box 1168, Records of the Adjutant General's Office, RG94, NA.

23. Cornelius C. Cusick, Oath of Office in the Military Service of the United States, Aug. 24, 1866, Exhibit F: Statement of the Military Service of Cornelius C. Cusick of the United States Army, compiled from the records of this office, Dec. 24, 1891, Army Retirement Book Records, Columbus, Ohio, Jan. 14, 1892, ACP Branch Document File 1888, Box 1168, Records of the Adjutant General's Office, RG94, NA.

24. Exhibit F: Statement of the Military Service of Cornelius C. Cusick; E. Roy Johnson, *Tuscaroras*, II, pp. 227–28; Armstrong, *Warrior in Two Camps*, p. 126; interview with Chief Edison Mt. Pleasant.

25. Jerome A. Greene, *Yellowstone Command: Colonel Nelson A. Miles and the Great Sioux War, 1876–1877* (Lincoln: Univ. of Nebraska Press, 1991), p. 293n. 13; Exhibit F: State-

ment of the Military Service of Cornelius C. Cusick; Cornelius C. Cusick Death Certificate, Jan. 2, 1904; Lizzie B. Cusick widow's pension application, Feb. 15, 1904; Lizzie B. Cusick's affidavit, June 9, 1904, widow's [of Cornelius C. Cusick] pension application 800,281, certificate 587,550, CWPR, NA.

26. J. S. Conrad, Efficiency Report in Case of C. C. Cusick, Captain, 22nd Infantry, ACP Branch Document File 1888, Box 1168, Records of the Adjutant General's Office, RG94, NA.

27. Alton B. Cusick to Commissioner of Pensions, June 20, 1921, Certificate of Marriage: Cornelius C. Cusick and Lizzie M. Barnes, June 19, 1879, Cleveland, Ohio, ACP Branch Document File 1888, Box 1168, Records of the Adjutant General's Office, RG94, NA.

4. "GRANT'S INDIAN": ELY S. PARKER AT THE BATTLE OF CHATTANOOGA

1. "General Ely S. Parker's Narrative" [of General Lee's Surrender at Appomattox], Ulysses S. Grant MSS, ser. 8, box 2, LC; Sylvanus Cadwalader, *Three Years with Grant*, ed. Benjamin P. Thomas (New York: Knopf, 1956), p. 323. See also Horace Porter, *Campaigning with Grant* (1897; paperback rpt. New York: Da Capo, 1986), pp. 33–34, 200, 207–8, 476–81; and John Y. Simon, ed., *The Papers of Ulysses S. Grant* (Carbondale: Southern Illinois Univ. Press, 1967–), 14:361, 374–78.

2. Armstrong, *Warrior in Two Camps*, pp. 1–60; Arthur C. Parker, *Life of General Ely S. Parker*, pp. 236–37.

3. Armstrong, *Warrior in Two Camps*, pp. 1–13.

4. Ibid., pp. 84–107.

5. Ibid., p. 87.

6. Reid Mitchell, *Civil War Soldiers: Their Expectations and Their Experiences* (New York: Viking, 1988), p. 107.

7. ESP to Nicholson Parker, Nov. 18, 1863, ESP MSS, APS.

8. Ibid.

9. Armstrong, *Warrior in Two Camps*, pp. 84–107.

10. ESP to Nicholson Parker, Nov. 18, 1863.

11. ESP to Caroline Parker Mountpleasant, Nov. 21, 1863, ESP MSS, APS.

12. Ibid.

13. Ibid. Oneidas who opposed removal held council with Ross in the 1830s and anti-removal Senecas praised his efforts at resisting Jacksonian attempts to remove the Cherokees. See Maris B. Pierce, *Address on the Present Condition and Prospects of the Aboriginal Inhabitants of North America with Particular Reference to the Seneca Nation* (published address presented in the Baptist Church of Buffalo, Aug. 28, 1838), Maris B. Pierce MSS, BECHS; and Gary E. Moulton, ed., *The Papers of Chief John Ross*, 2 vols. (Norman: Univ. of Oklahoma Press, 1985), 1:574.

14. ESP to Caroline Parker Mountpleasant, Dec. 2, 1863, ESP MSS, APS. For the Battle of Chattanooga see James Lee McDonough, *Chattanooga: A Death Grip on the Confederacy* (Knoxville: Univ. of Tennessee Press, 1984).

15. ESP to Caroline Parker Mountpleasant, Dec. 2, 1863.

16. ESP to Nicholson Parker, Jan. 25, 1864, ESP MSS, APS.

17. Ibid.

18. See Wallace, *Death and Rebirth of the Seneca*, pp. 30–34.

19. ESP to Nicholson Parker, Jan. 25, 1864.

20. Armstrong, *Warrior in Two Camps*, pp. 137–65.

21. Henry G. Waltmann, "Ely Samuel Parker, 1869–1871," in Robert Kvasnicka and Herman Viola, eds., *The Commissioners of Indian Affairs, 1824–1977* (Lincoln: Univ. of Nebraska Press, 1979), pp. 127–31.

22. U.S. Congress, House of Representatives, *House Report No. 39: Investigation into Indian Affairs,* 39th Cong., 3d sess., pp. i–vii, 32–33.

23. Waltmann, "Ely Samuel Parker," p. 131. See also Armstrong, *Warrior in Two Camps,* pp. 162–94.

24. Armstrong, *Warrior in Two Camps,* pp. 135, 137.

5. ORDINARY SEAMAN WILLIAM JONES IN WAR AND PEACE

1. William Jones Diary, RMSC; Invalid pension for William Jones, application 1,337 (Oct. 1865), certificate 2,693; Widow's pension (Maria Jones), application 6,953 (Aug. 1890), certificate 5,808, CWPR, NA.

2. Jones Diary; Declaration for Widow's Pension, Sept. 5, 1890, Widow's Declaration for Pension or Increase of Pension, May 12, 1890, General Affidavit of Warren Skye (Maria Jones's brother), May 12, 1890, William Jones Pension Records, CWPR, NA. The census of 1890 incorrectly lists Maria Jones as the widow of "marine" William Jones during the Civil War (Thomas Donaldson, comp., *The Six Nations of New York: Extra Census Bulletin* [Washington, D.C.: U.S. Government Printing Office, 1894], p. 15).

3. Jack A. Frisch, "Iroquois in the West," in Trigger, ed., *Handbook of North American Indians,* 15:544–46; John C. Ewers, "Iroquois Indians in the Far West," *Montana: The Magazine of Western History* 13 (1963): 2–10; Interview of George H. J. Abrams, Dec. 20, 1990. Abrams's great-grandfather, a Cornplanter heir, was killed in logging activities on the Allegheny River (Regimental Books, Company K, 57th Pennsylvania Volunteer Infantry, Records of the Adjutant General's Office, RG94, NA). For a good discussion of Senecas in Allegheny logging, see Diane B. Rothenberg, "Friends Like These: An Ethnohistorical Analysis of the Interaction Between Allegany Senecas and Quakers, 1798–1823" (Ph.D. diss., City Univ. of New York, 1976), pp. 99–101, 205, 212.

4. U.S. Bureau of the Census, *Population of the United States in 1860: Eighth Census* (Washington, D.C.: U.S. Government Printing Office, 1862), p. 605.

5. Betty Coit Prisch, *Aspects of Change in Seneca Iroquois Ladles A.D. 1600–1900* (Rochester, N.Y.: Rochester Museum and Science Center, Research Records No. 15, 1982), p. 56.

6. U.S.S. *Rhode Island* Logbook, Oct. 1864–Jan. 1865, U.S. War Department Records of the U.S. Navy, RG24; NA; William Jones Discharge Papers, Oct. 13, 1865, William Jones Pension Records, CWPR, NA; Jones Diary, RMSC.

7. Rowena Reed, *Combined Operations in the Civil War* (Annapolis: Naval Institute Press, 1978), pp. 329–35; Barrett, *Civil War in North Carolina,* pp. 262–64. For a recent study of the Battle of Fort Fisher, see Rod Gragg, *Confederate Goliath: The Battle of Fort Fisher* (New York: Harper Collins, 1991).

8. Rowena Reed, *Combined Operations,* pp. 336–37; Barrett, *Civil War in North Carolina,* pp. 265–67.

9. Rowena Reed, *Combined Operations,* pp. 337–42; Barrett, *Civil War in North Carolina,* pp. 264–70.

10. *OR,* ser. 1, vol. 11, pp. 340–41, 443.

11. Jones Diary, RMSC.

12. *OR*, ser. 1, vol. 11, pp. 442–44 and naval squadron maps inserted.

13. Ibid., pp. 144–45, 556–61, 597–99. See also Rowena Reed, *Combined Operations*, pp. 355–83.

14. Barrett, *Civil War in North Carolina*, pp. 279–83.

15. Rowena Reed, *Combined Operations*, p. 383.

16. Jones Diary, RMSC.

17. Application form for Navy Invalid Pension, Oct. 13, 1865, Invalid Pension certificate issued Nov. 18, 1865, Report [to Dr. Horwitz] of Medical Survey conducted by T. L. Smith and T. N. Leach [naval surgeons], Oct. 11, 1865, Claimant's Affidavit [William Jones], July 8, 1879, William Jones Pension Records, CWPR, NA. Jones Diary, RMSC.

18. Jones Diary, RMSC.

19. Ibid. I thank Barbara Graymont for sharing her special knowledge of Iroquois ceremonialism.

20. Ibid.

21. Examining Surgeon's Certificate, Sept. 25, 1871, Sept. 3, 1879, Feb. 18, 1880, Declaration for Restoration to the Rolls, Feb. 26, Sept. 12, 1879, Claimant's Affidavit, Apr. 2, July 8, 1879, William Jones Pension Records, CWPR, NA.

22. C. H. Avery (Erie County clerk) to L. J. McPartin, Aug. 13, 1889, General Affidavit of Warren Skye, May 12, Sept. 15, 1890, General Affidavit of William Smith and Elon Skye (both residents of Tonawanda Reservation), Sept. 5, 1890, Widow's Declaration for Pension or Increase of Pension, May 12, 1890, ibid.

6. THE ONEIDAS OF THE 14TH WISCONSIN VOLUNTEER INFANTRY

1. Robert Smith and Loretta Metoxen, "Oneida Traditions," Campisi and Hauptman, eds., *Oneida Indian Experience*, pp. 150–51; Reginald Horsman, "The Wisconsin Oneidas in the Preallotment Years," ibid., pp. 74–75; Jan Malcolm, "The Oneida Pentagon Report," MSS, Oneida Nation Museum, DePere, Wisc.; Frank L. Klement, *Wisconsin and the Civil War* (Madison: State Historical Society of Wisconsin, 1963), p. 42; USCIA, *Annual Report for 1865*, p. 52.

2. Joseph O. Powless and John Archiquette Diary, trans. by Oscar H. Archiquette, Manuscript Division, SHSW.

3. Horsman, "The Wisconsin Oneidas in the Preallotment Years," p. 74.

4. M. M. Davis to W. P. Dole, May 31, 1864, Green Bay Agency Records, 1861–64, OIA, M234, MR324, RG75, NA.

5. For the best treatments of Oneida history from 1776 to 1860, see Jack Campisi, "Ethnic Identity and Boundary Maintenance in Three Oneida Communities" (Ph.D. diss., State Univ. of New York, Albany, 1974), pp. 65–147, 262–75; and Campisi and Hauptman, eds., *Oneida Indian Experience*, pp. 31–82; Reginald Horsman, "The Origins of Oneida Removal to Wisconsin, 1815–1822," in Donald L. Fixico, ed., *An Anthology of Western Great Lakes Indian History* (Milwaukee: American Indian Studies Department of the University of Wisconsin, Milwaukee, 1987), pp. 203–32.

6. USCIA, *Annual Report for 1864*, p. 43.

7. Cornelius Hill et al. to W. P. Dole, Dec. 24, 1863, Green Bay Agency Records, 1861–64, OIA, M234, MR324, RG75, NA.

8. Horsman, "Wisconsin Oneidas in the Preallotment Years," p. 70.

9. USCIA, *Annual Report for 1861*, p. 42; ibid., *1863*, p. 34.

10. Richard N. Current, *The History of Wisconsin: The Civil War Era, 1848–1873* (Madison: State Historical Society of Wisconsin, 1976), pp. 319–23; Klement, *Wisconsin and the Civil War*, pp. 38–42.

11. For Civil War conscription, see Eugene C. Murdock, *Patriotism Limited, 1862–1865: The Civil War Draft and Bounty System* (Kent, Ohio: Kent State Univ. Press, 1967); and Murdock, *One Million Men: The Civil War Draft in the North* (Madison: State Historical Society of Wisconsin, 1971). See also James W. Geary, *We Need Men: The Union Draft in the Civil War* (De Kalb: Northern Illinois Univ. Press, 1991).

12. For the draft in Wisconsin, see Current, *History of Wisconsin*, pp. 311–35; E. B. Quiner, *The Military History of Wisconsin: A Record of the Civil and Military Patriotism of the State in the War for the Union* (Chicago: Clarke & Co., 1866), pp. 139–49; Klement, *Wisconsin and the Civil War*, pp. 33–39.

13. Eugene C. Murdock, *One Million Men*, pp. 30, 41, 76; Current, *History of Wisconsin*, p. 332; Geary, *We Need Men*, pp. 40, 105.

14. Current, *History of Wisconsin*, pp. 310–27.

15. Eugene C. Murdock, *One Million Men*, pp. 29–31, 40–41, 76; Current, *History of Wisconsin*, pp. 310–27.

16. Powless-Archiquette Diary, SHSW; USCIA, *Annual Report for 1864*, pp. 43, 443–44.

17. W. De Loss Love, *Wisconsin in the War of Rebellion* (New York: Love Publishing, 1866), pp. 787–90; Quiner, *Military History of Wisconsin*, pp. 598–612.

18. Charts 3a, 3b, and 4 were compiled from Regimental Muster and Descriptive Rolls, 14th Wisconsin Volunteer Infantry, State Militia, Red Book, Ser. 1144, MR 4, #P68-2492, and from State Militia, Blue Book, Ser. 1142, MR 10, #P68-2476, SHSW; and from Regimental Books, F and G Companies, 14th Wisconsin Volunteer Infantry, Records of the Adjutant General's Office, RG94, NA.

19. Quiner, *Military History of Wisconsin*, pp. 598–612.

20. Byron R. Abernethy, ed., *Private Elisha Stockwell, Jr., Sees the Civil War* (Norman: Univ. of Oklahoma Press, 1958), pp. 79–80.

21. Ibid., p. 88.

22. See charts 3a, 3b, and 4. See also Widow's [Evelina King] Pension Application, application 61,449, certificate 67,448 (1864), Simon King, CWPR, NA; Invalid Pension for Daniel Bread, application 102,617 (1866), CWPR, NA.

23. U.S. Department of War. Provost-General's Bureau. *Statistics, Medical and Anthropological* (Washington, D.C.: U.S. Government Printing Office, 1875), p. 473.

24. Quoted in Deborah B. Martin, *History of Brown County, Wisconsin: Past and Present* (Chicago: S. J. Clarke, 1913), p. 209.

25. Abernethy, ed., *Private Elisha Stockwell*, pp. 79–80.

26. *OR*, ser. 1, vol. 38, pp. 599–600.

27. *OR*, ser. 1, vol. 45, pp. 437–40.

28. See charts 3a, 3b, and 4; Quiner, *Military History of Wisconsin*, pp. 598–612.

29. Regimental Books, F and G Companies, 14th Wisconsin Volunteer Infantry, Records of the Adjutant General's Office, RG94, NA.

30. Ibid.; Robert Sterling, "Civil War Draft Resistance in the Middle West" (Ph.D. diss., Northern Illinois Univ., 1974), pp. 178–79, 259–74, 648; Judith Lee Hancock, "The Role of Community in Civil War Desertion," *Civil War History* 29 (June 1983): 125–26; Ella Lonn, *Desertion During the Civil War* (New York: Century, 1928); Eugene C. Murdock, *One Million Men*, p. 356; Paludan, *"A People's Contest,"* p. 168.

31. Regimental Books, F and G Companies, 14th Wisconsin Volunteer Infantry, Records of the Adjutant General's Office, RG94, NA.

32. Abernethy, ed., *Private Elisha Stockwell,* pp. 32–33.

33. Marlene Johnson, comp., *Iroquois Cookbook,* 2d ed. (Tonawanda Indian Reservation: Peter Doctor Memorial Indian Fellowship Foundation, 1989), p. 8, recipe of Amelia Williams (Tuscarora).

34. Stephen Ambrose, ed., *A Wisconsin Boy in Dixie: The Selected Letters of James K. Newton* (Madison: Univ. of Wisconsin Press, 1961), pp. 138–39.

35. Parker, Arthur C., *Parker on the Iroquois,* ed. William N. Fenton (Syracuse: Syracuse Univ. Press, 1968), pp. 73–74.

36. Powless-Archiquette Diary, SHSW.

37. Horsman, "Wisconsin Oneidas in the Preallotment Years," pp. 74–75.

38. Campisi, "Ethnic Identity and Boundary Maintenance," p. 141.

39. Interview with Norbert Hill, Sr., Oct. 17, 1978, Oneida, Wisc.

40. Horsman, "Wisconsin Oneidas in the Preallotment Years," pp. 75–78; Campisi, "Ethnic Identity and Boundary Maintenance," p. 146; Arlinda Locklear, "The Allotment of the Oneida Reservation and Its Legal Ramifications," in Campisi and Hauptman, eds., *Oneida Indian Experience,* pp. 83–94; and Laurence H. Hauptman, *The Iroquois and the New Deal* (Syracuse: Syracuse Univ. Press, 1981), pp. 70–74.

7. THE IROQUOIS IN INDIAN TERRITORY

1. For the Iroquois migrations, see William C. Sturtevant, "Oklahoma Seneca-Cayuga," in Trigger, ed., *Handbook of North American Indians,* 15:537–39, and Hauptman, *The Iroquois and the New Deal,* pp. 88–90; Foreman, *Last Trek of the Indians,* pp. 67–82, 322–36; Erminie Wheeler-Voegelin, "The 19th and 20th Century Ethnohistory of Various Groups of Cayuga Indians," MSS 7092, NAA.

2. Wheeler-Voegelin, "The 19th and 20th Century Ethnohistory of Various Groups of Cayuga Indians," pp. 62, 71.

3. Interview with Vernon Crow, former chief of the Seneca-Cayuga Tribe of Oklahoma, June 29, 1983, Miami, Okla. For Quantrill's activities, see Josephy, *The Civil War in the American West,* pp. 251, 358, 373–74, 380; Albert E. Castel, *A Frontier State at War: Kansas, 1861–1865* (Ithaca, N.Y.: Cornell Univ. Press, 1958), pp. 110–57; Richard S. Brownlee, *Gray Ghosts of the Confederacy: Guerrilla Warfare in the West, 1861–1865* (Baton Rouge: Louisiana State Univ. Press, 1958), chap. 7; Michael Fellman, *Inside War: The Guerrilla Conflict in Missouri During the American Civil War* (New York: Oxford Univ. Press, 1989), pp. 25, 41, 53, 206–7, 254; Jay Monaghan, *Civil War on the Western Border, 1854–1865* (Boston: Little, Brown, 1955), pp. 274–85.

4. USCIA, *Annual Report for 1861,* pp. 1, 36.

5. David A. Nichols, *Lincoln and the Indians: Civil War Policy and Politics* (Columbia: Univ. of Missouri Press, 1978), pp. 25–53. LeRoy H. Fischer, ed., *The Civil War in Indian Territory* (Los Angeles: Morrison, 1974), pp. 1–21; Robert M. Utley, *The Indian Frontier of the American West, 1846–1890* (Albuquerque: Univ. of New Mexico Press, 1984), pp. 73–75; Gary Moulton, *John Ross: Cherokee Chief* (Athens: Univ. of Georgia Press, 1979), pp. 167–72. Francis Paul Prucha, *The Great Father: The United States Government and the American Indians,* 2 vols. (Lincoln: Univ. of Nebraska Press, 1984), 1:415–36.

6. H. Craig Miner and William E. Unrau, *The End of Indian Kansas: A Study of Cultural Revolution, 1854–1871* (Lawrence: Regents Press of Kansas, 1978), pp. 1–54.

7. USCIA, *Annual Report for 1862,* pp. 7–8.

8. *OR,* ser. 4, vol. 1, pp. 359–61; Robert L. Duncan, *Reluctant General: The Life and*

Times of Albert Pike (New York: E. P. Dutton, 1961), pp. 168–83; Josephy, *The Civil War in the American West*, pp. 323–361; Walter L. Brown, "Albert Pike, 1809–1891" (Ph.D. diss., Univ. of Texas, 1955), p. 553; M. K. McNeil, "Confederate Treaties with the Tribes of Indian Territory," *Chronicles of Oklahoma* 42 (Winter 1964–65): 408–20; Kenny A. Franks, "An Analysis of the Confederate Treaties with the Five Civilized Tribes," *Chronicles of Oklahoma* 50 (Winter 1972–73): 458–73; Moulton, *John Ross*, pp. 168–74.

    9. Moulton, ed., *Papers of John Ross*, 2:168–74, 487.

   10. Ibid., pp. 487–88.

   11. Duncan, *Reluctant General*, p. 169.

   12. *OR*, ser. 4, vol. 1, pp. 647–66.

   13. Ibid.

   14. Ibid.

   15. Ibid.

   16. Ibid.

   17. Moulton, ed., *Papers of John Ross*, 2:491.

   18. Morris L. Wardell, *A Political History of the Cherokee Nation, 1838–1907* (1938; paperback rpt. Norman: Univ. of Oklahoma Press, 1977), pp. 149–50.

   19. W. Craig Gaines, *The Confederate Cherokees: John Drew's Regiment of Mounted Rifles* (Baton Rouge: Louisiana State Univ. Press, 1989), pp. 74–90; Edward C. Bearss, "The Battle of Pea Ridge," *Arkansas Historical Quarterly* 20 (Spring 1961): 74–94.

   20. Muriel H. Wright and LeRoy H. Fischer, *Civil War Sites in Oklahoma* (Oklahoma City: Oklahoma Historical Society, 1967), p. 18; Kenny A. Franks, *Stand Watie and the Agony of the Cherokee Nation* (Memphis: Memphis State Univ. Press, 1979), p. 128.

   21. USCIA, *Annual Report for 1862*, pp. 143–45.

   22. Edmund J. Danziger, Jr., "The Office of Indian Affairs and the Problem of Civil War Refugees in Kansas," *Kansas Historical Quarterly* 35 (Autumn 1969): 257–75; and Danziger, *Indians and Bureaucrats: Administering the Reservation Policy During the Civil War* (Urbana: Univ. of Illinois Press, 1974), pp. 133–36. See also Dean Banks, "Civil War Refugees from Indian Territory in the North, 1861–1864," *Chronicles of Oklahoma* 41 (Autumn 1963): 286–98; Nichols, *Lincoln and the Indians*, pp. 34–63.

   23. John Melton (and George Herron) to Commissioner of Indian Affairs, Sept. 2, 1862, Neosho Agency Records, 1862–65, MR 533, RG75, NA.

   24. Wheeler-Voegelin, "The 19th and 20th Century Ethnohistory of Various Groups of Cayuga Indians," pp. 68, 74.

   25. Annie Heloise Abel, *The American Indian as Participant in the Civil War* (Cleveland: Arthur H. Clark, 1919), pp. 204–5.

   26. *OR*, ser. 4, vol. 2, p. 354.

   27. Quoted in Wilcomb E. Washburn, ed., *The American Indian and the United States: A Documentary History*, 4 vols. (Westport, Conn.: Greenwood, 1973), 1:115.

   28. USCIA, *Annual Report for 1864*, pp. 32, 330–31.

   29. USCIA, *Annual Report for 1865*, pp. 32–35, 202–3, 334, 479–522. For Ely S. Parker's role, see Armstrong, *Warrior in Two Camps*, pp. 114–16. For a brief sketch of Cooley, see Gary L. Roberts, "Dennis Nelson Cooley, 1865–1866," in Kvasnicka and Viola, eds., *Commissioners of Indian Affairs*, pp. 98–108. For this remarkable setting, see Edward C. Bearss and Arrell M. Gibson, *Fort Smith: Little Gibraltar on the Arkansas* (Norman: Univ. of Oklahoma Press, 1969).

   30. USCIA, *Annual Report for 1865*, pp. 34–35.

   31. Ibid., pp. 334.

   32. Ibid.

33. Kappler, comp., *Indian Affairs*, pp. 960–69.
34. Ibid.
35. Ibid. See Bert Anson, *The Miami Indians* (Norman: Univ. of Oklahoma Press, 1970), pp. 243–44; James H. Howard, *Shawnee* (Athens: Ohio Univ. Press, 1981), pp. 21–22; Miner and Unrau, *End of Indian Kansas*, pp. 107–41; Keith Murray, *The Modocs and Their War* (Norman: Univ. of Oklahoma Press, 1971). There had been plans to "resettle" the Wyandots on Seneca lands since 1859. See USCIA, *Annual Report for 1866*, p. 56.

8. CHIEF SAMUEL GEORGE, IROQUOIS CONFEDERACY SPOKESMAN

1. Whipple Report, p. 390.
2. For Albert Cusick, see William M. Beauchamp, Notebook: Sketches of Onondagas of Note, pp. 219–21, William M. Beauchamp MSS, SC17369, Box 3, NYSL.
3. Frederick Houghton, *The History of the Buffalo Creek Reservation*, Publications of the Buffalo Historical Society, no. 24 (Buffalo, 1920), pp. 1–181; Beauchamp, Notebook, pp. 172–73; Samuel George's Pension Application, New York State Division of Military and Naval Affairs, Adjutant General's Office, Claims, Applications and Awards for Service in the War of 1812, ca. 1857–61, NYSA; Snyder, ed., *Red and White on the New York Frontier*, p. 30.
4. Wallace, *Death and Rebirth of the Seneca*, pp. 239–337.
5. Anthony F. C. Wallace, "Origins of the Longhouse Religion," in *Handbook of North American Indians*, ed. Trigger, 15:447.
6. There is a need for a major study of the Iroquois in the War of 1812. For their participation in the conflict, see Snyder, ed., *Red and White on the New York Frontier*; Arthur C. Parker, "The Senecas in the War of 1812," *Proceedings of the New York State Historical Association* 15 (1916): 78–90; Elias Johnson, *Legends, Traditions and Laws*, pp. 165–70; New York State Adjutant General's Office, *Index of Awards*, pp. 563–73; Charles M. Johnston, ed., *The Valley of the Six Nations: A Collection of Documents on the Indian Lands of the Grand River* (Toronto: Champlain Society, 1964), pp. 193–228; Carl F. Klinck and James J. Talman, eds., *The Journal of Major John Norton, 1816* (Toronto: Champlain Society, 1970), pp. 349–53; G. F. G. Stanley, "The Significance of the Six Nations Participation in the War of 1812," *Ontario History* 55 (1963): 215–63; Beauchamp, Notebook, pp. 159–60; Jasper Parrish to Peter B. Porter, July 27, 1814, Asa Landforth to Peter B. Porter, Sept. 7, 1814, MR 2, Peter B. Porter MSS, BECHS; E. A. Cruikshank, ed., *The Documentary History of the Campaign upon the Niagara Frontier, 1812–1814* (Welland, Ontario: Lundy's Lane Historical Society, 1896–1908), 2:338–89, 406, 448; 3:145. For Indian casualties at the Battle of Chippewa, see John Brannon, comp., *Official Letters of the Military and Naval Officers of the United States During the War with Great Britain . . .* (Washington, D.C.: Way and Gideon, 1823), pp. 368–73; "General Peter B. Porter's Description of the Battle of Chippawa," *Public Papers of Daniel D. Tompkins: Governor of New York*, ed. Hugh Hastings (New York: Wynkoop, Hallenbeck and Crawford State Printers, 1898), 1:86–92.
7. Beauchamp, Notebook, p. 173; "Clifton" Letter to Narragansett weekly quoted in *Syracuse Standard*, July 26, 1858, newsclipping in Sanford Thayer File (relative to portrait of Captain George), OHA.
8. Orlando Allen, "Personal Recollections of Captains Jones and Parrish," *Publications of the Buffalo Historical Society* 6 (1903): 544.
9. Morgan, *League of the Iroquois*, p. 441.
10. For more on Iroquois runners, Peter Nabokov, *Indian Running: Native American History and Tradition* (Santa Fe, N.M.: Ancient City, 1981), pp. 18, 84, 178.

11. Samuel George, Pension Application, War of 1812 Pension Records, NYSA.

12. Manley, "Buying Buffalo from the Indians," pp. 313–29. For the text of the Treaty of Buffalo Creek, see Kappler, comp., *Indian Affairs*, 2:502–16.

13. Sam George and David Smith to the Chiefs at Cattaraugus, June 8, 1850, Maris B. Pierce MSS, BECHS.

14. Jabez Backus Hyde, "A Teacher Among the Senecas: Historical and Personal Narrative of Jabez Backus Hyde," *Publications of the Buffalo Historical Society* 6 (1903): 247; Donaldson, comp., *The Six Nations in New York*, pp. 6–9; Laurence M. Hauptman, "Foreword" to Dennis Connors, ed., *Onondaga: Portrait of a Native People* (Syracuse: Syracuse Univ. Press, 1986), pp. 5–10; Harold Blau, Jack Campisi, and Elisabeth Tooker, "Onondaga," in *Handbook of North American Indians*, ed. Trigger, 15:495–97.

15. For Captain Cold, sometimes referred to as Captain Cole (Tayatoaque or Ut-ha-wah), see Beauchamp, Notebook, pp. 165–66; Elisabeth Tooker, "The League of the Iroquois: Its History, Politics and Ritual," in *Handbook of North American Indians*, ed. Trigger, 15:436. In Schoolcraft's Indian Census, 1845, George is listed under "Senecas of Cattaraugus Reservation," entry 170, NYSL.

16. Annemarie Shimony, "Conflict and Continuity: An Analysis of an Iroquois Uprising," in *Extending the Rafters: Interdisciplinary Approaches to Iroquoian Studies*, ed. Jack Campisi, Michael Foster, and Marianne Mithun (Albany: State Univ. of New York Press, 1984), p. 154; Morgan, *League of the Ho-de-no-sau-nee, or Iroquois*, p. 65; Tooker, "League of the Iroquois," pp. 424–25; William N. Fenton, "The Roll Call of the Iroquois Chiefs: A Study of a Mnemonic Cane from the Six Nations Reserve," *Smithsonian Miscellaneous Collections* 111 (1950): 1–73.

17. Onondaga Chiefs to Nathan Bristow, Apr. 3, 1853, ESP MSS, APS.

18. Ibid.; David Hill to Ebenezer Meriam, Feb. 16, 1853, Nov. 17, 1854, Jan. 4, 1855, and Thomas LaFort to Meriam, May 31, 1853, Letters of Onondaga Indians, 1850–55 MSS, APS.

19. For the draft in New York State, see Eugene C. Murdock, *Patriotism Limited*, pp. vii–41.

20. For Iroquois conscription in World War II and Vietnam, see Hauptman, *Iroquois Struggle for Survival*, pp. 1–9.

21. INP to Sara Jemison Parker, Feb. 26, 1863, INP MSS, BECHS.

22. "An Onondaga Chief at Washington" and "Affairs of the Six Nations," Nov. 25, 1863, newsclipping in Samuel George File, OHA; Herman J. Viola, *Diplomats in Buckskin: A History of Indian Delegations in Washington City* (Washington, D.C.: Smithsonian Institution Press, 1981), pp. 95–96.

23. Roy Basler, ed., *Collected Works of Abraham Lincoln*, 8 vols. (New Brunswick, N.J.: Rutgers Univ. Press, 1953), 7:27; E. D. Townsend and C. S. Christinsen, Special Order No. 542, Dec. 7, 1863, New York Agency Records, OIA, M234, MR590, RG75, NA; quote in Abstracts of Civil War Muster Rolls: 13th New York Heavy Artillery — James Big Kettle (p. 242), Cornelius Fatty (p. 1058), James Halfwhite (p. 1381), Seth Jacob (p. 1669), Jesse Kenjockety (p. 1797), Wooster King (p. 1838), Young King (p. 1840), Murphy Longfinger (p. 1969), Stephen Ray (p. 2672), Martin Red Eye (p. 2678), Thomas Scrogg (p. 2879), Nathaniel Strong (p. 3165), and Dennis Titus (p. 3275); 86th New York Volunteers: John Thomas (p. 1939), ser. 13775, Records of the New York State Adjutant General's Office, NYSA.

24. Seneca Residing at Cattaraugus Petition to Abraham Lincoln, June 4, 1864, and Samuel George to William Dole, July 5, 1864, New York Agency Records, OIA, M234, MR590, RG75, NA.

25. See chapter 2 for Williams. E. R. S. Canby to J. P. Usher, Jan. 14, 1864, E. Townsend

Special Order No. 126, Mar. 24, 1864, N. T. Strong to General Sprague, Apr. 12, 1864, J. Stonehouse to Edwin Stanton, Apr. 1, 1864, John Sprague to William P. Doyle [sic], Apr. 13, 1864, Samuel George to President of the United States, June 16, 1864, New York Agency Records, OIA, M234, MR590, RG75, NA; Abstract, Muster Rolls: 24th New York Cavalry: John Bennett (p. 122), Ira Pierce (p. 1453); John B. Williams (p. 2046), 97th New York Volunteers: Titus Mohawk (p. 1616); and 14th New York Heavy Artillery: Oliver Silverheels (p. 374), Ser. 13775, Division of Military and Naval Affairs, NYSA.

26. Hauptman, *The Iroquois and the New Deal*, p. 1–18; Hauptman, *Iroquois Struggle for Survival*, pp. 205–43.

27. USCIA, *Annual Report for 1862*, p. 43.

28. Harry Kelsey, "Charles Mix," in *Commissioners of Indian Affairs*, ed. Kvasnicka and Viola, pp. 77–79.

29. Kappler, *Indian Affairs*, 2:767–71.

30. Transcript of "A Council of the Six Nations," May 11, 1864, PYM, AB 3.2 (8), Box 2, QC, HC; USCIA, *Annual Report for 1862*, pp. 456–68. See also Thomas Abler, "The Kansas Connection, the Seneca Nation and the Iroquois Confederacy Council," in *Extending the Rafters*, ed. Campisi, Foster, and Mithun, p. 89.

31. Transcript of "A Council of the Six Nations," May 11, 1864.

32. USCIA, *Annual Report for 1862*, pp. 460–64; transcript of "A Council of the Six Nations," May 11, 1864.

33. USCIA, *Annual Report for 1862*, pp. 460–64.

34. USCIA, *Annual Report for 1862*, pp. 457–60. For the Kansas claim, see Petition of Daniel Two Guns, Nathaniel T. Strong, et al. to Commissioner of Indian Affairs, Feb. 19, 1864, Petition of Peter Wilson, Maris B. Pierce, Israel Jimieson, et al. to President Abraham Lincoln, Apr. 6, 1864, Secretary of the Interior Usher to Commissioner of Indian Affairs Dole, May 31, 1864, New York Agency Records, OIA, M234, MR590, RG75, NA.

35. Chiefs of the St. Regis Indians, Louis Chubb, Mitchell Garrow, and Thomas Tarbell, Chiefs of St. Regis Indians, to the Department of the Interior, June 18, 1864, New York Agency Records, OIA, M234, MR590, RG75, NA. These chiefs expressed dissatisfaction with Wilson and indicated that he did not represent Mohawk interests. Harrison Halftown (Seneca Nation clerk) Resolution of Seneca Nation, Nov. 20, 1868, ibid. For provisions of the failed treaty of 1868 attempting to resolve the claim, see PYM, IR, AA 4.16 (6), QC, HC.

36. Abler, "Kansas Connection," pp. 88–92; Campisi, "Consequences of the Kansas Claims to Oneida Tribal Identity," pp. 35–47.

37. Samuel George to Governor John J. Hoffman, Mar. 5, June 18, 1870, MS Items No. 17605 and 17606, NYSL.

38. Beauchamp, Notebook, p. 174.

39. Ibid., pp. 173–74; "Captain George's Speech at the Fourth of July Dinner," *Syracuse Journal*, July 6, 1865, newsclippings in George File, OHA.

40. Morgan, *League of the Ho-de-no-sau-nee, or Iroquois*, p. 107.

41. "Funeral of an Indian Chief," newsclipping, Sept. 1873, and "Ho-no-we-ye-ach-te: Death of Capt. George, Head Chief of the Onondagas," *Syracuse Journal*, Sept. 25, 1873, George File, OHA.

9. RAILROADING

1. U.S. Bureau of the Census, *Ninth Census: The Statistics of the Population of the United States* (Washington, D.C.: U.S. Government Printing Office, 1872), 1:209–10, 215.

2. Asher Wright to George T. Trimble, May 8, 1862, Benjamin Hallowell to William C.

White, July 5, 1862, N. H. Pierce to George T. Trimble, July 23, Aug. 4, 1862, NYYM, HRR; *Whipple Report*, 1:415; Robert E. Bieder and Christopher Plant, "Annuity Census as a Source for Historical Research: The 1858 & 1869 Tonawanda Seneca Annuity Censuses," *American Indian Culture and Research Journal* 5, no. 3 (1981): 38; USCIA, *Annual Report for 1866*, p. 61.

3. The following discussion of leases grows out of new historical research based on my testimony before the U.S. House of Representatives Subcommittee on Interior and Insular Affairs on Sept. 13, 1990, and the U.S. Senate Select Committee on Indian Affairs on Sept. 18, 1990 (testimony on H.R. 5367 and S. 2895, the Seneca Nation Settlement Act of 1990, signed into law on Nov. 3, 1990). For my earlier writings on the subject, see Laurence M. Hauptman, "The Historical Background to the Present-Day Seneca Nation–Salamanca Lease Controversy: The First Hundred Years, 1851–1951," Nelson A. Rockefeller Institute of Government, *Working Paper No. 20* (Fall 1985), reprinted in *Iroquois Land Claims*, ed. Vecsey and Starna, pp. 101–22. I have also dealt with the Seneca leases in *The Iroquois Struggle for Survival*, pp. 15–43; *Formulating American Indian Policy in New York State*, pp. xi, 4, 14–17, 25–26, 113; and "Compensatory Justice: The Seneca Nation Settlement Act," *National Forum* 71 (Spring 1991): 31–33.

4. Abrams, *Seneca People*, p. 70; Thomas E. Hogan, "City in a Quandary: Salamanca and the Allegany Leases," *New York History* 55 (Jan. 1974): 84. For railroad politics in New York, see Harry H. Pierce, *Railroads of New York: A Study of Government Aid, 1826–1875* (Cambridge, Mass.: Harvard Univ. Press, 1953); Frederick C. Hicks, ed., *High Finance in the Sixties: Chapters from the Early History of the Erie Railroad* (1929; rpt. Port Washington, N.Y.: Kennikat, 1967); Lee Benson, *Merchants, Farmers, and Railroads: Railroad Regulation and New York Politics, 1850–1887* (Cambridge, Mass.: Harvard Univ. Press, 1955); and Edward Hungerford, *Men of Erie: A Story of Human Effort* (New York: Random House, 1946).

5. Hogan, "City in a Quandary," p. 84.

6. Hungerford, *Men of Erie*, pp. 189–95; Abrams, *Seneca People*, p. 72. Hogan ("City in a Quandary," p. 84) claims the leases were legal because the New York State legislature confirmed them. This is incorrect.

7. Thomas Wistar, "Report of the Committee on the Civilization and Improvement of the New York Indians," *Friend* 38 (June 10, 1865): 325.

8. Hungerford, *Men of Erie*, pp. 192–95; John P. Herrick, *Empire Oil: The Story of Oil in the Empire State* (New York: Dodd, Mead, 1949), pp. 57–58; Thomas S. Abler, "Factional Dispute and Party Conflict in the Political System of the Seneca Nation (1845–1895): An Ethnohistorical Analysis" (Ph.D. diss., Univ. of Toronto, 1969), pp. viii, 169–73; Hogan, "City in a Quandary," pp. 79–101; Hogan, "A History of the Allegany Reservation, 1850–1900" (Master's thesis, State Univ. of New York, College at Fredonia, 1974), p. 8.

9. U.S. Bureau of the Census, *Ninth Census*, 1:207, for comparison of 1860 and 1870 population figures for Salamanca, Bucktooth, and Red House.

10. Society of Friends, Philadelphia Yearly Meeting, *A Brief Sketch of the Efforts* . . . (Philadelphia: Indian Committee of the Philadelphia Yearly Meeting of Friends, 1866), pp. 20, 53. For a discussion of the impact of leasing, see Laurence M. Hauptman, "Senecas and Subdividers: Resistance to Allotment of Indian Lands in New York, 1875–1906," *Prologue: The Journal of the National Archives* 9 (Summer 1977): 105–16.

11. Abler, "Seneca Nation Factionalism," pp. 25–26; Abrams, *Seneca People*, pp. 68–88.

12. Abrams, *Seneca People*, pp. 68–88.

13. USCIA, *Annual Report for 1864*, p. 45.

14. Abler, "Seneca Nation Factionalism," pp. 25–26; Abrams, *Seneca People*, pp. 68–88.

15. William Dole to Henry Silverheels, Nov. 16, 1864, Asher Wright to Benjamin

Hallowell, Nov. 14, 1864, Misc. MSS, 11 mo. 16, FHL, SC; Hallowell to William Dole, Nov. 10, 1864, Dole to Hallowell, Dec. 1, 1864, FHL, SC; Israel Jimeson to Joseph Elkinton, Nov. 9, 1864, PYM, IR, AB 3.2 (8), 1858–70, box 2, QC, HC. See also Abler, "Seneca Nation Factionalism," p. 26; Abrams, *Seneca People*, pp. 80–82.

16. Hogan, "City in a Quandary," pp. 85–88.

17. Ibid.; Wistar, "Report of the Committee on the Civilization and Improvement of the Indians," p. 325.

18. John W. Street (general attorney and claim agent for the Atlantic and Great Western Railroad) to the Commissioner of Indian Affairs, Aug. 29, 1874, New York Agency Records, OIA, M234, MR592, RG75, NA. For early attempts to acquire Indian lands, see chap. 1. For the Ogden Land Company's preemptive claim, which continued to save the Senecas from allotment, see Hauptman, "Senecas and Subdividers," pp. 105–16.

19. New York State Legislature, *Laws of New York*, 88th sess., chap. 133 (Mar. 16, 1865) and chap. 211 (Mar. 25, 1865) (Albany, N.Y., 1865), pp. 234–35, 346.

20. John Hoffman (governor of New York State), Letter of Transmittal of Joint Legislative Resolution of New York State Legislature, Jan. 18, 1871, New York Agency Records, OIA, M234, MR591, RG75, NA; U.S. Congress, Senate, Select Committee on Indian Affairs, *Report No. 101-511: Providing for the Renegotiation of Certain Leases of the Seneca Nation, and for Other Purposes*, 101st Cong., 2d sess., p. 5. I thank Pete Taylor, special counsel for the Senate Select Committee on Indian Affairs, for providing me with this document.

21. Hudson Ansley to Commissioner of Indian Affairs, Feb. 6, 1871, with resolution of Cattaraugus County Board of Supervisors, Nov. 30, 1870, New York Agency Records, OIA, M234, MR571, RG75, NA.

22. Street to Commissioner of Indian Affairs, Aug. 29, 1874; Hogan, "City in a Quandary," pp. 88–89.

23. Hudson Ansley to Secretary of the Interior, July 10, 1873, Records of the New York Agency, OIA, M234, MR571, RG75, NA.

24. Hogan, "City in a Quandary," pp. 91–92.

25. Quoted in *Congressional Record*, Senate, 43d Cong., 2d sess., pt. 2, Feb. 2, 1875, pp. 913–14. During this period, the Seneca Nation's attorney received his salary from an appropriation from the New York State legislature. For Sherman's later activities, see Abrams, *Seneca People*, pp. 80–83.

26. U.S. Congress, Senate, *Misc. Doc. No. 122: Protest of the President, Councilors, and People of the Seneca Nation of Indians Made in Their National Council Against the Passage of the Bill (H.R. No. 3080) to Authorize the Seneca Nation to Lease Their Lands Within the Cattaraugus and Allegany Reservations, and to Confirm Existing Leases, June 3, 1874*, 43d Cong., 1st sess. This document is reprinted in *Senate Report No. 101-511*, pp. 9–10.

27. Hauptman, "Senecas and Subdividers," pp. 105–16.

28. Ibid.

29. *Congressional Record*, Feb. 2, 1875, pp. 911–12. For a brief summary of Bogy's career, see William E. Unrau, "Lewis Vital Bogy, 1860–1867," in *Commissioners of Indian Affairs*, ed. Kvasnicka and Viola, pp. 109–14.

30. *Congressional Record*, Senate, 43d Cong., 2d sess., pt. 2, pp. 909–10, 913–14, 919.

31. Ibid., pp. 908–9, 914–15, 918.

32. Ibid., p. 920.

33. 18 *Stat.*, 330 (Feb. 19, 1875). The Society of Friends Philadelphia Yearly Meeting warned the Senecas against further leasing and called for honest tribal leadership to take advantage of the "considerable income" derived from the 1875 act. They feared that the growing pressures for oil and mining leases would "bring many white men to settle on the reserva-

tion, and give them claims upon it; and you know from past experience, that this always leads at last to the white man getting possession of the land altogether, and to the Indians going away homeless." They warned that the reservation "belongs to the nation, as a whole; and the leases should never have been made to white men, without the consent of the nation; but have always been a source of trouble, as you know" (Henry Wood, Jacob Edge, George J. Scattergood, Joseph S. Elkinton et al. to the Indians of the Seneca Nation, Jan. 6, 1879, PYM, IR, AB 1.2 [1869–1979], QC, HC).

34. 26 *Stat.*, 558 (Sept. 30, 1890).

35. See Hauptman, "Historical Background to the Present-Day Seneca Nation–Salamanca Lease Controversy."

36. *Public Law 101-503*, Nov. 3, 1990. New York State is also to provide $16 million in direct cash payment and $9 million in economic development funds to the Seneca Nation of Indians.

37. The new leases are described in *Senate Report 101-511*, pp. 17–31.

10. WOMEN AT WAR

1. For Iroquois women in the American Revolution, see Graymont, *The Iroquois in the American Revolution*, pp. 132, 141, 188; also see the sections on Oneida traditions by Gloria Halbritter and Loretta Metoxen in *Oneida Indian Experience*, ed. Campisi and Hauptman, pp. 145–46. Iroquois women in the War of 1812 are mentioned in the following: New York Adjutant-General's Office, *Index of Awards*, pp. 563–73 (pension 9,990 – Susan Jacob; 15,075 – Julia John; 10,025 – Polly Cooper; and 10,001 – Dolly Skanandoah). The famous "Aunt" Dinah John lived until 1883 and was one of the most illustrious Iroquois women of the nineteenth century. She received a pension from New York State in the 1870s. See Whipple Report, 1:447, 2:1225; William Beauchamp, Notebook, pp. 171–72; Richard G. Case, "Woman's Portrait Puzzles Historians," *Syracuse Herald Journal*, Apr. 30, 1975; Aunt Dinah John File, OHA.

2. See, for example, Wallace, *Death and Rebirth of the Seneca*, pp. 28–30; Nancy Bonvillain, "Iroquoian Women," in *Studies on Iroquoian Culture*, ed. Bonvillain, Occasional Publications in Northeastern Anthropology, no. 6 (Rindge, N.H.: *Man in the Northeast*, 1980), pp. 47–58; J. N. B. Hewitt, "Status of Women in Iroquois Polity Before 1784," *Smithsonian Institution Annual Report for 1932* (Washington, D.C., 1932), pp. 475–88; Alexander Goldenweiser, "Functions of Women in Iroquois Society," *American Anthropologist* 16 (1915): 376–77.

3. Joseph François Lafitau, *Customs of the American Indians* (1724), 2 vols., trans. and ed. William N. Fenton and Elizabeth Moore (Toronto: Champlain Society, 1974), 1:69.

4. Judith K. Brown, "Economic Organization and the Position of Women Among the Iroquois," *Ethnohistory* 17 (Summer–Fall 1970): 151–67.

5. Elisabeth Tooker, "Women in Iroquois Society," in *Extending the Rafters*, ed. Campisi, Foster, and Mithun, pp. 109–23. For an important recent analysis of Iroquois women in the mid- and late nineteenth century, see Nancy Shoemaker, "The Rise and Fall of Iroquois Women," *Journal of Women's History* 2 (Winter 1991): 39–57; and Shoemaker, "From Longhouse to Loghouse: Household Structure Among the Senecas in 1900," *American Indian Quarterly* 15 (Summer 1991): 329–338.

6. Wallace, "Origins of the Longhouse Religion," pp. 445–48. Not all these efforts were welcomed or accepted. See Diane Rothenberg, "The Mothers of the Nation: Seneca Resistance to Quaker Intervention," in *Women and Colonization: Anthropological Perspectives*, ed. Mona Etienne and Eleanor Leacock (New York: Praeger, 1980), pp. 63–87.

7. Wistar, "Report of the Committee on the Civilization and Improvement of the New York Indians," p. 324.

8. Lydia Ann Thorne to the New York Yearly Meeting of Friends, May 26, 1863, NYYM, HRR.

9. Wistar, "Report of the Committee on the Civilization and Improvement of the Indians," p. 324. The Friends' early efforts at the Tunesassa Boarding School can be found in the following: Joseph Elkinton "to our brethren the Indian natives of the Seneca Nation," Nov. 1852, PYM, IR, AB 3.2, Box 1, File 6, 1849–52, QC, HC; Catherine Lee to Thomas Wistar, Mar. 26, 1867 [re: curriculum], PYM, IR, Bound Correspondence, 1860–83, D 10.3, QC, HC; Sarah Elkinton to Joseph Elkinton, Feb. 10, Aug. 4, 1854, May 16, 1856, Sarah Elkinton to Ephraim Elkinton, Dec. 22, 1855, Elkinton Family MSS, ser. 3, box 5, File: Sarah Elkinton Smith and Ephraim Elkinton Corresp., FHL, SC. For a recent portrait of the Friends' work, see Lois Barton, *A Quaker Promise Kept: Philadelphia Friends' Work with the Allegany Senecas, 1795–1860* (Eugene, Ore.: Spencer Butte, 1990).

10. NYS, SPI, *Annual Reports*, 1861–65 (Albany, 1861–65).

11. New York State, *Census of the State of New York for 1865*, comp. Franklin B. Hough (Albany: Charles Van Benthuysen & Son, 1867), pp. 603–7.

12. New York State, *Census of the State of New York for 1875*, comp. C. W. Seaton (Albany: Weed, Parsons & Co., 1877), p. 465. Shoemaker, "The Rise and Fall of Iroquois Women," pp. 39–57.

13. William H. Glasson, *Federal Military Pensions in the United States* (New York: Oxford Univ. Press, 1918), pp. 123, 235, 273; Glasson, *History of Military Pension Legislation in the United States* (New York: Columbia Univ. Press, 1900), p. 86.

14. Amy E. Holmes, "'Such Is the Price We Pay': American Widows and the Civil War Pension System," in *Toward a Social History of the American Civil War*, ed. Maris A. Vinovskis, p. 173.

15. Donaldson, comp., *Extra Census Bulletin. Indians. The Six Nations of New York.* (Washington, D.C.: U.S. Census Printing Office, 1892), p. 16.

16. Simon King Pension Record, widow's [Evelina] pension application 51,449, certificate 67,448; Paul Doxtator Pension Record, widow's [Christine] application 94,976, certificate 76,402; Abraham Antoin [Antoine] Pension Record, mother's [Susan] pension application 72,418, certificate 55,270; Peter Bread Pension Record, widow's [Sarah] pension application 1,100,502, certificate 845,492, CWPR, NA.

17. Paul C. Doxtator Pension Record, invalid pension, application 559,449, certificate 489,633; widow's [Mary] pension application 1,173,143, certificate 910,919. "This man deserted on or about Nov. 23, 1864 but as he returned to the service on or about April 1, 1865 under the President's Proclamation dated Mar. 11, 1865 and appears to have complied with the conditions thereof (so far as not waived by the Government) the *charge* of desertion no longer stands against him. The second of the *fact* that he was absent in desertion from on or about Nov. 23, 1864, to on or about April 1, 1865, cannot, however, be expunged" (R. C. Drum, Adjutant General, to Commissioner of Pensions, Mar. 30, 1887, Paul C. Doxtator Pension Record, CWPR, NA). Peter Johnson, another Oneida deserter, went from his Wisconsin community to live in New York (Donaldson, comp., *Extra Census Bulletin. Indians. The Six Nations of New York*, p. 16).

18. Thomas Baird Pension Record, widow's [Mary] pension application 60,477, minor's application 192,869, certificate 725,587, CWPR, NA.

19. E. B. Goodenough to Joseph H. Barrett (pension commissioner), July 18, 1866, Moses Webster, Peter Bread, et al. affidavit, Mar. 20, 1890, J. J. Woodward (assistant surgeon, U.S. Army) to Record and Pension Bureau, Mar. 2, 1866, C. S. Breck (assistant adjutant general)

to the Commissioner of Pensions, Jan. 17, 1866, Thomas Antone [Anthony] Pension Record, minor's [Sallie] pension application 115,883, CWPR, NA.

20. William E. McLean (deputy commissioner), M. Butterfield (reviewer), A. S. Coleman (chief of Special Examination Division), "TO BE DROPPED," Oct. 31, 1885, Deposition, Case of Celinda Danforth, Cobus Danforth Pension Record, widow's [Celinda] pension application 68,662, certificate 45,723, CWPR, NA.

21. William Kennedy Pension Record, CWPR, NA.

22. Peter Snow, John Baldwin, and Joseph Smith (notarized by Asher Wright and Nicholson H. Parker), Affidavit, Apr. 16, 1866, Thomas B. Green statement of 1865, Asher Wright to Joseph Barrett, May 3, 1866, Foster J. Hudson Pension Record, CWPR, NA.

23. *Senate Report No. 2214*, 59th Cong., 1st sess., Apr. 2, 1906 (approved May 8, 1906), Cornelius C. Cusick Pension Record, CWPR, NA.

24. Jerome Bread to Harold Ickes, Apr. 25, 1933, Bread to George Brown, Sept. 24, 1933, Catherine Cornelius to "Dear Sir," Dec. 10, 1935, E. L. Bailey to Catherine Cornelius, May 28, 1936, Peter Bread Pension Record, CWPR, NA.

25. Affidavits of Philip Fatty, Willie C. Hoag, and Mary King, Sept. 22, 1896, Wooster King Pension Record, invalid pension application 204,183, certificate 136,935, widow's [Mary] pension application 603,782, certificate 448,288, CWPR, NA.

26. Cornelius Plummer Pension Record, mother's [Sally] pension application 7,065, certificate 38,155, CWPR, NA; Thomas Shongo Pension Record, wife's [Achsah Halftown Shongo] pension application 510,551, certificate 848,451, CWPR, NA.

11. CHILDREN AT WAR

1. Thomas Baird Pension File, Minor pension application 192,869, certificate 725,587, CWPR, NA.

2. Whipple Report, 2:907–12.

3. For a survey of state educational policies, see Hauptman, *Formulating American Indian Policy in New York State*, pp. 9–11.

4. New York State, Superintendent of Common Schools, *Annual Report* (Albany, 1849), p. 17.

5. NYS, SPI, *10th Annual Report* (Albany, 1863), pp. 98–99; NYS, SPI, *11th Annual Report* (Albany, 1864), pp. 97–99; *12th Annual Report* (Albany, 1865), pp. 98–99; *13th Annual Report* (Albany, 1867), pp. 97–98.

6. NYS, SPI, *12th Annual Report*, p. 28 and app. C; *9th Annual Report* (Albany, 1862), app. C.

7. New York State Department of Education, Native American Indian Education Unit, *Indian Education in New York State* (Albany, n.d.). This is an informational handout distributed by the Native American Indian Education Unit, periodically updated since it was first prepared by Ruth Birdseye in the mid-1950s.

8. NYS, SPI, *9th Annual Report*, app. D; *13th Annual Report*, pp. 93–105. The Friends Tunesassa Boarding School also had problems of students running away from the school for at least the first fifteen years of its operation. See Catherine Lee to Thomas Wistar, PYM, IR, Bound Correspondence, 1860–83, D. 10.3, QC, HC.

9. NYS, SPI, *13th Annual Report*, app. D. These figures are calculated from charts on pp. 93, 96, 101, and 103.

10. NYS, SPI, *9th Annual Report*, p. 30.

11. D. W. Pierce to Joseph Elkinton, Aug. 8, 1863, PYM, IR, Bound Correspondence, 1860–83, D. 10.3, QC, HC. Pierce reported on the eight state schools at Cattaraugus. See NYS, SPI, *13th Annual Report,* app. D; *13th Annual Report,* pp. 93, 101.

12. NYS, SPI, *13th Annual Report,* p. 101.

13. NYS, SPI, *9th Annual Report,* app. D; *11th Annual Report,* p. 90.

14. NYS, SPI, *9th Annual Report,* app. D.

15. NYS, SPI, *13th Annual Report,* pp. 98–99.

16. New York State, *Census of the State of New York for 1855,* comp. Franklin B. Hough (Albany: Charles Van Benthuysen, 1857), pp. 500–519; New York State, *Census of 1865,* pp. 600–607.

17. NYS, SPI, *9th Annual Report,* app. D; USCIA, *Annual Report for 1865,* p. 61.

18. NYS, SPI, *10th Annual Report,* p. 105.

19. Wistar, "Report of the Committee on Civilization and Improvement of the Indians," p. 324; Rayner W. Kelsey, *Friends and the Indians, 1655–1917* (Philadelphia: Associated Executive Committee of Friends on Indian Affairs, 1917), pp. 96–130. See Barton, *Quaker Promise Kept,* pp. 15–21, 29, and passim.

20. See Hauptman, *The Iroquois and the New Deal,* pp. 92–95, 209n. 23, 24, 25.

21. USCIA, *Annual Report for 1864,* pp. 443–44.

22. William N. Fenton, "Toward the Gradual Civilization of the Indian Natives: The Missionary and Linguistic Work of Asher Wright (1803–1875) Among the Senecas of Western New York," *Proceedings of the American Philosophical Society* 100 (1956): 567–81.

23. Asher Wright to D. E. Sill, Feb. 6, 1864, New York Agency Records, OIA, M234, 590, RG75, NA.

24. NYS, SPI, *12th Annual Report,* p. 92.

25. Asher Wright to George T. Trimble, May 9, 1862, NYYM, HR.

26. NYS, SPI, *9th Annual Report,* app. C; *22nd Annual Report, 1875* (Albany, 1875), pp. 97–98; interview with Pauline L. Seneca, July 15, 1982, Cattaraugus Indian Reservation. The late Mrs. Seneca was a teacher at the Thomas School. She also attended the Friends' Tunesassa Boarding School. I have learned much about the school from Professor Frederick Stefon of Pennsylvania State University at Wilkes-Barre, who is preparing an administrative history of the Thomas School. See Frederick Stefon, "The Thomas Indian School as a Crucible for Change," paper delivered at the Annual Meeting of the American Society for Ethnohistory, Nov. 11–13, 1988; Alberta Austin, comp., *Ne Ho Ni Yo De: No—That's What It Was Like,* 2 vols. (New York: Rebco Enterprises, 1986–89). Austin's work, a compilation of oral histories, contains much information about the Thomas School. I have also learned much about the school from Marlene Johnson, a former tribal councillor of the Seneca Nation and current director of the Higher Education Opportunity Program at St. Bonaventure University. Johnson attended the Thomas School and is preparing a book of personal reminiscences about it.

27. NYS, SPI, *9th Annual Report,* p. 31.

28. Asher Wright to John Manley, Sept. 30, 1864, New York Agency Records, OIA, M234, MR590, RG75, NA.

29. USCIA, *Annual Report,* 1864, app. NYS, SPI, *11th Annual Report,* p. 85.

30. Wright to Manley, Sept. 30, 1864.

31. Hauptman, *Iroquois Struggle for Survival,* pp. 12–14; and *Formulating American Indian Policy in New York State,* pp. 9, 12, 71–72; Fenton, "Toward the Gradual Civilization of the Indian Natives," pp. 567–81.

12. TWO WARS

1. USCIA, *Annual Report for 1864*, p. 454.
2. Powless-Archiquette Diary, SHSW.
3. Col. T. S. Strohecker to My Dear Comrade (Willett Pierce), Postcard reminder of "annual reunion of the 57th Regiment, Pennsylvania Veteran Volunteer Infantry, Oct. 17, 1901," Civil War Collection, SINM. See the photographs of Oneida Civil War veterans in this book.
4. For the GAR, see Mary R. Dearing, *Veterans in Politics: The Story of the G.A.R.* (Baton Rouge: Louisiana State Univ. Press, 1952); Stuart McConnell, "Who Joined the Grand Army? Three Case Studies in the Construction of Union Veteranhood, 1866-1900," in *Toward a Social History of the American Civil War*, ed. Maris A. Vinovskis, pp. 139-70. For the GAR in New York State, see George J. Lankevich, "The Grand Army of the Republic in New York State, 1865-1898" (Ph.D. diss., Columbia Univ., 1967).
5. McConnell, "Who Joined the G.A.R." pp. 140-41.
6. Donaldson, comp., *The Six Nations of New York*, p. 16.
7. For Parker, see Armstrong, *Warrior in Two Camps*, pp. 192-93, and caption of photograph on p. 193. For Cusick, see Order of Indian Wars of the United States, *Circular ser.* No. 1 (1904), Cornelius C. Cusick Muster Rolls for the 132d NYS Volunteer Infantry, NYS Archives.
8. Linas Pierce to Willard [Willett?] Pierce, May 5, 1901, SINM.
9. Reid Mitchell, "The Northern Soldier and His Community," in *Toward a Social History of the American Civil War*, ed. Vinovskis, p. 80.
10. Joseph Elkinton and his family were strongly opposed to war, including the Civil War. See Joseph Elkinton and Sons to Merick and Sons, Oct. 30, 1861, Elkinton Family MSS, Correspondence, 1817-62, ser. 3, box 3, FHL.
11. Wilbur H. Siebert, *The Underground Railroad* (1898; rpt. New York: Arno Press and the New York Times, 1968), p. 203; Alice H. Henderson, "The History of the New York State Anti-Slavery Society" (Ph.D. diss., Univ. of Michigan, 1963), pp. 389-406. See also Larry Gara, *The Liberty Line: The Legend of the Underground Railroad* (Lexington: Univ. Press of Kentucky, 1961); Ena L. Farley, "The African American Presence in the History of Western New York," *Afro-Americans in New York Life and History* 14 (Jan. 1990): 81-82.
12. Abraham [Abram] Elm Pension Record, invalid application 983,742, certificate 771,598, CWPR, NA; *U.S.* v. *Elm*, 25 Fed. Cas. 1006 (Dec. 24, 1877); Interview with Ray Elm, May 6, 1990, and June 13, 1991, Onondaga Indian Reservation. See Society of American Indians, *Proceedings of the First Annual Convention, October, 1911* (Columbus, Ohio: Society of American Indians (1911), group photograph. Ray Elm is Abraham Elm's grandson.
13. 25 Fed. Cas. 1006.
14. Whipple Report, 1:555-59.
15. Ibid., pp. 41-45, 68, 73-74, 78-79, 405-6. For Sims, see pp. 406-17. For Cusick, see pp. 456-83, 506.
16. Ibid., p. 421.
17. For the best work on Indian education in this era, see Frederick Hoxie, *A Final Promise: The Campaign to Assimilate the Indians, 1880-1920* (Lincoln: Univ. of Nebraska Press, 1984).
18. Hauptman, *The Iroquois and the New Deal*, pp. 70-74, 88-97.
19. For New York State efforts at securing jurisdiction, see Hauptman, *Formulating American Indian Policy in New York State*, pp. 3-17, and *Iroquois Struggle for Survival*, pp. 15-64.

Bibliography

ARCHIVES/MANUSCRIPT COLLECTIONS

American Philosophical Society, Philadelphia.
William N. Fenton MSS.
Ely S. Parker MSS.
Letters of Onondaga Indians.
Buffalo and Erie County Historical Society, Buffalo, N.Y.
Arthur C. Parker MSS.
Ely S. Parker MSS.
Isaac Newton Parker MSS in the Roy Nagle Collection.
Maris B. Pierce MSS.
Peter B. Porter MSS.
Miscellaneous Scrapbook Dealing with Indians and Slavery, 1859–70.
Wilkeson Family MSS (Letters Concerning Indian Volunteers).
Haverford College. Quaker Collection, Haverford, Pa.
Records of the Philadelphia Yearly Meeting of Friends. Indian Committee.
Records of the Baltimore Yearly Meeting. Special Committee on Indian Concerns.
Library of Congress. Manuscript Division, Washington, D.C.
Thomas Francis Bayard MSS.
Ulysses S. Grant MSS.
Andrew Johnson MSS.
Abraham Lincoln MSS.
Patrick Ryan Diary.
Theodore Edgar Saint John MSS.
James Wadsworth (and Wadsworth Family) MSS.
National Archives, Washington, D.C. U.S. Department of the Interior. Bureau of Indian Affairs. RG75.
Green Bay Agency Records, 1824–80.
Neosho Agency Records, 1831–75.

New York Agency Records, 1829–80.
New York Agency Emigration Records, 1829–51.
Seneca Agency in New York Records, 1824–32.
Six Nations Agency Records, 1824–34.
Southern Superintendency Records, 1861–65.
Special Case File No. 29: Kansas Claims by New York Indians.
National Archives. U.S. War Department. Civil War Pension Records.
New York State Units. 13th and 14th Heavy Artillery; 24th New York Cavalry; 86th, 98th, 132d, and 154th Volunteer Infantry.
Pennsylvania Unit. 57th Volunteer Infantry.
Wisconsin Unit. 14th Volunteer Infantry.
National Archives. U.S. War Department. Records of the Adjutant General's Office. RG94.
Appointment, Commission, and Personnel Branch.
Compiled Service Records.
Regimental Books:
Clothing Books.
Morning Reports.
Order Books.
Letter Books.
Regimental Description Books [Muster Rolls].
Regimental Letter Books.
National Archives. U.S. War Department Records of the U.S. Navy. RG24.
Log Book of *USS Rhode Island.*
Muster Rolls of *USS Rhode Island.*
Newberry Library. D'Arcy McNickle Center for the History of the American Indian, Chicago.
Iroquois Indians: A Documentary History of the Six Nations and Their League. Francis Jennings et al., eds. 50 microfilm reels.
New York State Archives, Albany. Records of the Division of Military and Naval Affairs.
War of 1812 Pension Records [Applications].
Civil War Records.
Abstracts of Civil War Muster Rolls of New York Units:
13th and 14th Heavy Artillery; 24th New York Cavalry; 86th, 98th, 132d, and 154th Volunteer Infantry.
Correspondence and Petition Files of the Adjutant General's Office, 1821–96.
Register of Letters Received by the Adjutant General's Office, 1862–66.
Town Clerks' Registers of Officers, Soldiers, and Seamen.
Records of the Thomas Indian School.
Records of the New York State Board of Charities.
New York State Library. Manuscript Division, Albany.
William M. Beauchamp MSS.
Bliss Family MSS.

Grand Army of the Republic Collection.
Franklin B. Hough MSS.
Indian Census (Schoolcraft) of 1845.
Arthur C. Parker MSS.
New York Yearly Meeting of Friends. Haviland Record Room, New York City.
Records of the New York Yearly Meeting of Friends, Joint Indian Committee,
1835–63.
Oklahoma Historical Society, Oklahoma City.
Grant Foreman Papers (WPA), Indian-Pioneer History.
Quapaw Agency Records.
Oneida Nation of Indians of Wisconsin.
MSS in Oneida Indian Museum.
List: "The Following Are Civil War Veterans Who Never Came Back to
Oneida, Wisconsin."
"Pentagon Report," compiled by Jan Malcolm, 1990.
Language Department Records: The Oneida Language and Folklore Project
Stories (WPA), 1938–41.
Onondaga Historical Association, Syracuse, N.Y.
Sanford Thayer File.
Newsclipping Files Relative to Onondaga Indians.
Samuel George.
Aunt Dinah John.
Pennsylvania State Archives. Harrisburg, Pa.
Civil War Records.
RG 19: Department of Military Affairs: Muster Rolls and Related Records
of the 57th Pennsylvania Volunteer Infantry.
MGGO: Grand Army of the Republic Collection.
Rochester Museum and Science Center, Rochester, N.Y.
William Jones Diary.
Seneca-Iroquois National Museum, Salamanca, N.Y.
Civil War Collection: Letters of Seneca Soldiers.
Smithsonian Institution. National Anthropological Archives, Washington, D.C.
J. N. B. Hewitt MSS.
Erminie Wheeler-Voegelin. "The 19th and 20th Century Ethnohistory of Vari-
ous Groups of Cayuga Indians," MSS 7092.
State Historical Society of Wisconsin, Madison.
Powless, Joseph, and John Archiquette Diary. Trans. by Oscar Archiquette.
Wisconsin Adjutant General. Descriptive Muster Rolls for 14th Wisconsin
Volunteer Infantry. 2 microfilm reels.
Swarthmore College. Friends Historical Library, Swarthmore, Pa.
Elkinton Family MSS.
Journals of Ebenezer Worth, Sr., 1843–75.
Records of the Baltimore Yearly Meeting. Standing Committee on the Indian
Concern.
Records of the Philadelphia Yearly Meeting. Indian Committee.

Records of the Joint Committee on Indian Affairs.
University of Rochester. Rush Rhees Library, Rochester, N.Y.
    Lewis Henry Morgan MSS.
    Arthur C. Parker MSS.
    Ely S. Parker MSS.
    William Seward MSS.
    James Wadsworth MSS.

GOVERNMENT PUBLICATIONS

Congressional Globe, 1848–73.
Congressional Record, 1873–75.
Donaldson, Thomas, comp. *Extra Census Bulletin. Indians. The Six Nations of New York.* Prepared for the Eleventh Census, 1890. Washington, D.C.: U.S. Government Printing Office, 1894.
Hastings, Hugh, ed. *Public Papers of Daniel D. Tompkins: Governor of New York, 1807–1817.* 3 vols. New York: Wynkoop, Hallenbeck & Crawford State Printers, 1898.
Kappler, Charles J., comp. *Indian Affairs: Laws and Treaties.* 5 vols. Washington, D.C.: U.S. Government Printing Office, 1903–41.
New York State. *Census of the State of New York for 1855.* Compiled by Franklin B. Hough. Albany: Charles Van Benthuysen, 1857.
New York State. *Census of the State of New York for 1865.* Compiled by Franklin B. Hough. Albany: Charles Van Benthuysen & Son, 1867.
New York State. *Census of the State of New York for 1875.* Compiled by C. W. Seaton. Albany: Weed, Parsons & Co., 1877.
New York State. Department of Education. Native American Unit. *Indian Education in New York State.* Albany, n.d.
New York State. Legislature. *Laws of the State of New York,* 1840–80.
New York State. Legislature. Assembly. *Report of the Special Committee to Investigate the Indian Problem of the State of New York.* Appointed by the Assembly of 1888. 2 vols. Albany: Troy Press, 1889.
New York State. Superintendent of Common Schools. *Annual Report for 1849.* Albany, 1849.
New York State. Superintendent of Public Instruction. *Annual Reports,* 1854–75.
New York State Adjutant General's Office. *Index of Awards: Soldiers of the War of 1812.* Baltimore: Genealogical Publishing Co., 1969.
New York State Historian (Hugh Hastings). *2nd Annual Report.* Albany, 1897.
Phisterer, Frederick, comp. *New York in the War of the Rebellion, 1861 to 1865.* 3d ed. 5 vols. Albany: J. B. Lyon Co. State Printers, 1912.
U.S. Bureau of the Census. *Ninth Census: The Statistics of the Population of the United States.* Washington, D.C.: U.S. Government Printing Office, 1872.
———. *Population of the United States in 1860: Eighth Census.* Washington, D.C.: U.S. Government Printing Office, 1864.

————. *Preliminary Report on the Eighth Census*. Washington, D.C.: U.S. Government Printing Office, 1862.

U.S. Congress. House of Representatives. *House Report No. 39: Investigation into Indian Affairs*. 39th Cong., 3d sess.

U.S. Congress. Senate. *Misc. Doc. No. 122: Protest of the President, Councillors, and People of the Seneca Nation of Indians Made in Their National Council Against the Passage of the Bill (H.R. No. 3080): To Authorize the Seneca Nation to Lease Lands Within the Cattaraugus and Allegany Reservations and to Confirm Existing Leases, June 3, 1874*. 43d Cong., 1st sess.

————. Select Committee on Indian Affairs. *Report 101–511: Providing for the Renegotiation of Certain Leases of the Seneca Nation, and for Other Purposes*. 101st Cong., 2d sess.

U.S. Department of the Interior. Commissioner of Indian Affairs. *Annual Reports*, 1860–75.

U.S. Navy Department. *Official Records of the Union and Confederate Navies in the War of the Rebellion*. 30 vols. Washington, D.C.: U.S. Government Printing Office, 1894–1922.

United States. *Public Law 101–503: The Seneca Nation Settlement Act of 1990* (Nov. 3, 1990).

United States War Department. Provost-General's Bureau. *Statistics, Medical and Anthropological*. Washington, D.C.: U.S. Government Printing Office, 1857.

U.S. War Department. *The War of the Rebellion: A Compilation of the Official Records of the Union and Confederate Armies*. 128 vols. Washington, D.C.: U.S. Government Printing Office, 1880–1901.

Wisconsin Adjutant General's Office. *Roster of Wisconsin Volunteers: War of the Rebellion, 1861–1865*. 2 vols. Madison: Democrat Printing Co. State Printers, 1886.

BOOKS, BOOKLETS, AND PAMPHLETS

Abel, Annie Heloise. *The American Indian as Participant in the Civil War*. Cleveland: Arthur H. Clark, 1919.

————. *The American Indian as Slaveholder and Secessionist*. Cleveland: Arthur H. Clark, 1915.

————. *The American Indian Under Reconstruction*. Cleveland: Arthur H. Clark, 1919.

Abernethy, Byron R., ed. *Private Elisha Stockwell, Jr., Sees the Civil War*. Norman: Univ. of Oklahoma Press, 1958.

Abler, Thomas S., ed. *Chainbreaker: The Revolutionary War Memoirs of Governor Blacksnake as Told to Benjamin Williams*. Lincoln: Univ. of Nebraska Press, 1989.

Abrams, George H. J. *The Seneca People*. Phoenix: Indian Tribal Series, 1976.

Adams, William, ed. *Historical Gazetteer and Biographical Memorial of Cattaraugus County, N.Y.* Syracuse, N.Y.: Lyman, Horton, 1893.

Alcott, Louisa May. *Hospital Sketches.* Boston: J. Redpath, 1863.

Ambrose, Stephen, ed. *A Wisconsin Boy in Dixie: The Selected Letters of James K. Newton.* Madison: Univ. of Wisconsin Press, 1961.

Anson, Bert. *The Miami Indians.* Norman: Univ. of Oklahoma Press, 1970.

Armstrong, William H. *Warrior in Two Camps: Ely S. Parker, Union General and Seneca Chief.* Syracuse: Syracuse Univ. Press, 1978.

Austin, Alberta, comp. *Ne Ho Ni Yo De: No—That's What It Was Like.* 2 vols. New York: Rebco Enterprises, 1986–89.

Axtell, James. *The Invasion Within: The Contest of Cultures in Colonial North America.* New York: Oxford Univ. Press, 1985.

Baird, W. David. *The Quapaw Indians.* Norman: Univ. of Oklahoma Press, 1980.

———, ed. *A Creek Warrior for the Confederacy: The Autobiography of Chief G. W. Grayson.* Norman: Univ. of Oklahoma Press, 1988.

Barnes, David M. *The Draft Riots in New York: July, 1863. The Metropolitan Police: Their Services During Riot Week. Their Honorable Record.* New York: Baker & Goodwin, 1863.

Barrett, John G. *The Civil War in North Carolina.* Chapel Hill: Univ. of North Carolina Press, 1963.

Barton, Lois. *A Quaker Promise Kept: Philadelphia Friends' Work with the Allegany Senecas, 1795–1960.* Eugene, Ore.: Spencer Butte, 1990.

Basler, Roy, ed. *Collected Works of Abraham Lincoln.* 8 vols. New Brunswick, N.J.: Rutgers Univ. Press, 1953.

Bates, Samuel P. *History of Pennsylvania Volunteers.* 5 vols. Harrisburg, Pa.: B. Singerly, 1869–71.

Bauer, K. Jack. *Soldiering: The Civil War Diary of Rice C. Bull.* Novato, Calif.: Presidio Press, 1977.

Bearss, Edward C., and Arrell M. Gibson. *Fort Smith: Little Gibraltar on the Arkansas.* Norman: Univ. of Oklahoma Press, 1969.

Beauchamp, William M. *A History of the New York Iroquois.* New York State Museum *Bulletin* 78, Albany, N.Y., 1905.

Benson, Lee. *Merchants, Farmers, and Railroads: Railroad Regulation and New York Politics, 1850–1887.* Cambridge, Mass.: Harvard Univ. Press, 1955.

Bernstein, Iver. *The New York City Draft Riots: Their Significance for American Society and Politics in the Age of the Civil War.* New York: Oxford Univ. Press, 1990.

Bieder, Robert E. *Science Encounters the Indian: The Early Years of American Ethnology.* Norman: Univ. of Oklahoma Press, 1986.

Bloomfield, J. K. *The Oneidas.* New York: Alden Bros., 1907.

Bonvillain, Nancy, ed. *Studies on Iroquoian Culture.* Occasional Publications in Northeastern Anthropology, 6. Rindge, N.H.: *Man in the Northeast,* 1980.

Brannon, John, comp. *Official Letters of the Military and Naval Officers of the United States During the War with Great Britain in the Years, 1812, 13, 14, 15. . . .* Washington, D.C.: Way & Gideon, 1823.

Britton, Wiley. *The Union Indian Brigade in the Civil War*. Kansas City, Mo.: Franklin Hudson, 1922.

Brownlee, Richard S. *Gray Ghosts of the Confederacy: Guerrilla Warfare in the West, 1861–1865*. Baton Rouge: Louisiana State Univ. Press, 1958.

Brummer, Sidney D. *Political History of New York State During the Period of the Civil War*. New York: Longman, Green, 1911.

Burton, William L. *Melting Pot Soldiers: The Union's Ethnic Soldiers*. Ames: Iowa State Univ. Press, 1989.

Cadwalader, Sylvanus. *Three Years with Grant*. Edited by Benjamin P. Thomas. New York: Knopf, 1956.

Campisi, Jack, Michael Foster, and Marianne Mithun, eds. *Extending the Rafters: Interdisciplinary Approaches to Iroquoian Studies*. Albany: State Univ. of New York Press, 1984.

Campisi, Jack, and Laurence M. Hauptman, eds. *The Oneida Indian Experience: Two Perspectives*. Syracuse: Syracuse Univ. Press, 1988.

Castel, Albert E. *A Frontier State at War: Kansas, 1861–1865*. Ithaca, N.Y.: Cornell Univ. Press, 1958.

———. *General Sterling Price and the Civil War in the West*. Baton Rouge: Louisiana State Univ. Press, 1968.

Catton, Bruce. *Glory Road: The Bloody Route from Fredericksburg to Gettysburg*. Garden City, N.Y.: Doubleday, 1952.

———. *Reflections on the Civil War*. Edited by John Leekley. 1981. Paperback reprint. New York: Berkeley, 1982.

———. *A Stillness at Appomattox*. Garden City, N.Y.: Doubleday, 1953.

———. *Terrible Swift Sword*. Garden City, N.Y.: Doubleday, 1963.

Chazanof, William. *Joseph Ellicott and the Holland Land Company of Western New York*. Syracuse: Syracuse Univ. Press, 1970.

Congdon, Charles E. *Allegany Ox-Bow*. Little Valley, N.Y.: N.p., 1967.

Conners, Dennis, ed. *Onondaga: Portrait of a Native People*. Syracuse: Syracuse Univ. Press, 1986.

Cook, Adrian. *The Armies of the Streets: The New York City Draft Riots of 1863*. Lexington: Univ. Press of Kentucky, 1974.

Cooper, Alonzo. *In and Out of Rebel Prisons*. Oswego, N.Y.: R. J. Oliphant, 1888.

Cornish, Dudley T. *The Sable Army: Negro Troops in the Union Army, 1861–1865*. New York: Longman, Green, 1956.

Cruikshank, E. A., ed. *The Documentary History of the Campaign upon the Niagara Frontier, 1812–1814*. 9 vols. Welland, Ontario: Lundy's Lane Historical Society, 1896–1908.

Current, Richard N. *The History of Wisconsin: The Civil War Era, 1848–1873*. Madison: State Historical Society of Wisconsin, 1976.

Cusick, David. *Sketches of Ancient History of the Six Nations. . . .* 1827; 2d ed. Lockport, N.Y.: Cooley & Lothrop, 1828.

Dale, Edward Everett, and Gaston Litton, eds. *Cherokee Cavaliers: Forty Years of*

Cherokee History as Told in Correspondence of the Ridge-Boudinot Family. Norman: Univ. of Oklahoma Press, 1939.

Danziger, Edmund J., Jr. *Indians and Bureaucrats: Administering the Reservation Policy During the Civil War.* Urbana: Univ. of Illinois Press, 1974.

Dearing, Mary R. *Veterans in Politics: The Story of the G.A.R.* Baton Rouge: Louisiana State Univ. Press, 1952.

Dollard, John. *Fear in Battle.* New Haven: Institute for Human Relations, Yale University, 1943.

Dornbusch, Charles E. *Military Bibliography of the Civil War.* 4 vols. Cornwallville, N.Y.: Hope Farm Press, 1961–87.

Doty, Lockwood L. *A History of Livingston County.* Geneseo, N.Y.: E. E. Doty, 1876.

Duncan, Robert L. *Reluctant General: The Life and Times of Albert Pike.* New York: E. P. Dutton, 1961.

Dunkelman, Mark H., and Michael J. Winey. *The Hardtack Regiment: An Illustrated History of the 154th Regiment New York State Infantry Volunteers.* Rutherford, N.J.: Fairleigh Dickinson Univ. Press, 1981.

Dunlay, Thomas W. *Wolves for the Blue Soldiers: Indian Scouts and Auxiliaries with the United States Army, 1860–1890.* Lincoln: Univ. of Nebraska Press, 1982.

Dyer, Frederick H. *A Compendium of the War of the Rebellion.* 3 vols. New York: Thomas Yoselof, 1959.

Ellis, Franklin. *History of Cattaraugus County, New York.* Philadelphia: L. H. Everts, 1879.

Ernst, Robert. *Immigrant Life in New York City, 1825–1863.* New York: Columbia Univ. Press, 1949.

Etienne, Mona, and Eleanor Leacock, eds. *Women and Colonization: Anthropological Perspectives.* New York: Praeger, 1980.

Evans, W. McKee. *To Die Game: The Story of the Lowry Band, Indian Guerrillas of Reconstruction.* Baton Rouge: Louisiana State Univ. Press, 1971.

Fellman, Michael. *Inside War: The Guerrilla Conflict in Missouri During the American Civil War.* New York: Oxford Univ. Press, 1989.

Fenton, William N. *The Iroquois Eagle Dance: An Offshoot of the Calumet Dance.* Bulletin 156. Washington, D.C.: Bureau of American Ethnology, 1953.

———. *An Outline of Seneca Ceremonies at Coldspring Longhouse.* Publications in Anthropology 9. New Haven: Yale Univ., 1936.

Fischer, LeRoy H., ed. *The Civil War in Indian Territory.* Los Angeles: Morrison, 1974.

Fixico, Donald L., ed. *An Anthology of Western Great Lakes Indian History.* Milwaukee: American Indian Studies Department of the University of Wisconsin, Milwaukee, 1987.

Foote, Shelby. *The Civil War: A Narrative.* 3 vols. New York: Random House, 1958–74.

Foreman, Grant. *The Last Trek of the Indians.* 1946. Reprint. New York: Russell & Russell, 1972.

Fox, William F. *Regimental Losses in the American Civil War, 1861–1865.* Albany, N.Y.: Albany Publishing Co., 1889.

Franks, Kenny A. *Stand Watie and the Agony of the Cherokee Nation.* Memphis, Tenn.: Memphis State Univ. Press, 1979.

Futch, Ovid. *History of Andersonville Prison.* Gainesville: Univ. of Florida Press, 1968.

Gaines, W. Craig. *The Confederate Cherokees: John Drew's Regiment of Mounted Rifles.* Baton Rouge: Louisiana State Univ. Press, 1989.

Gara, Larry. *The Liberty Line: The Legend of the Underground Railroad.* Lexington: Univ. Press of Kentucky, 1961.

Gates, Paul Wallace. *Fifty Million Acres: Conflicts over Kansas Land Policy, 1854–1890.* Ithaca, N.Y.: Cornell Univ. Press, 1954.

Geary, James W. *We Need Men: The Union Draft in the Civil War.* De Kalb: Northern Illinois Univ. Press, 1991.

Gehring, Charles T., and William A. Starna, eds. and trans. *A Journey into Mohawk and Oneida Country, 1634–1635.* Syracuse: Syracuse Univ. Press, 1988.

Gibson, Arrell, ed. *America's Exiles: Indian Colonization in Oklahoma.* Oklahoma City: Oklahoma Historical Society, 1976.

Glasson, William H. *Federal Military Pensions in the United States.* New York: Oxford Univ. Press, 1918.

———. *History of Military Pension Legislation in the United States.* New York: Columbia Univ. Press, 1900.

Glatthaar, Joseph T. *Forged in Battle: The Civil War Alliance of Black Soldiers and White Officers.* New York: Free Press, 1990.

———. *The Mach to the Sea and Beyond: Sherman's Troops in the Savannah and Carolina Campaigns.* New York: New York Univ. Press, 1985.

Gould, Benjamin A. *Investigations in the Military and Anthropological Statistics of American Soldiers.* Cambridge, Mass.: Hurd & Houghton, 1869.

Gragg, Rod. *Confederate Goliath: The Battle of Fort Fisher.* New York: Harper Collins, 1991.

Grant, Ulysses S. *Personal Memoirs of U. S. Grant.* 2 vols. New York: C. L. Webster, 1885–86.

Graymont, Barbara. *The Iroquois in the American Revolution.* Syracuse: Syracuse Univ. Press, 1972.

———, ed. *Fighting Tuscarora: The Autobiography of Chief Clinton Rickard.* Syracuse: Syracuse Univ. Press, 1973.

Greene, Jerome A. *Yellowstone Command: Colonel Nelson A. Miles and the Great Sioux War, 1876–1877.* Lincoln: Univ. of Nebraska Press, 1991.

Grinnell, George Bird. *The Story of the Indian.* New York: Macmillan, 1911.

Hagerman, Edward. *The American Civil War and the Origins of Modern Warfare: Ideas, Organization and Field Command.* Bloomington: Indiana Univ. Press, 1988.

Hale, Horatio E. *The Iroquois Book of Rites.* 2 vols. Philadelphia: D. G. Brinton, 1883.

Haller, John S., Jr. *Outcasts from Evolution: Scientific Attitudes of Racial Inferiority, 1859–1900*. Urbana: Univ. of Illinois Press, 1971.

Hauptman, Laurence M. *Formulating American Indian Policy in New York State, 1970–1986*. Albany: State Univ. of New York Press, 1988.

———. *The Iroquois and the New Deal*. Syracuse: Syracuse Univ. Press, 1981.

———. *The Iroquois Struggle for Survival: World War II to Red Power*. Syracuse: Syracuse Univ. Press, 1986.

Herrick, John P. *Empire Oil: The Story of Oil in the Empire State*. New York: Dodd, Mead, 1949.

Hesseltine, William B. *Civil War Prisons: A Study in War Psychology*. Columbus: Ohio State Univ. Press, 1930.

Hewitt, J. N. B. *Iroquoian Cosmology*. Bureau of American Ethnology, *Annual Report*. Washington, D.C.: Bureau of American Ethnology, 1928.

Hicks, Frederick C., ed. *High Finance in the Sixties: Chapters from the Early History of the Erie Railroad*. 1929. Reprint. Port Washington, N.Y.: Kennikat Press, 1967.

Houghton, Frederick. *The History of the Buffalo Creek Reservation*. Buffalo Historical Society Publications, 24, Buffalo, N.Y., 1920.

Howard, Jones H. *Shawnee*. Athens: Ohio Univ. Press, 1981.

Hoxie, Frederick, *A Final Promise: The Campaign to Assimilate the Indians, 1880–1920*. Lincoln: Univ. of Nebraska Press, 1984.

Hungerford, Edward. *Men of Erie: A Story of Human Effort*. New York: Random House, 1946.

Hunt, George T. *The Wars of the Iroquois: A Study in Intertribal Trade Relations*. Madison: Univ. of Wisconsin Press, 1940.

Jackson, Harry F., and Thomas F. O'Donnell, eds. *Back Home in Oneida: Hermon Clarke and His Letters*. Syracuse: Syracuse Univ. Press, 1965.

Jennings, Francis. *The Ambiguous Iroquois Empire*. New York: Norton, 1984.

———. *Empire of Fortune: Crowns, Colonies and Tribes in the Seven Years War in America*. New York: Norton, 1988.

——— et al., eds. *The History and Culture of Iroquois Diplomacy: An Interdisciplinary Guide to the Treaties of the Six Nations and Their League*. Syracuse: Syracuse Univ. Press, 1985.

Jimerson, Randall C. *The Private Civil War: Popular Thought During the Sectional Conflict*. Baton Rouge: Louisiana State Univ. Press, 1988.

Johnson, E. Roy. *The Tuscaroras: History — Traditions — Culture*. 2 vols. Murfreesboro, N.C.: Johnson Publishing Co., 1968.

Johnson, Elias. *Legends, Traditions and Laws, of the Iroquois or Six Nations, and History of the Tuscarora Indians*. Lockport, N.Y.: Union Printing and Publishing, 1881.

Johnson, Marlene, comp. *Iroquois Cookbook*. 2d ed. Tonawanda Indian Reservation: Peter Doctor Memorial Fellowship Foundation, 1989.

Johnston, Charles M., ed. *The Valley of the Six Nations: A Collection of Documents on the Indian Lands of the Grand River*. Toronto: Champlain Society, 1964.

Josephy, Alvin M., Jr. *The Civil War in the American West*. New York: Knopf, 1991.

Keegan, John. *The Face of Battle*. New York: Viking, 1976.

———. *The Mask of Command*. New York: Viking, 1987.

Kelley, Daniel G. *What I Saw and Suffered in Rebel Prisons*. Buffalo, N.Y.: Thomas, Howard & Johnson, 1868.

Kelsay, Isabel Thompson. *Joseph Brant, 1743–1807: Man of Two Worlds*. Syracuse: Syracuse Univ. Press, 1984.

Kelsey, Rayner W. *Friends and the Indians, 1655–1917*. Philadelphia: Associated Executive Committee of Friends on Indian Affairs, 1917.

Ketchum, William. *An Authentic Comprehensive History of Buffalo*. 2 vols. Buffalo, N.Y.: Rockwell, Baker & Hill, 1864–65.

[Joseph] Kittinger Diary, 1861–1865. Buffalo, N.Y.: Kittinger Co. in cooperation with the Buffalo and Erie County Historical Society, n.d.

Klement, Frank L. *The Limits of Dissent*. Lexington: Univ. Press of Kentucky, 1970.

———. *Wisconsin and the Civil War*. Madison: State Historical Society of Wisconsin, 1963.

Klinck, Carl F., and James J. Talman, eds. *The Journal of Major John Norton, 1816*. Toronto: Champlain Society, 1970.

Kreutzer, William. *Notes and Observations Made During Four Years of Service with the 98th New York Volunteers*. Philadelphia: Grant, Faire & Rogers, 1878.

Kvasnicka, Robert, and Herman Viola, eds. *The Commissioners of Indian Affairs, 1824–1977*. Lincoln: Univ. of Nebraska Press, 1979.

Lafitau, Joseph François. *Customs of the American Indians* (1724). 2 vols. Translated and edited by William N. Fenton and Elizabeth Moore. Toronto: Champlain Society, 1974.

Larned, Josephus N. *A History of Buffalo, Delineating the Evolution of the City*. 2 vols. New York: Progress of the Empire State Company, 1911.

Liberty, Margot, ed. *American Indian Intellectuals*. St. Paul, Minn.: American Ethnological Society, 1978.

Linderman, Gerald F. *Embattled Courage: The Experience of Combat in the American Civil War*. New York: Free Press, 1987.

Livermore, Thomas. *Numbers and Losses in the Civil War in America, 1861–1865*. 2d ed. Boston: Houghton Mifflin, 1901.

Long, Everett B. *The Civil War Day by Day: An Almanac, 1861–1865*. Garden City, N.Y.: Doubleday, 1971.

Lonn, Ella. *Desertion During the Civil War*. New York: Century, 1928.

Love, W. De Loss. *Wisconsin in the War of Rebellion*. New York: Love Publishing, 1866.

Lurie, Nancy O. and Eleanor Leacock, ed. *North American Indians in Historical Perspective*. New York: Random House, 1971.

McDonough, James Lee. *Chattanooga: A Death Grip on the Confederacy*. Knoxville: Univ. of Tennessee Press, 1984.

McFeeley, William S. *Grant: A Biography*. New York: Norton, 1981.

McKay, Ernest A. *The Civil War and New York City*. Syracuse: Syracuse Univ. Press, 1990.

McKelvey, Blake. *Rochester on the Genesee: The Growth of a City*. Syracuse: Syracuse Univ. Press, 1973.

McPherson, James M. *Battle Cry of Freedom: The Civil War Era*. New York: Oxford Univ. Press, 1988.

————. *The Negro's Civil War*. New York: Pantheon Books, 1965.

————. *Ordeal by Fire: The Civil War and Reconstruction*. New York: Knopf, 1982.

Martin, Deborah B. *History of Brown County, Wisconsin: Past and Present*. Chicago: S. J. Clarke, 1913.

Maxwell, William Quentin. *Lincoln's Fifth Wheel: The Political History of the United States Sanitary Commission*. New York: Longmans Green, 1956.

Merk, Frederick. *Economic History of Wisconsin During the Civil War Decade*. Madison, Wisc., 1916.

Miner, H. Craig. *The Corporation and the Indian: Tribal Sovereignty and Industrial Civilization in Indian Territory*. Columbia: Univ. of Missouri Press, 1976.

Miner, H. Craig, and William E. Unrau. *The End of Indian Kansas: A Study of Cultural Revolution, 1854–1871*. Lawrence: Regents Press of Kansas, 1978.

Mitchell, Reid. *Civil War Soldiers: Their Expectations and Their Experiences*. New York: Viking Press, 1988.

Mitchell, Stewart. *Horatio Seymour of New York*. Cambridge, Mass.: Harvard Univ. Press, 1938.

Monaghan, Jay. *Civil War on the Western Border, 1854–1865*. Boston: Little, Brown, 1955.

Morgan, Lewis Henry. *The League of the Ho-de-no-sau-nee, or Iroquois*. 1851. Paperback reprint. New York: Corinth Books, 1962.

Moulton, Gary E. *John Ross: Cherokee Chief*. Athens: Univ. of Georgia Press, 1979.

————, ed. *The Papers of John Ross*. 2 vols. Norman: Univ. of Oklahoma Press, 1975.

Murdock, Eugene C. *One Million Men: The Civil War Draft in the North*. Madison: State Historical Society of Wisconsin, 1971.

————. *Patriotism Limited, 1862–1865: The Civil War Draft and Bounty System*. Kent, Ohio: Kent State Univ. Press, 1967.

Murray, Keith. *The Modocs and Their War*. Norman: Univ. of Oklahoma Press, 1971.

Mushkat, Jerome. *The Reconstruction of New York Democracy, 1861–1874*. Madison, N.J.: Fairleigh Dickinson Univ. Press, 1981.

————. *Tammany: The Evolution of a Political Machine, 1789–1865*. Syracuse: Syracuse Univ. Press, 1971.

Nabokov, Peter. *Indian Running: Native American History and Tradition*. Santa Fe, N.M.: Ancient City Press, 1981.

Nevins, Allan, ed. *Diary of the Civil War, 1860–1865: George Templeton Strong*. New York: Macmillan, 1962.

Newton, James K. *A Wisconsin Boy in Dixie: The Selected Letters of James K. Newton.* Edited by Stephen E. Ambrose. Madison: Univ. of Wisconsin Press, 1961.

Nichols, David A. *Lincoln and the Indians: Civil War Policy and Politics.* Columbia: Univ. of Missouri Press, 1978.

Paludan, Phillip S. *"A People's Contest": The Union and Civil War, 1861–1865.* New York: Harper & Row, 1988.

———. *Victims: A True Story of the Civil War.* Knoxville: Univ. of Tennessee Press, 1981.

Parker, Arthur C. *The Life of General Ely S. Parker, Last Grand Sachem of the Iroquois and General Grant's Military Secretary.* Publications of the Buffalo Historical Society, 23. Buffalo, 1919.

———. *Parker on the Iroquois.* Ed. William M. Fenton. Syracuse: Syracuse Univ. Press, 1968.

Parker, David B. *A Chautauqua Boy in '61 and Afterward: Reminiscence.* Edited by Torrance Parker. Boston, Small, Maynard, 1912.

Parrish, William E. *A History of Missouri.* Vol. 3: 1860 to 1875. Columbia: Univ. of Missouri Press, 1973.

Pickett, George E. *Soldier of the South: General Pickett's War Letters to His Wife.* Edited by Arthur C. Inman. Boston: Houghton Mifflin 1928.

Pierce, Harry H. *Railroads of New York: A Study of Government Aid, 1826–1875.* Cambridge, Mass.: Harvard Univ. Press, 1953.

Porter, Horace. *Campaigning with Grant.* 1897. Paperback reprint. New York: De Capo, 1986.

Prisch, Betty Coit. *Aspects of Change in Seneca Iroquois Ladles A.D. 1600–1900.* Rochester, N.Y.: Rochester Museum and Science Center, Research Record No. 15, 1982.

Prucha, Francis Paul. *The Great Father: The United States Government and the American Indians.* 2 vols. Lincoln: Univ. of Nebraska Press, 1984.

Quiner, E. B. *The Military History of Wisconsin: A Record of the Civil and Military Patriotism of the State in the War for the Union.* Chicago: Clarke, 1866.

Rampp, Lary C., and Donald L. *The Civil War in Indian Territory.* Austin, Tex.: Presidial Press, 1975.

Reed, Rowena. *Combined Operations in the Civil War.* Annapolis, Md.: Naval Institute Press, 1978.

Reed, William H. *Hospital Life in the Army of the Potomac.* Boston: William V. Spencer, 1866.

Resek, Carl. *Lewis Henry Morgan: American Scholar.* Chicago: Univ. of Chicago Press, 1960.

Richards, Cara E. *The Oneida People.* Phoenix, Ariz.: Indian Tribal Series, 1974.

Richter, Daniel K., and James H. Merrell, eds. *Beyond the Covenant Chain: The Iroquois and Their Neighbors in Indian North America, 1600–1800.* Syracuse: Syracuse Univ. Press, 1987.

Robertson, James I., Jr. *Soldiers: Blue and Gray.* Columbia, S.C.: Univ. of South Carolina Press, 1988.

Satz, Ronald N. *American Indian Policy in the Jacksonian Era.* Lincoln: Univ. of Nebraska Press, 1975.

Schoolcraft, Henry R. *Notes on the Iroquois, or Contributions to American History, Antiquities, and General Ethnology.* Albany, N.Y.: Erastus H. Pense, 1847.

Seaver, James E., comp. *A Narrative of the Life of Mrs. Mary Jemison.* Reprint with introduction by George H. J. Abrams. Syracuse: Syracuse Univ. Press, 1990.

Shannon, Fred. *The Organization and Administration of the Union Army.* 2 vols. Cleveland: Arthur H. Clark, 1928.

Shaw, Charles A., comp. *A History of the 14th Regiment New York Heavy Artillery in the Civil War from 1863 to 1865.* Mount Kisco, N.Y.: North Westchester Publishing Co., 1918.

Shimony, Annemarie A. *Conservatism Among the Iroquois at the Six Nations Reserve.* Publications in Anthropology 65. New Haven: Yale University, 1961.

Siebert, Wilbur H. *The Underground Railroad.* 1898. Reprint. New York: Arno Press and the New York Times, 1968.

Simon, John Y., ed. *The Papers of Ulysses S. Grant.* 15 vols. Carbondale: Southern Illinois Univ. Press, 1967–.

Smith, Adelaide W. *Reminiscences of an Army Nurse During the Civil War.* New York: Greaves, 1911.

Snyder, Charles M., ed. *Red and White on the New York Frontier: Insights from the Papers of Erastus Granger, Indian Agent, 1807–1819.* Harrison, N.Y.: Harbor Hill Books, 1978.

Society of Friends. Joint Committee on Indian Affairs. *The Case of the Seneca Indians in the State of New York.* 1840. Reprint. Stanfordville, N.Y.: Earl M. Coleman, 1979.

———. Philadelphia Yearly Meeting. *A Brief Sketch of the Efforts of [the] Philadelphia Yearly Meeting of the Religious Society of Friends to Promote the Civilization and Improvement of the Indians; also of the Present Conditions of the Tribes in the State of New York.* Philadelphia: Indian Committee of the Philadelphia Yearly Meeting of Friends, 1866.

———. *A Brief Statement of the Rights of the Seneca Indians in the State of New York to Their Lands in That State.* Philadelphia: W. H. Pile, 1877.

Stearns, Amos E. *The Civil War Diary of Amos E. Stearns: A Prisoner at Andersonville.* East Rutherford, N.J.: Fairleigh Dickinson Univ. Press, 1981.

Steiner, Paul E. *Disease in the Civil War: Natural Biological Warfare in 1861–1865.* Springfield, Ill.: C. C. Thomas, 1968.

Sutherland, Daniel E. *The Expansion of Everyday Life, 1860–1876.* New York: Harper & Row, 1989.

Thomas, Howard. *Boys in Blue from the Adirondack Foothills.* New York: Prospect Books, 1960.

Thornton, Russell. *American Indian Holocaust and Survival: A Population History Since 1492.* Norman: Univ. of Oklahoma Press, 1987.

Tooker, Elisabeth. *The Iroquois Ceremonial of Midwinter.* Syracuse: Syracuse Univ. Press, 1970.

———, ed. *Proceedings of the 1965 Conference on Iroquois Research.* Albany: New York State Museum and Science Service, 1967.

Town of Brant, N.Y.: Records of Soldiers and Officers in the Military Service, 1861–1865. N.p., n.d.

Trigger, Bruce G., ed. *Handbook of North American Indians.* Vol. 15: *Northeast.* Washington, D.C.: Smithsonian Institution, 1978.

Turner, George E. *Victory Rode the Rails: The Strategic Place of the Railroads in the Civil War.* New York: Bobbs-Merrill, 1953.

Utley, Robert M. *Frontier Regulars: The United States Army and the Indian, 1866–1891.* New York: Macmillan, 1973.

———. *The Indian Frontier of the American West, 1846–1890.* Albuquerque: Univ. of New Mexico Press, 1984.

Vecsey, Christopher, and William A. Starna, eds. *Iroquois Land Claims.* Syracuse: Syracuse Univ. Press, 1988.

Viola, Herman J. *Diplomats in Buckskin: A History of Indian Delegations in Washington City.* Washington, D.C.: Smithsonian Institution Press, 1981.

Vinovskis, Maris A., ed. *Toward a Social History of the American Civil War: Exploratory Essays.* Cambridge: Cambridge Univ. Press, 1990.

Wallace, Anthony F. C. *The Death and Rebirth of the Seneca.* New York: Knopf, 1970.

Wardell, Morris L. *A Political History of the Cherokee Nation, 1838–1907.* 1938. Paperback reprint. Norman: Univ. of Oklahoma Press, 1977.

Washburn, Wilcomb E., ed. *The American Indian and the United States: A Documentary History.* 4 vols. Westport, Conn.: Greenwood, 1973.

Weighley, Russell. *The American Way of War: A History of United States Military Strategy and Policy.* New York: Macmillan, 1973.

Welcher, Frank J. *The Union Army, 1861–1865: Organization and Operations.* Vol. 1: *The Eastern Theatre.* Bloomington: Indiana Univ. Press, 1989.

Wiley, Bell Irvin. *The Life of Billy Yank: The Common Soldier of the Union.* Indianapolis: Bobbs-Merrill, 1952.

Wooster, Robert. *The Military and United States Indian Policy, 1865–1903.* New Haven: Yale Univ. Press, 1988.

Wright, Muriel H., and LeRoy H. Fischer, *Civil War Sites in Oklahoma.* Oklahoma City: Oklahoma Historical Society, 1967.

ARTICLES

Abler, Thomas S. "Friends, Factions and the Seneca Nation Revolution of 1848." *Niagara Frontier* 21 (Winter 1974): 74–79.

———. "The Kansas Connection: The Seneca Nation and the Iroquois Confederacy Council." In *Extending the Rafters: Interdisciplinary Approaches to Iroquoian*

Studies, edited by Jack Campisi, Michael Foster, and Marianne Mithun, 81–94. Albany: State Univ. of New York Press, 1984.

———. "Seneca Nation Factionalism: The First Twenty Years." In *Iroquois Culture, History and Prehistory: Proceedings of the 1965 Conference on Iroquois Research*, edited by Elisabeth Tooker, 25–26. Albany: New York State Museum and Science Service, 1967.

Allen, Orlando. "Personal Recollections of Captains Jones and Parrish." *Publications of the Buffalo Historical Society* 6 (1903): 544.

Banks, Dean. "Civil War Refugees from Indian Territory in the North, 1861–1864." *Chronicles of Oklahoma* 41 (Autumn 1963): 286–98.

Barsh, Russel Lawrence. "American Indians in the Great War." *Ethnohistory* 38 (Summer 1991): 276–303.

Bearss, Edwin C. "The Battle of Pea Ridge." *Arkansas Historical Quarterly* 20 (Spring 1961): 74–94.

———. "The Civil War Comes to Indian Territory: The Flight of Opothleyahola." *Journal of the West* 11 (January 1972): 9–42.

Bieder, Robert E., and Christopher Plant. "Annuity Census as a Source for Historical Research: The 1858 and 1869 Tonawanda Seneca Annuity Censuses." *American Indian Culture and Research Journal* 5, no. 1 (1981): 33–46.

Blassingame, John. "The Union Army as an Educational Institution." *Journal of Negro Education* 34 (Spring 1965): 152–59.

Blau, Harold, Jack Campisi, and Elisabeth Tooker. "Onondaga." In *Handbook of North American Indians*, vol. 15: *Northeast*, edited by Bruce G. Trigger, 491–99. Washington: D.C.: Smithsonian Institution, 1978.

Bonvillain, Nancy. "Iroquoian Women." In *Studies on Iroquoian Culture*, edited by Nancy Bonvillain, 47–58. Occasional Publications in Northeastern Anthropology, No. 6. Rindge, N.H.: *Man in the Northeast*, 1980.

Brown, Judith K. "Economic Organization and the Position of Women Among the Iroquois." *Ethnohistory* 17 (Summer-Fall 1970): 151–67.

Cain, Marvin R. "A 'Face of Battle' Needed: An Assessment of Motives and Men in Civil War Historiography." *Civil War History* 28 (Mar. 1982): 5–27.

Campisi, Jack. "Consequences of the Kansas Claims to Oneida Tribal Identity." In *Proceedings of the First Congress, Canadian Ethnology Society*, edited by Jerome H. Barkow, 35–47. Ottawa: Canadian National Museum of Man, Ethnology Division, Mercury Series Paper 17, 1974.

———. "From Stanwix to Canandaigua: National Policy, States' Rights, and Indian Land." In *Iroquois Land Claims*, edited by Christopher Vecsey and William A. Starna, 49–66. Syracuse: Syracuse Univ. Press, 1988.

———. "National Policy, States' Rights, and Indian Sovereignty: The Case of the New York Iroquois." In *Extending the Rafters: Interdisciplinary Approaches to Iroquoian Studies*, edited by Jack Campisi, Michael Foster, and Marianne Mithun, 95–108. Albany: State Univ. of New York Press, 1984.

———. "New York–Oneida Treaty of 1795: A Finding of Fact." *American Indian Law Review* 4 (Summer 1976): 71–82.

Chernow, Barbara A. "Robert Morris: Genesee Land Speculator." *New York History* 58 (Apr. 1977): 195–220.

Danzinger, Edmund J., Jr. "The Office of Indian Affairs and the Problem of Civil War Refugees in Kansas." *Kansas Historical Quarterly* 35 (Autumn 1969): 257–75.

Davies, Wallace E. "The Problem of Race Segregation in the Grand Army of the Republic." *Journal of Southern History* 13 (Aug. 1947): 354–72.

Dean, Eric T. "'We Will All Be Lost and Destroyed': Post-Traumatic Stress Disorder and the Civil War." *Civil War History* 37 (June 1991): 138–51.

Elder, Glen H., Jr. "Military Times and Turning Points in Men's Lives." *Developmental Psychology* 22 (Mar. 1986): 233–45.

Ewers, John C. "Iroquois Indians in the Far West." *Montana: The Magazine of Western History* 14 (1963): 2–10.

Farley, Ena L. "The African American Presence in the History of Western New York." *Afro-Americans in New York Life and History* 14 (Jan. 1990), 27–89.

Fenton, William N. "The Iroquois in History." In *North American Indians in Historical Perspective,* edited by Nancy O. Lurie and Eleanor Leacock, 160–61. New York: Random House, 1971.

———. "The Roll Call of the Iroquois Chiefs: A Study of a Mnemonic Cane from the Six Nations Reserve." *Smithsonian Miscellaneous Collections* 111 (1950): 1–73.

———. "Toward the Gradual Civilization of the Indian Natives: The Missionary and Linguistic Work of Asher Wright (1803–1875) Among the Seneca of Western New York." *Proceedings of the American Philosophical Society* 100 (Dec. 1956): 567–81.

———, ed. "Answers to Governor Cass's Questions by Jacob Jameson, a Seneca (ca. 1821–1825)." *Ethnohistory* 16, no. 2 (1969): 113–39.

———. "A Further Note on Jacob Jameson's Answers to the Lewis Cass Questionnaire." *Ethnohistory* 17, no. 1–2 (1970): 91–92.

———. "Seneca Indians by Asher Wright (1859)." *Ethnohistory* 4, no. 3 (1957): 302–21.

Franks, Kenny A. "An Analysis of the Confederate Treaties with the Five Civilized Tribes." *Chronicles of Oklahoma* 50 (Winter 1972/1973): 458–73.

———. "The Confederate States and the Five Civilized Tribes: A Breakdown of Relations." *Journal of the West* 12 (July 1973): 439–54.

———. "The Implementation of the Confederate Treaties with the Five Civilized Tribes." *Chronicles of Oklahoma* 51 (Spring 1973): 21–33.

Frisch, Jack A. "Iroquois in the West." In *Handbook of North American Indians,* vol. 15: *Northeast,* edited by Bruce G. Trigger, 544–46. Washington, D.C.: Smithsonian Institution, 1978.

Geary, James W. "Civil War Conscription in the North: A Historiographic Review." *Civil War History* 32 (1986): 208–28.

Gibson, Arrell M. "Native Americans and the Civil War." *American Indian Quarterly* 9 (Fall 1985): 385–410.

Graves, William H. "Indian Soldiers for the Gray Army: Confederate Recruitment in Indian Territory." *Chronicles of Oklahoma* 60 (Summer 1991): 134–45.

Graymont, Barbara. "New York State Indian Policy after the Revolution." *New York History* 57 (October 1976): 438–74.

———. "The Tuscarora New Year Festival." *New York History* 50 (Apr. 1969): 143–63.

Gunther, Gerald. "Governmental Power and New York Indian Lands—A Reassessment of a Persistent Problem of Federal-State Relations." *Buffalo Law Review* 7 (Fall 1958): 1–14.

Goldenweiser, Alexander, "Functions of Women in Iroquois Society." *American Anthropologist* 16 (1915): 376–77.

Haller, John S. "Civil War Anthropometry: The Making of a Racial Ideology." *Civil War History* 16 (Dec. 1970): 309–24.

Hallock, Judith Lee. "The Role of the Community in Civil War Desertion." *Civil War History* 29 (June 1983): 123–34.

Harris, Emily J. "Sons and Soldiers: Deerfield, Massachusetts and the Civil War." *Civil War History* 30 (June 1984): 157–71.

Hauptman, Laurence M. "Compensatory Justice: The Seneca Nation Settlement Act of 1900." *National Forum* (Auburn University) 71 (Spring 1991): 31–33.

———. "Governor Theodore Roosevelt and the Indians of New York State." *Proceedings of the American Philosophical Society* 199 (Feb. 1975): 1–7.

———. "The Historical Background to the Present-Day Seneca Nation—Salamanca Lease Controversy." In *Iroquois Land Claims.* edited by Christopher Vecsey and William A. Starna, 67–86. Syracuse: Syracuse Univ. Press, 1988.

———. "Samuel George (1795–1873): A Study of Onondaga Conservatism." *New York History* 70 (Jan. 1989): 4–22.

———. "Senecas and Subdividers: The Resistance to Allotment of Indian Lands in New York, 1875–1906." *Prologue: The Journal of the National Archives* 9 (Summer 1977): 105–16.

———. "The Tuscarora Company: An Iroquois Unit in the American Civil War." *Turtle Quarterly* (Spring 1988): 10–12.

Hewitt, J. N. B. "Status of Women in Iroquois Polity Before 1784." In *Smithsonian Institution Annual Report for 1932,* 475–78. Washington, D.C.: Smithsonian Institution, 1932.

Hogan, Thomas E. "City in a Quandary: Salamanca and the Allegany Leases." *New York History* 55 (Jan. 1974): 79–101.

Holm, Tom. "Fighting a White Man's War: The Extent and Legacy of American Indian Participation in World War II." *Journal of Ethnic Studies* 9 (Summer 1981): 69–81.

Holmes, Amy E. "'Such Is the Price We Pay': American Widows and the Civil War Pension System." In *Toward a Social History of the American Civil War: Exploratory Essays,* edited by Maris A. Vinovskis, 171–95. New York: Cambridge Univ. Press, 1990.

Horsman, Reginald. "The Origins of Oneida Removal to Wisconsin, 1815–1822."

In *An Anthology of Western Great Lakes Indian History,* edited by Donald L. Fixico, 203–32. Milwaukee: American Indian Studies Department of the Univ. of Wisconsin, Milwaukee, 1987.

————. "The Wisconsin Oneidas in the Preallotment Years." In *The Oneida Indian Experience: Two Perspectives,* edited by Jack Campisi and Laurence M. Hauptman, 65–82. Syracuse: Syracuse Univ. Press, 1988.

Hyde, Jabez Backus. "A Teacher Among the Senecas: Historical and Personal Narrative of Jabez Backus Hyde." *Publications of the Buffalo Historical Society* 6 (1903): 247.

Katz, Michael, Michael J. Doucet, and Mark S. Stern. "Migration and the Social Order in Erie County, New York: 1855." *Journal of Interdisciplinary History* 8 (Spring 1978): 669–701.

Kelsey, Harry. "Charles Mix." In *The Commissioners of Indian Affairs, 1824–1977,* edited by Robert Kvasnicka and Herman Viola, 89–98. Lincoln: Univ. of Nebraska Press, 1979.

————. "William P. Dole and Mr. Lincoln's Indian Policy." *Journal of the West* 10 (July 1971): 484–92.

Landy, David. "Tuscarora Among the Iroquois." In *Handbook of North American Indians,* vol. 15: *Northeast,* edited by Bruce G. Trigger, 518–24. Washington, D.C.: Smithsonian Institution, 1978.

————. "Tuscarora Tribalism and National Identity." *Ethnohistory,* 5, no. 3 (1958): 250–84.

Larsen, Lawrence H. "Draft Riot in Wisconsin, 1862." *Civil War History* 7, no. 4 (1961): 421–27.

Levine, Peter. "Draft Evasion in the North During the Civil War, 1863–1865." *Journal of American History* 67 (Mar. 1981): 816–34.

Locklear, Arlinda. "The Allotment of the Oneida Reservation and Its Legal Ramifications." In *The Oneida Indian Experience: Two Perspectives,* edited by Jack Campisi and Laurence M. Hauptman, 83–93. Syracuse: Syracuse Univ. Press, 1988.

McConnell, Stuart. "Who Joined the Grand Army? Three Cases in the Construction of Union Veteranhood, 1866–1900." In *Toward a Social History of the American Civil War: Exploratory Essays,* edited by Maris Vinovskis, 139–70. New York: Cambridge Univ. Press, 1990.

McNeil, M. K. "Confederate Treaties with the Tribes of Indian Territory." *Chronicles of Oklahoma* 42 (Winter 1964–1965): 408–20.

Manley, Henry S. "Buying Buffalo from the Indians." *New York History* 28 (July 1947): 313–29.

————. "Indian Reservation Ownership in New York." *New York State Bar Bulletin* 32 (Apr. 1960): 134–38.

————. "Red Jacket's Last Campaign." *New York History* 31 (Apr. 1950): 149–68.

Mitchell, Reid. "The Northern Soldier and His Community." In *Toward a Social History of the American Civil War: Exploratory Essays,* edited by Maris A. Vinovskis, 78–92. Cambridge: Cambridge Univ. Press, 1990.

Moulton, Gary E. "John Ross and W. P. Dole: A Case Study of Lincoln's Indian Policy." *Journal of the West* 12 (July 1973): 414–23.

Newman, Marshall T. "The Physique of the Seneca Indians of Western New York State." *Journal of the Washington Academy of Sciences* 17 (Nov. 1957): 357–62.

Otterbein, Keith F. "Huron v. Iroquois: A Case Study in Inter-tribal Warfare." *Ethnohistory* 26 (Spring 1979): 141–52.

———. "Why the Iroquois Won: An Analysis of Iroquois Military Tactics." *Ethnohistory* 11 (Winter 1964): 56–63.

Parker, Arthur C. "The Senecas in the War of 1812." *Proceedings of the New York State Historical Association* 15 (1916): 78–90.

Pound, Cuthbert W. "Nationals Without a Nation: The New York State Tribal Indians." *Columbia Law Review* 22 (Feb. 1922): 97–102.

Quaife, Milo M. "The Panic of 1862 in Wisconsin." *Wisconsin Magazine of History* 4 (Dec. 1920): 166–95.

Richter, Daniel. "War and Culture: The Iroquois Experience." *William and Mary Quarterly*, 3d ser., vol. 40, no. 4 (1983): 537–44.

Roberts, Gary L. "Dennis Nelson Cooley, 1865–1866." In *The Commissioners of Indian Affairs, 1824–1977*, edited by Robert Kvasnicka and Herman Viola, 99–108. Lincoln: Univ. of Nebraska Press, 1979.

Rorabaugh, W. J. "Who Fought for the North in the Civil War? Concord, Massachusetts, Enlistments." *Journal of American History* 73 (Dec. 1986): 695–701.

Rothenberg, Diane. "The Mothers of the Nation: Seneca Resistance to Quaker Intervention." In *Women and Colonization: Anthropological Perspectives*, edited by Mona Etienne and Eleanor Leacock, 63–87. New York: Praeger, 1980.

Seraile, William. "The Struggle to Raise Black Regiments in New York State, 1861–1864." *New-York Historical Society Quarterly* 58 (July 1974): 215–33.

Shimony, Annemarie. "Conflict and Continuity: An Analysis of an Iroquois Uprising." In *Extending the Rafters: Interdisciplinary Approaches to Iroquoian Studies*, edited by Jack Campisi, Michael Foster, and Marianne Mithun, 153–64. Albany: State Univ. of New York Press, 1984.

Shoemaker, Nancy. "From Longhouse to Loghouse: Household Structure among the Senecas in 1900." *American Indian Quarterly* 15 (Summer 1991): 329–38.

———. "The Rise and Fall of Iroquois Women." *Journal of Women's History* 2 (Winter 1991): 39–57.

Smith, Robert, and Loretta Metoxen. "Oneida Traditions." In *The Oneida Indian Experience: Two Perspectives*, edited by Jack Campisi and Laurence M. Hauptman, 150–51. Syracuse: Syracuse Univ. Press, 1988.

Snyderman, George S. "Behind the Tree of Peace: A Sociological Analysis of Iroquois Warfare." *Pennsylvania Archaeologist* 38 (Fall 1948): 3–93.

Stanley, George F. G. "The Significance of the Six Nation Participation in the War of 1812." *Ontario History* 55 (Dec. 1963): 215–31.

Tooker, Elisabeth. "Ely S. Parker: Seneca, ca. 1828–1895." In *American Indian Intellectuals*, edited by Margot Liberty, pp. 15–30. St. Paul, Minn.: West Publishing Co. for the American Ethnological Society, 1978.

————. "The League of the Iroquois: Its History, Politics, and Ritual." In *Handbook of North American Indians*, vol. 15: *Northeast*, edited by Bruce G. Trigger, 418–41. Washington, D.C.: Smithsonian Institution, 1978.

————. "Women in Iroquois Society." In *Extending the Rafters*, edited by Jack Campisi, Michael Foster, and Marianne Mithun, 109–23. Albany: State Univ. of New York Press, 1984.

Unrau, William E. "Lewis Vital Bogy, 1860–1867." In *The Commissioners of Indian Affairs, 1824–1977*, edited by Robert Kvasnicka and Herman Viola, 109–14. Lincoln: Univ. of Nebraska Press, 1979.

Vernon, Howard. "The Cayuga Claims: A Background Study." *American Indian Research and Culture Journal* 4 (Fall 1980): 21–35.

Vinovskis, Maris A. "Have Social Historians Lost the Civil War? Some Preliminary Demographic Speculations." *Journal of American History* 76 (June 1989): 34–58.

Wallace, Anthony F. C. "Origins of the Longhouse Religion." In *Handbook of North American Indians*, vol. 15: *Northeast*, edited by Bruce G. Trigger, 442–48. Washington, D.C.: Smithsonian Institution, 1978.

Waltmann, Henry G. "Ely Samuel Parker, 1869–1871." In *The Commissioners of Indian Affairs, 1824–1977*, edited by Robert Kvasnicka and Herman Viola, 123–34. Lincoln: Univ. of Nebraska Press, 1979.

Wheeler, Gerald E., and A. Stuart Pitt. "The 53d New York: A Zoo-Zoo Tale." *New York History* 37 (Oct. 1956): 415–20.

Wilkinson, Norman B. "Robert Morris and the Treaty of Big Tree." *Mississippi Valley Historical Review* 60 (Sept. 1953): 257–78.

Wistar, Thomas. "Report on the Committee on the Civilization and Improvement of the New York Indians." *Friend* 38 (June 10, 1865): 324–27.

Zobel, Hiller B. "Enlisted for Life." *American Heritage* 37 (June–July 1986): 56–64.

DISSERTATIONS AND THESES

Abler, Thomas S. "Factional Dispute and Party Conflict in the Political System of the Seneca Nation (1845–1895): An Ethnohistorical Analysis." Ph.D. diss., Univ. of Toronto, 1969.

Boyce, Douglas W. "Tuscarora Political Organization, Ethnic Identity and Sociohistorical Demography, 1711–1825." Ph.D. diss., Univ. of North Carolina, 1973.

Brown, Walter L. "Albert Pike, 1809–1891." Ph.D. diss. Univ. of Texas, 1955.

Campisi, Jack. "Ethnic Identity and Boundary Maintenance in Three Oneida Communities." Ph.D. diss., State Univ. of New York, Albany, 1974.

Henderson, Alice H. "The History of the New York State Anti-Slavery Society." Ph.D. diss., Univ. of Michigan, 1963.

Hogan, Thomas E. "A History of the Allegany Reservation, 1850–1900." Master's thesis, State Univ. of New York, College at Fredonia, 1974.

Lankevich, George J. "The Grand Army of the Republic in New York State, 1865–1898." Ph.D. diss., Columbia Univ., 1967.

Rothenberg, Diane B. "Friends Like These: An Ethnohistorical Analysis of the Interaction Between Allegany Senecas and Quakers, 1798–1823." Ph.D. diss., City Univ. of New York, 1976.

Sterling, Robert. "Civil War Draft Resistance in the Middle West." Ph.D. diss., Northern Illinois Univ., 1974.

Van Hoeven, James W. "Salvation and Indian Removal: The Career Biography of the Rev. John Freeman Schermerhorn, Indian Commissioner." Ph.D. diss., Vanderbilt Univ., 1972.

Index

THE IROQUOIS IN THE CIVIL WAR

was composed in 10 on 12 Palatino on Digital Compugraphic equipment
by Metricomp;
printed by sheet-fed offset on 50-pound, acid-free Natural Hi Bulk,
Smyth-sewn and bound over binder's boards in Holliston Roxite B,
and with dust jackets printed
by Braun-Brumfield, Inc.;
and published by
SYRACUSE UNIVERSITY PRESS
SYRACUSE, NEW YORK 13244-5160

Laurence M. Hauptman, Series Editor

This series presents a wide range of scholarship — archaeology, anthropology, history, public policy, sociology, women's studies — that focuses on the indigenous peoples of Northeastern North America. The series encourages more awareness and a broader understanding of the Iroquois Indians — the Mohawk, Oneida, Onondaga, Cayuga, Seneca, and Tuscarora — and their Native American neighbors and provides a forum for scholars to elucidate the important contributions of the first Americans from prehistory to the present day.

Selected titles in the series include:

Schmitt